**PRAISE FOR**

**AWARDS**

*Winner*

**2020 Prime Minister's Literary Award**
**2020 Victorian Premier's Literary Award**
**2019 New South Wales Premier's General History Award**

*Finalist*

**2020 Phi Beta Kappa Ralph Waldo Emerson Award**
**2019 Mountbatten Maritime Award for Best Book**
**2019 Sigurd F. Olson Nature Writing Award**
**2019 Queensland Literary Award**

"Magnificent. . . . A grand, symphonic, beautifully written book. . . . *Sea People* is an archive-researched historical account that has the page-turning qualities of an all-absorbing mystery."  —*Boston Globe*

"*Sea People* is a roaring success. . . . A deeply interesting read and at points incredibly moving."  —NPR

"Compelling. . . . These pages will unleash the imagination [and] spark insight."  —*National Geographic*

"*Sea People* is a rich compendium of the ways Polynesia has been pinned down on the maps of geography, history, and culture through the centuries. As Thompson so eloquently shows, such descriptions are only half of a story."  —*Harper's Magazine*

"Christina Thompson . . . is perhaps ideally placed to try to answer the question [of Polynesian origins]—and in *Sea People*, her fascinating and satisfying addition to an already considerable body of Polynesian literature, she succeeds admirably."  —*New York Times Book Review*

"Christina Thompson's outstanding study brims with detail." —*Nature*

"Superb. . . . An illuminating read for amateur sleuths and professional scholars alike." —*The Spectator* (London)

"The supra theme of *Sea People* is a vision of knowledge systems intertwined—the outcome of history, cultural tolerance, and a grasp of misunderstandings. Thompson's tone is perfectly tuned for such enlightenment, as is the life-position from which she writes."
—*Sydney Morning Herald* (Australia)

"A triumph. . . . *Sea People* deserves a wide audience, one well beyond those who are from, or conduct research in, the region. . . . Infused with curiosity and respect, *Sea People* is everything historical nonfiction should be." —*Australian Book Review*

"A rewarding chronicle that spans centuries of investigations . . . [Thompson] shows us how we know what we know about the peopling of nearly a quarter of the Earth's surface." —*Smithsonian*

"Who hasn't stayed up late reading South Sea tales? Christina Thompson's *Sea People*—the exploration and settlement of the vast Pacific Ocean by stone-age Polynesians—is a South Sea tale to top them all, and every word is true. It's a compelling story, beautifully told, the best exploration narrative I've read in years."
—Richard Rhodes, author of *Energy: A Human History* and the Pulitzer Prize–winning *The Making of the Atomic Bomb*

"I loved this book. I found *Sea People* the most intelligent, empathic, engaging, wide-ranging, informative, and authoritative treatment of Polynesian mysteries that I have ever read. Christina Thompson's gorgeous writing arises from a deep well of research and succeeds in conjuring a lost world."
—Dava Sobel, bestselling author of *Longitude* and *The Glass Universe*

"To those of the Western Hemisphere, the Pacific represents a vast unknown, almost beyond our imagining; for its Polynesian island peoples, this fluid, shifting place is home. Christina Thompson's wonderfully researched and beautifully written narrative brings these two stories together, gloriously and excitingly. Filled with teeming grace and terrible power, her book is a vibrant and revealing new account of the watery part of our world."
—Philip Hoare, author of *RisingTideFallingStar*

"I have rarely read so exciting and companionable a narrative as Christina Thompson's *Sea People*. In her capable hands this saga of Polynesia's scattered islands becomes a comprehensive and dramatic history of our planet and the ways its peoples, creatures, vegetation, land forms, and waters interacted over the centuries and eons since the world began."
—Megan Marshall, Pulitzer Prize–winning author of *Margaret Fuller: A New American Life* and *Elizabeth Bishop: A Miracle for Breakfast*

"With a flair for making the past live again, Christina Thompson gives us a comprehensive story of Polynesia and of those who have studied it. *Sea People* tells the story of a unique geographic, cultural, and intellectual voyage across water and through time. Essential reading for anyone seeking to understand Polynesia, the Pacific, or the spread of humanity around the globe."
—Jack Weatherford, bestselling author of *Genghis Khan and the Making of the Modern World*

"*Sea People* teems with compelling insights as it explores the age-old mysteries of Polynesian origins. We don't just visit the turreted cliffs of the Marquesas with Mendaña, the cloud-wrapped peaks of Hawaii with Cook, or the treacherous reefs of Raroia with Heyerdahl. We envision the whole panorama of European exploration and colonization against the even greater grandeur of Polynesian inventiveness, dignity, and self-determination. Thanks to Thompson's vision, we encounter an authentic global mystery that proves as vast and luminous as the Pacific itself."
—Paul Fisher, author of *House of Wits: An Intimate Portrait of the James Family*

"Thoroughly researched and engagingly written, Thompson's account shows how the science of human history, despite occasional wrong turns and dead ends, slowly but steadily advances. A must read for anyone fascinated by the Polynesians or interested in the history of science."
—Patrick V. Kirch, author of *On the Road of the Winds*

"A luminous, beautifully rendered account of Polynesian navigation and exploration, and the lives and knowledge that built and populated an astonishing Oceanian civilization. Thompson captures the remarkable deep history of a world shaped between land and sea."
—Matt K. Matsuda, author of *Pacific Worlds*

ALSO BY CHRISTINA THOMPSON

*Come on Shore and We Will Kill and Eat You All*

# SEA

# PEOPLE

*The Puzzle of Polynesia*

**CHRISTINA**

**THOMPSON**

HARPER

NEW YORK • LONDON • TORONTO • SYDNEY

# HARPER

A hardcover edition of this book was published in 2019 by HarperCollins Publishers.

HarperCollins books may be purchased for educational, business, or sales promotional use. For information, please email the Special Markets Department at SPsales@harpercollins.com.

FIRST HARPER PAPERBACKS EDITION PUBLISHED 2022.

*Designed by Fritz Metsch*
*Map design by Laura Healy*

Library of Congress Cataloging-in-Publication Data has been applied for.

ISBN 978-0-06-206088-4

24 25 26 27 28 LBC 6 5 4 3 2

*For Tauwhitu*

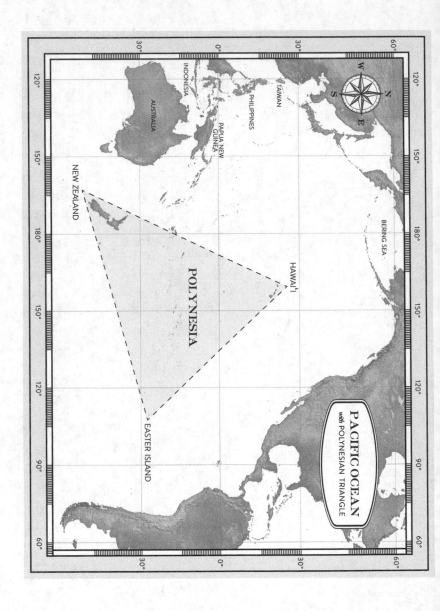

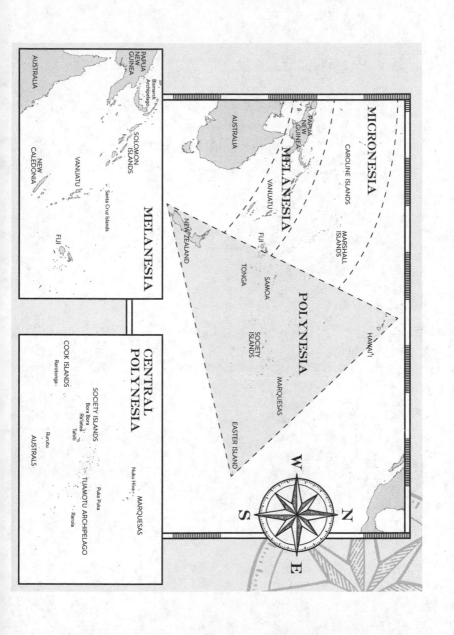

*For we are dear to the immortal gods,*
*Living here, in the sea that rolls forever,*
*Distant from other lands and other men.*

—Homer, the *Odyssey*
(translated by Robert Fitzgerald)

# Contents

*In which we follow the trail of the earliest European explorers as they attempt to cross the Pacific for the first time, encountering a wide variety of islands and meeting some of the people who live there.*

Part II: CONNECTING THE DOTS
(1764–1779)

*In which we travel with Captain Cook to the heart of Polynesia, meet the Tahitian priest and navigator Tupaia, and sail with the two of them to New Zealand, where Tupaia makes an important discovery.*

Part III: WHY NOT JUST ASK THEM?
(1779–1920)

*In which we look at some of the stories that Polynesians told about themselves and consider the difficulty nineteenth-century Europeans had trying to make sense of them.*

*Part IV:* THE RISE OF SCIENCE
(1920–1959)
*In which anthropologists pick up the trail of the ancient Polynesians,
bringing a new, quantitative approach to the questions of who, where,
and when.*

*Part V:* SETTING SAIL
(1947–1980)

*In which we set off on an entirely new tack, taking to the sea with a crew of experimental voyagers as they attempt to reenact the voyages of the ancient Polynesians.*

*Part VI:* WHAT WE KNOW NOW
(1990–2018)

*In which we review some of the latest scientific findings and think about what it takes to answer big questions about the deep past.*

# Contents

# List of Plates

was given in 1839. From Richard Owen, *Memoirs on the extinct wingless birds of New Zealand* (London, 1879). Wikimedia Commons.

11. Moa egg found by Jim Eyles at Wairau Bar in 1939. Photograph by Norman Heke, Museum of New Zealand Te Papa Tongarewa.

12. Necklace of moa bone reels and stone "whale tooth" pendant, discovered at Wairau Bar. Canterbury Museum, Christchurch, New Zealand.

13. "The Arrival of the Maoris in New Zealand" by Louis John Steele and Charles F. Goldie (1898), Auckland Art Gallery Toi o Tāmaki, gift of the late George and Helen Boyd, 1899. Based on Théodore Géricault's *The Raft of the Medusa* (1818–19), this painting depicts a vision of Polynesian voyaging not unlike that implied by drift voyaging theories.

14. Reconstructed three-thousand-year-old Lapita pot from Teouma, Efate Island, Vanuatu. Photograph by Philippe Metois, courtesy Stuart Bedford and Matthew Spriggs.

15. Micronesian stick chart from the Marshall Islands. Denver Museum of Nature and Science.

16. *Hōkūleʻa* passing the Statue of Liberty in 2016 on the Mālama Honua voyage around the world. Photo by Naʻalehu Anthony, courtesy ʻŌiwi TV and the Polynesian Voyaging Society.

# PROLOGUE

## *Kealakekua Bay*

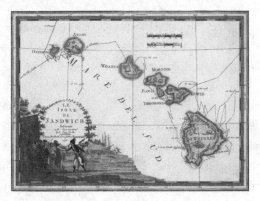

Map of the Sandwich Islands by Giovanni Cassini (Rome, 1798),
based on Cook's chart of Hawai'i.
STORY OF HAWAII MUSEUM, KAHULUI, MAUI.

KEALAKEKUA BAY LIES on the west, or leeward, side of the Big Island
of Hawai'i, in the rain shadow cast by the great volcano Mauna Loa.
It is a smallish bay about a mile wide, open to the southwest, with
a bit of flat land at either end and a great wall of cliffs along the
middle, where in ancient times the bodies of Hawaiian chiefs were
hidden in secret caves. The name of the bay, Kealakekua, means
in Hawaiian "the Path of the God," and in the final centuries of
Polynesian isolation, before the arrival of Europeans, it was a seat
of power and the ancestral home of no less a personage than the
first Hawaiian monarch, Kamehameha I.

   To get to Kealakekua Bay, you take the main road south from
Kailua, leaving behind the more heavily settled areas of the Kona
Coast and passing through a series of small towns. The highway
on this part of the island runs along the shoulder of the mountain,

and the drive down to sea level is a steep one. Turning off at the Napoʻopoʻo Road, you wind down through an arid landscape of mesquite and lead trees interspersed with ornamental plantings of hibiscus and plumeria. Taking a right at the bottom and following the road to its end, you come at last to a little cul-de-sac under a pair of spreading jacarandas. The beach, with its jumble of boulders, is a stone's throw away, the high red rampart of the Pali looms on the right, and, squinting into the distance, you can just make out the low, scrubby outline of the farther shore.

Immediately adjacent rises the wall of the Hikiau Heiau, a large rectangular platform neatly built of close-fitting lava stones. The first time we visited this spot, my husband, Seven, and I were at the end of a long trip across the Pacific with our three sons. We had seen these sorts of structures before, coming upon them half-hidden in the forests of Nuku Hiva and high on a headland on Oʻahu's North Shore, and once on a beach like this on the island of Raʻiatea. In many parts of Polynesia they are known as *marae*, and in the days before Europeans reached the Pacific they were places of great mystery and supernatural power. Presided over by chiefs and priests and dedicated to particular gods, they were sites of sacrifice—including, occasionally, of humans—and propitiation to ensure safe voyaging or good health or plentiful food or success in war. They were decorated with scaffoldings and carved wooden images, and often with skulls, and were governed by the incontestable law of *kapu* (known elsewhere as *tapu* and the source of our word "taboo"), the system of rules and prohibitions linking everyday existence to the world of the numinous, which permeated every aspect of ancient Polynesian life.

We picked our way around the outside of the *heiau*, trying to get a sense of what was there. What remained of the original structure was a raised dry-stone platform more than a hundred feet long and about half as wide, rising to a height of ten feet at the beach end. It was said to have been nearly twice this size when it was first seen by Europeans, in the late 1700s, and would have been an imposing edifice with a commanding view of the bay. Or so we imagined. The stone stairway up to the top of the platform was roped off, and no fewer than three separate signs reminded us that no trespassing was allowed. Visitors were admonished not to wrap or to remove any of the stones or to climb on the walls or in any other way to disrespect the site. *Heiau* on the islands of Hawai'i have more signage than similar structures on other islands, and, given the number of visitors, it's easy to see why. But encounters with the past are different when they are mediated in this way, and I was glad that our first experience of such places had been deep in a forest in the Marquesas, where we had wandered freely among the ruins, ruminating after our own fashion upon the passage of time.

Directly in front of the *heiau* was an obelisk built of the same black lava rock but cemented in a very un-Polynesian way. It was about ten or twelve feet high and was mounted with a bronze commemorative plaque that read:

> In this heiau, January 28, 1779,
> Captain James Cook R. N.
> read the English burial service
> over William Whatman, seaman,
> the first recorded Christian service
> in the Hawaiian Islands.

Here was a completely different story from the one the *heiau* had to tell. On the surface, it was the story of poor Whatman, dead of a stroke, whose last wish had been to be buried on shore, and of the almost accidental arrival of Christianity, the rippling effect of which would be felt in these islands for centuries to come. But the much larger story, only obliquely indicated here, was of the coming of Europeans to the Pacific—the most consequential thing to have happened in these islands since the arrival of the Polynesians themselves. And so, while we might have come simply to see the *heiau*, with its tantalizing glimpse of a remote and cryptic Polynesian past, it was, in fact, the intersection of these two histories that had brought us to Kealakekua Bay.

COOK'S ARRIVAL IN the Hawaiian Islands marks a turning point in the history of European understanding of the Pacific. It was January 1778, and he was a year and a half into his third voyage. In the course of the first two, Cook had explored much of the South Pacific, laying down the east coast of Australia, circumnavigating New Zealand, charting many of the major island groups, even making the first crossing below the Antarctic Circle. On his third and final voyage, he was headed into new territory: that part of the Pacific that lies north of the equator. He had set his sights on one of the great chimerical objects of European geography, the Northwest Passage, and when he chanced upon the island of Kauaʻi, he was bound for Nootka Sound.

At the time, the Hawaiian Islands were not yet marked on any European map. In hindsight, it is quite surprising that they remained undiscovered as long as they did. For more than two hundred years, beginning as early as the 1560s, Spanish galleons had plied the North Pacific, sailing from Acapulco to Manila and back again once or twice a year, passing just south of Hawaiʻi on the westward journey and just north of it as they sailed back east, without ever realizing that the islands were there. Cook, on the other hand, was sailing north from Tahiti, along what would eventually be recognized as an ancient Polynesian sea road, when he accidentally encountered the Hawaiian chain in what would prove to be the last great Pacific discovery by any European explorer.

Cook stopped only briefly on this first pass. The window for northern explorations was narrow, and he had no time to spare. But that autumn, when the northern ice began to close in, he returned to examine the islands more carefully. Falling in with the north coast of Maui, toward the end of November, Cook turned east and saw the great island of Hawaiʻi rising before him, its summit unexpectedly covered with snow. He decided to sail around the island in order to put its great bulk between him and the strong northeasterly winds and to look along the leeward side for a place where he might refresh his crew. The weather was squally and his progress slow, and for nearly two months the British ships crept round the Big Island. Finally, toward the end of January 1779, they reached Kealakekua Bay. And here something rather peculiar happened.

Cook at this moment probably knew more about the Pacific than any living European. He had made three voyages in ten years, each of several years' duration, and had visited every major island group in Polynesia. He had witnessed dozens, perhaps hundreds, of gatherings, many occasioned by the arrival of his own ships, but nowhere, he wrote, had he ever seen so many people assembled in one place at one time. Cook estimated that no fewer than a thousand canoes came out to meet them, while "all the Shore of the bay was covered with people and hundreds were swimming about the Ships like shoals of fish." But it was not just the numbers that impressed him; it was the mood. Early encounters between Europeans and Pacific Islanders were frequently tense; often there were skirmishes, sometimes people were killed. On this occasion, however, the atmosphere seemed strangely festive. As Cook and his officers noted with some surprise, the islanders were not even armed.

As soon as the Englishmen landed, they were escorted up the beach to the *heiau*, preceded by heralds who called out, "Orono, Orono." Spectators, who had gathered in the hundreds along the shore, flung themselves to the ground as the strangers approached, prostrating themselves before the procession. Cook was led up onto the platform, draped in a red cloth, and presented with offerings of cooked pig. A pair of priests chanted, alternately addressing Cook and a collection of wooden images, while the crowd intoned "Orono" at intervals. Even within Cook's extensive experience, this reception was unique, and it quickly became clear to everyone present—as it has been to every historian and anthropologist since then—that something quite out of the ordinary was going on.

There have been varying interpretations of these events over the years, but the most widely accepted view is that, by sheer chance, Cook had arrived in the Hawaiian Islands during a seasonal ritual cycle known as the Makahiki. The central event of this festival, which runs from October to February, is the return of the god Lono, who arrives from Kahiki (the Hawaiian name for Tahiti but also a word meaning "a faraway place") and is ritualistically borne around the island in a clockwise fashion, visiting each district in turn and collecting tributes. Lono, a god of peace and fertility, is represented in this procession by a long pole with a crosspiece draped with white cloth.

By the queerest twist of fate, Cook himself had been slowly sailing around the island in a clockwise direction, in a ship with tall masts and white sails, during precisely these months and had come ashore at a place specifically consecrated to the god Lono. Thus it was that he was received as a temporal embodiment of the god. This is not to say that Cook was "mistaken" for the god Lono—a crude, if common, misinterpretation—but rather that, coming as he did, when he did, he was understood to be cloaked in the mantle of the deity's power.

For two weeks, Cook's ships remained in Kealakekua Bay, and for two weeks the extraordinary obeisances continued. At the end of January, Whatman died and was buried in the *heiau* with both Christian and Hawaiian honors, Cook reading the burial service and the Hawaiian priests contributing a pig to the grave. Three days later, the ships weighed anchor and sailed away. And that should have been the end of the story. But a few days out, the foremast of Cook's ship split in a gale and he turned back to Kealakekua to make repairs. This time almost no one came out to meet them.

Cook himself had the feeling that they had outstayed their welcome, but what he could not have known was that there was a deeper, more metaphysical problem. As the embodiment of Lono, he was supposed to leave at the end of the Makahiki season, with a promise to return—but not until the following year. When, instead, he returned almost immediately, his reappearance proved

impossible to explain. The then-reigning chief of Hawai'i, Kala-
ni'ōpu'u, dismissed the Englishmen's account of technical difficulties, insisting, rather, that on his earlier visit Cook had "amused
them with Lies."

The air of festivity that had characterized the Makahiki was
now at an end, and the mood in the bay was marked by irritability
and mistrust. On shore, the carpenters worked away at the mast,
but there were thefts and disagreements, punishments and dis-
putes. Then, on the third day, in one of those fracases that so often
erupted in these situations—a shout and a shove and a discharged
weapon—Cook was killed. It was almost absurdly accidental, and
it might so easily have happened at any time, in more or less this
way, on any of a number of islands. But this was how and where it
did happen, here in Kealakekua Bay.

THE SPOT WHERE Cook was killed lies about a mile from the *heiau*,
across the bay at a place called Ka'awaloa. A twenty-five-foot-high
white obelisk, erected there in his memory in 1874, appears to the
naked eye as a small white object on a low green promontory, or,
with a bit of magnification, like the top of a tiny white church
buried up to its steeple in the ground. There is no road down to
Ka'awaloa, and the only ways to reach the monument are by hiking
down from the highway or sailing or motoring into the bay or paddling across in a kayak from the nearby Napo'opo'o pier.

Seven and the boys were curious about the kayaks, so we drove
over to Napo'opo'o to have a look. Unlike the *heiau*, which retains
much of the solemnity of a church, the Napo'opo'o pier is a hive of activity. The parking lot was full of vans loading and unloading kayaks
in every imaginable color. Tanned, athletic-looking tourists milled
about in bathing suits and life jackets while big Hawaiian guys with
tattooed calves sauntered back and forth with armloads of bright yellow paddles. It was clear that the Hawaiians were in charge of the
rentals, so Seven went over to have a word with one of them.

"Hey," he said, "how much for a kayak?"

"Thirty dollars," the guy replied. And then, "Twenty for you, brother."

At this point, we had been traveling in the Pacific for almost eight weeks. We had had our passports stamped in six different countries, touched down on fourteen different islands, learned how to say hello in eight different (albeit closely related) languages, and in every single place there had been an encounter like this. *Hey, brother, how's it going? Hey, brother, where you from? Hey, brother, you need something?* In Tonga, a man with whom we had only the most distant connection loaned us his car. In Hawai'i, the cousin of an acquaintance offered us her house. On islands all over the Pacific, people stopped to ask my husband who he was and where he was from.

The reason for this is that Seven is Polynesian. He is Māori, which is to say that he belongs to the branch of the Polynesian family that settled the islands of New Zealand around the beginning of the second millennium A.D. Hawaiians are also Polynesians: they belong to the branch of the family that settled the Hawaiian Islands a bit earlier, around the end of the first millennium. Both groups can trace their roots back to the islands of central Polynesia—to Tahiti and the Society Islands, the Marquesas, and the Cooks— which were settled, in turn, by voyagers from islands farther to the west. So rapid and complete was this expansion, and so vast the territory across which it spread, that, until the era of mass migration, Polynesians were both the most closely related and the most widely dispersed people in the world.

Seven's encounter with the kayak dealer was a legacy of this prehistoric diaspora, and, like the stonework of the Hikiau Heiau, we had encountered it before, thousands of miles away in the Tuamotus, on Tahiti, and Tongatapu. But the amazing thing is that we could have gone on traveling for thousands more miles and visited hundreds more islands and the experience would have been the same. Because the fact is that Seven can get on a plane in the country of his birth, fly for nine hours, and get off in a completely different country where he will be treated by the locals as one of their own. Then, if he wants, he can get on another plane, fly for nine hours in an entirely different direction, get off, and still be treated like a local. And then, if he wants to go back to where he started, it's still another nine hours by plane.

This is what is meant by the Polynesian Triangle, an area of ten million square miles in the middle of the Pacific Ocean defined by the three points of Hawai'i, New Zealand, and Easter Island. All the islands inside this triangle were originally settled by a clearly identifiable group of voyagers: a people with a single language and set of customs, a particular body of myths, a distinctive arsenal of tools and skills, and a "portmanteau biota" of plants and animals that they carried with them wherever they went. They had no knowledge of writing or metal tools—no maps or compasses—and yet they succeeded in colonizing the largest ocean on the planet, occupying every habitable rock between New Guinea and the Galápagos, and establishing what was, until the modern era, the largest single culture area in the world.

**FOR MORE THAN** a thousand years, Polynesians occupied these islands, and until the arrival of explorers like Captain Cook, they were the only people ever to have lived there. There are not many places on earth about which one can say this, and yet it is true of every island in Polynesia. Until the arrival of European explorers—of Mendaña in the Marquesas and Tasman in New Zealand and Roggeveen on Easter Island—every one of these Polynesian cultures existed in splendid isolation from the rest of the world. This long sequestration is part of what makes Polynesia so fascinating to outsiders—a natural laboratory, some have called it, for the study of language change and genetic diversity and social evolution.

What it means for insiders, on the other hand, is that there exists a great web of interconnectedness that continues to this day. According to New Zealand tradition, Seven, whose real name is Tauwhitu—*whitu*, or some cognate thereof (*fitu, hitu, itu, hiku*), being the universal word for "seven" in Polynesia—is descended from a voyager named Puhi, who sailed to New Zealand from the ancestral homeland of Hawaiki in one of a fleet of eight great canoes. Whether or not this is really what happened, it is certainly true that his ancestors came to Aotearoa (the Polynesian name for New Zealand) from an island in eastern Polynesia and that their ancestors came to that island from another island before that. The simplicity of this genealogy is stunning. No chaotic mixture of raiders and conquerors; no muddle of Vikings and Normans and Jutes. For centuries Polynesians were the only people in this region of the world, and thus the only people Seven *can* be descended from are the ones who figured out how to cross thousands of miles of open ocean in double-hulled voyaging canoes.

To me—and not just to me—this is a big part of the fascination with this story. Few of us can trace our own lineages with such certainty going back so far, and it pleases me to think that my children share in this breathtaking genealogy. But what makes the whole thing truly fantastic is what their ancestors *had to do* in order to find and colonize all of these islands. There is a reason the remote Pacific was the last place on earth to be settled by humans: it was the most difficult, more daunting even than the deserts or the ice. And yet, somehow, Polynesians managed not just to find but to colonize every habitable island in this vast sea.

We know they did it because when the first Europeans arrived in the Pacific, they found these islands inhabited. But we also know that by the time Europeans arrived, the epic phase of Polynesian history—the age of exploration and long-distance voyaging—was already over. The world of the ancient voyagers had blossomed, flourished, and passed away, leaving behind a group of closely related but widely scattered daughter cultures that had been developing in isolation from one another for hundreds of years. Once explorers and migrants, they had become settlers and colonists; they knew themselves less as Voyagers of the Great Ocean than, as in the Marquesan formulation, Enata

Fenua ("People of the Land"). Of course, they were still a sea people, traveling within and in some cases among archipelagoes, taking much of their living from the sea. But at far reaches of the Polynesian Triangle—in New Zealand, Hawai'i, Easter Island, even the Marquesas—they retained only a mythic sense of having ever come from someplace else.

To Europeans, who had themselves only just begun to master the enormous expanses of the Pacific, and then only at the cost of great suffering and loss of life, the discovery of people on these small and widely scattered islands was a source of wonderment. There seemed to be no obvious explanation for how they had gotten there, and, in the absence of any direct evidence, Europeans had difficulty envisioning a scenario that would explain how a people without writing or metal tools could, in the words of Cook, have "spread themselves over all the isles in this Vast Ocean." This conundrum, which came to be known as "the problem of Polynesian origins," emerged as one of the great geographical mysteries of mankind.

Over the past three hundred years, all kinds of people have taken a stab at solving this mystery, and many harebrained theories have been proposed: that the islands of Polynesia are the peaks of a drowned continent and the inhabitants the survivors of a great deluge; that Polynesians are Aryans or American Indians or the descendants of a tribe of wandering Jews; that the islands were settled by castaways or fishermen blown thither by capricious winds. But the truth, if you stop to think about it, can hardly be less astonishing; as the New Zealand ethnologist Elsdon Best once put it, "Could the story of the Polynesian voyagers be written in full, then would it be the wonder-story of the world."

The problem, of course, is that we are talking about *prehistory.* It is hard enough to know what happened in the past when there exists a documentary record, but there is no written record of these events. Here, the evidence is all partial, ambiguous, open to widely differing interpretations, and in some cases so technical that it is difficult for a layperson to judge. When I first set out to write this book, I imagined I would be recounting the tale of the voyagers themselves, those daring men and women who crossed such stupendous tracts of sea and whose exploits constitute one of the greatest adventures in human history. But, almost immediately, it dawned on me that one could tell such a story only by pretending to know more than can actually be known. This realization quickly led me to another: that the story of the Polynesian settlement of the Pacific is not so much a story about *what happened* as a story about *how we know.*

The evidence for what happened in the Pacific has taken different forms in different eras. In the sixteenth, seventeenth, and eighteenth centuries, it consisted of the eyewitness reports of European explorers, who left sketchy but fascinating accounts of Polynesian cultures before they had begun to change under the influence of the outside world. From the nineteenth century we have a different type of source material: Polynesian oral traditions, or what the islanders had to say about themselves. Then, starting in the early twentieth century, science began to deliver up whole new bodies of information based on biometrics, radiocarbon dating, and computer simulations. And, finally, in the 1970s, an experimental voyaging movement emerged, which added a completely different dimension to the story.

Because this evidence is complex—not to mention partial, fragmentary, and perennially open to reinterpretation—the story of what happened in Polynesia has not followed a single bearing to certainty from doubt. In fact, if you were to map it, it would look a lot like the track of a ship under sail, zigzagging and backtracking, haring off in one direction, only to turn and work its way back to an earlier course. There are difficulties with every kind of data— linguistic, archaeological, biological, folkloric—and aspects of the story that have nothing to do with the Pacific at all, for many of the arguments made about Polynesia have been driven by preoccupations originating in Oxford or Berlin.

But these, too, are part of the story, for the history of the Pacific is not just a tale of men and women (and dogs and pigs and chickens) in boats. It is also the story of all those who have wondered who Polynesians were, where they came from, and how they managed to find all those tiny islands scattered like stars in the emptiness of space. Thus, the book you have before you: a tale not just of the ancient mariners of the Pacific but of the many people who have puzzled over their history—the sailors, linguists, archaeologists, historians, ethnographers, folklorists, biologists, and geographers who have each, as it were, put in their oar.

*Part I*

# THE

# EYEWITNESSES

# (1521–1722)

*In which we follow the trail of the earliest European
explorers as they attempt to cross the Pacific for the
first time, encountering a wide variety of islands and
meeting some of the people who live there.*

# A VERY GREAT SEA

## *The Discovery of Oceania*

*Globe showing the Pacific Ocean.*

**IF YOU WERE** to look at the Pacific Ocean from space, you might notice that you would not be able to see both sides of it at the same time. This is because at its widest, the Pacific is nearly 180 degrees across—more than twelve thousand miles, or almost half the circumference of the earth. North to south, from the Aleutian Islands to the Antarctic, it stretches another ten thousand miles. Taken as a whole, it is so big that you could fit all the landmasses of earth inside it and there would still be room for another continent as large as North and South America combined. It is not simply the largest body of water on the planet—it is the largest single feature.

For most of human history, no one could have known any of this. They could not have known how far the ocean extended or what bodies of land it might or might not contain. They could not have known that the distances between islands, comparatively small at the ocean's western edge, would stretch and stretch until they were thousands of miles wide. They could not have known that parts of the great ocean were completely empty, containing no land at all, or that the winds and weather in one region might be quite different from—even the reverse of—what was to be met with in another part of the sea. For tens of thousands of years, long after humans had colonized its edges, the middle of the Pacific Ocean remained beyond the reach of man.

The first people to reach any of the Pacific's islands did so during the last ice age, when sea levels were as much as four hundred feet lower than they are today and the islands of Southeast Asia were a continent known as Sundaland. This meant that people could walk across most of what is now Indonesia, though only as far as Borneo and Bali; east of that, they had to paddle or swim. No one really knows how the first migrants did it—or, for that matter, who they were—but by sixty-five thousand years ago they had reached the large islands of Australia and New Guinea, which were then joined together in a separate continent called Sahul.

They crossed water again between New Guinea and the islands of the Bismarck Archipelago, reaching as far east as the Solomon Islands, where their progress appears to have been arrested. Perhaps they were stopped by rising sea levels or by the growing gaps of water between bodies of land or by the increasing poverty of plant and animal species as they moved farther out into the sea. Or perhaps they just petered out, like the Norse who tried to settle the island of Greenland and died there or gave up and retreated. In any case, this is how things stood for something like twenty to thirty thousand years. They had pushed out, as it were, to the edge of the shelf, but the vast expanse of the world's largest ocean remained an insurmountable barrier.

Then, about four thousand years ago, a new group of migrants appeared in the western Pacific. A true seagoing people, they were the first to leave behind the chains of intervisible islands and sail out into the open ocean. They were perhaps the closest thing to a sea people the world has known, making their homes on the shores of small islands, always preferring beaches, peninsulas, even sand-spits to valleys, highlands, and hills. They inhabited one of the rich-est marine environments in the world, with warm, clear tropical waters and mazes of coral in which hundreds of edible species lived. Most of their food came from the ocean: not just fish and shellfish, but eels, porpoises, turtles, octopuses, and crustaceans. They fished the quiet lagoon waters for reef species and trolled the open ocean for pelagic fish like tunas. They gathered sea snails and bivalves, *Turbo*, *Tridacna*, and *Spondylus* oysters, harvested slug-like sea cu-cumbers from the ocean floor, and pried spiny sea urchins from crevices in the rocks.

All their most ingenious technology—their lures, nets, weirs, and especially canoes—were designed for life at the water's edge. They made hand nets and casting nets, weighted seine nets with sinkers and buoyed them with pumice floats. They shaped hooks and lures from turtle shell and the pearly conical shell of the *Tro-chus* snail. We refer to the vessels they built as "canoes," but this barely begins to capture their character, something of which is re-flected in the language they used. They had words for lash, plank, bow, sail, strake, keel, paddle, boom, bailer, thwart, anchor, mast, and prop. They had words for cargo, for punting and tacking, for embarking, sailing to windward, and steering a course. They had words for decking, for figureheads, and rollers; they even had a term, *katae*, for the free side of a canoe—the one opposite the out-rigger—a concept for which we have no convenient expression.

They lived on the margin between land and sea, and their lan-guage was, not surprisingly, rich in terms for describing the litto-ral. Two of their key distinctions were between the lee side and the weather side of an island and between the inside and the outside of the reef. The principal axis of the directional system they used on land was toward and away from the ocean, and they had another system based on winds for when they were out at sea. They had countless words for water under the action of waves—foam, froth, billow, breaker, swell—and a metaphor in which open water was "alive" and sheltered water "dead." They had a word for the kind of submerged or hidden coral that was attractive to fish but dangerous for boats, and another for smooth or rounded coral that translated literally as "blossom of stone." They had words for pools, passages, and channels, and one for islets that was derived from the verb "to break off." They had a word for the gap between two points of land (as in a passage through the reef), which evolved into a word for the distance between any two points (as in the distance between islands) and which, as these distances expanded, eventually came to mean the far, deep ocean, and even space itself.

The one thing they do not seem to have had is a name for the ocean as a whole, nothing that would correspond to our "Pacific Ocean." They probably had names for parts of it, like their descendants the Tahitians, who referred to a region west of their islands as Te Moana Urifa, meaning "the Sea of Rank Odor," and a region to the east as Te Moana o Marama, meaning "the Sea of the Moon." But they seem not to have conceptualized the ocean in its entirety. Indeed, they could hardly be expected to have conceived of it as a discrete and bounded entity when, for them, it was not so much a thing apart as the medium in which they lived. It was *tasik*, meaning "tide" or "sea" or "salt water"; or it was *masawa*, meaning "deep or distant ocean" or "open sea."

EUROPEAN UNDERSTANDING OF the Pacific has been quite different, in part, because it has a recorded starting point. It begins on the 25th (or possibly the 27th) of September 1513, when the Spanish conquistador Vasco Núñez de Balboa climbed over the Isthmus of Panama and caught sight of what he called the Mar del Sur. He referred to it as *la otra mar*, meaning "the other sea," and for Europeans, who were already acquainted with both the Atlantic and Indian Oceans, this is precisely what the Pacific was. It was *another* ocean, defined by its relationship to already known bodies of water and land. If the Atlantic, also known as the Mar del Norte, was the ocean between Europe and the Americas, then the Mar del Sur was the ocean between the New World and the East. This was an essentially geographical perspective, and from the very beginning the principal questions for Europeans were: How big was this ocean, where were its boundaries, and how difficult might it be to cross?

The first European to cross the Pacific was the Portuguese navigator Ferdinand Magellan, who set sail from Spain in 1519 in search of a western route to the Spice Islands. Magellan had an idea that there might be a passage through South America, and after crossing the Atlantic, he picked up the South American coastline near what is now Rio de Janeiro and followed it south. He was at 52 degrees south latitude, nearly to the tip of the continent, before he found it: the winding, tortuous strait that now bears his name. To the north lay Patagonia, or the Land of Giants; to the south, Tierra del Fuego, or the Land of Fire. After thirty-eight difficult days, he emerged into an ocean that, thanks to a rare spell of good weather, was surprisingly calm. It was Magellan who gave the Pacific the name by which it is still known (though many storm-tossed travelers have since disputed its fitness).

But this was only the beginning of Magellan's journey. Like other navigators of his era, he labored under a misapprehension about the size of the earth and the relationships of its landmasses to one another. He believed that once he reached the Mar del Sur it would be but a short distance to the Indies. In fact, it was a very great distance indeed. For over three months they sailed without sight of land, excepting a glimpse of two little atolls, that he named Los Desventurados, or the Unfortunate Isles. They had been short of provisions when they began their crossing; before it was over, the crew was reduced to eating rats, sawdust, and the leather on the ships' yards. The voyage was marked by every possible calamity— mutiny, shipwreck, scurvy, starvation, not to mention the death of its commander, in a melee on an island in the Philippines. When, three years later, the expedition finally returned, it was with just one of the five original ships and eighteen of the original 188 men. They had, however, crossed the Pacific and discovered just how big it really was. They had also established that it was possible to reach the Indies by traveling west from Europe, though to do so, one would have to traverse "a sea so vast that the human mind can scarcely grasp it."

And not only so vast, but so empty. Maps of the Pacific can give the impression that parts of the great ocean are filled with bits of land. But what looks like a V-shaped scattering of islands concentrated in the west and stretching across the tropics—as if some giant standing on the Asian mainland had taken a handful of earth and tossed it out in the direction of Peru—is really a kind of cartographic illusion. While there are a great many islands in the Pacific—some twenty to twenty-five thousand, depending on what you count—the vast majority are so minuscule that on most maps, if they were represented to scale, they would be too small to see. Indeed, the space taken up by the names of these islands is often times greater than the land area they represent, and there are enormous stretches of ocean to the north, south, and east where there are no islands at all. So, while much is often made of the fact that Magellan managed to "miss everything" between the coast of Chile and the Philippines (and it is true that he succeeded in threading a number of archipelagoes without spotting any of the islands they contain), when you truly grasp how very little land there is and how much water, it's almost more surprising that anyone ever found anything at all.

One of the few survivors of Magellan's voyage, Antonio Pigafetta, wrote an account of his experience; it is from him that we know about the rats—traded, he tells us, at half an écu apiece— and the weevily biscuit powder, and the rank, revolting water they had to drink. His description of this part of the voyage is economical, as though perhaps it had been more horrible than he cared to recall, and he ends his chapter on the crossing of the Pacific with the following remark: "If our Lord and the Virgin Mother had not aided us . . . we had died in this very great sea. And I believe that nevermore will any man undertake to make such a voyage." In this, however, he was mistaken. Magellan was followed into the Pacific by a series of navigators from several European nations. Drawn both by the known wealth of the Indies and by the tantalizing prospect of the unknown, they embarked on an ocean about which they knew almost nothing. But each one who returned brought back new information, and little by little, over the course of the next few centuries, a picture of the Pacific began to emerge.

THE PACIFIC WAS so large, and its exploration so difficult, that it took Europeans nearly three hundred years to complete it, and during this period the contact between islanders and outsiders was random and sporadic. Nevertheless, the accounts of these early explorers—our first eyewitnesses—have a unique value. Privileged observers, they see Polynesia at the moment of contact with the outside world, and they can tell us things that are hard to discover in any other way.

Take, for example, the size of Polynesian populations. This has been an enduringly difficult number to pin down, in part because one of the things outsiders brought to the Pacific was disease. Epidemics—of smallpox, influenza, measles, scarlet fever, dysentery—affected virtually every island group and dramatically increased Polynesian mortality. So, even before any kind of official census could be taken, many island populations were already in decline. But we can look to the early eyewitnesses for a sense of how densely populated the islands were before any of this had happened. Their estimates are hardly scientific, and scholars continue to debate their validity, but they are a key piece of evidence nonetheless.

We can see other things, too, through the eyes of the early explorers. It is helpful, for example, to learn what animals they found on different islands. Polynesians brought four main animals with them into the remote Pacific: the pig, the dog, the chicken, and the rat. These animals, sometimes referred to as "commensals" because they exist in a symbiotic relationship with people, are an interesting proxy for human movement in the Pacific. Since they were unable to travel from island to island on their own, their presence tells you something about where the people who must have transported them went.

Not all of these animals made it to all of the islands. There were only rats and chickens on Easter Island when Europeans arrived (no pigs or dogs), and only rats and dogs (no pigs or chickens) in New Zealand. In the Marquesas, they had pigs, chickens, and rats, but there is no early record of dogs. And then there are the islands on which Europeans puzzlingly found dogs but no people. On some islands, the animals may have died out (this appears to have been the case with the Marquesan dog, which turns up in archaeological digs); in other cases, they may never have arrived. Either way, their absence suggests something about the difficulty of successfully transporting animals about the Pacific. It may also tell us something about the frequency of prehistoric voyaging, because if you were missing both chickens and pigs and you had the chance to get them from another island, wouldn't you do it?

Of course, there were lots of things the early explorers did *not* see, and many of their accounts are maddeningly superficial. Early visitors to the Marquesas saw none of the monumental architecture and sculpture that links that archipelago to both Tahiti and Easter Island. Early visitors to Easter Island reported the presence of "stone giants" but were confusing on the question of how easy it was to grow food. And the first European visitors to New Zealand saw nothing, being too scared of the Māori to go ashore.

Much has been made in histories of the Pacific about the problem of observer bias. Early European explorers saw the world through lenses that affected how they interpreted what they found. The Catholic Spanish and Portuguese of the sixteenth century were deeply concerned with the islanders' heathenism; the mercantile Dutch, in the seventeenth century, were preoccupied by what they had to trade; the French, coming along in the eighteenth century, were most interested in their social relations and the idea of what constituted a "state of nature." Still, the project on which these explorers were embarked was, very broadly speaking, an empirical one; their primary task was to discover what was out there and report back about what they had seen. Naturally, there were other agendas: territorial expansion, political advantage, conquest, commerce. But on a quite fundamental level, the project was one of observation and reportage, and, for the most part, they got better at it as the centuries wore on.

There was, however, one really big mistake that all the early European explorers in the Pacific made, one that blinded them to the true character of the region for ages. It was essentially a geographical error, and the best way to understand it is by looking at early European maps.

THE FIRST EUROPEAN maps of the world, the so-called Ptolemaic maps of the fifteenth century, do not even include Oceania, or what Cook would later call "the fourth part" of the globe. Their focus is on the known, inhabited regions of the world, which means, at this stage of history, that there is nothing west of Europe, east of Asia, or south of the Tropic of Capricorn. This all changed with the discovery of the Americas, and maps of the sixteenth century show a world that is already quite recognizable. The outlines of Europe, Asia, and Africa all look surprisingly correct, and even the New World, though distorted, bears a better-than-passing resemblance to North and South America as we know them today.

The Pacific in this period is still something of a cipher. Virtually all the major archipelagoes are missing, California is sometimes depicted as an island, and the continent of Australia is often drawn as though it were a peninsula of something else. The large island of New Guinea is frequently represented at twice its real size, and the Solomon Islands, discovered in 1568 and then lost for almost exactly two hundred years, are not only grossly exaggerated but seemingly untethered. On some maps they are located in the western Pacific, where they belong, but on others they have floated right out into the middle of the ocean, a clear reflection of the fact that for centuries no one had the foggiest idea where they actually were.

But the most remarkable feature of maps from this period is the presence of an enormous landmass, greater than all North America, Europe, and Asia combined, wrapped around the southern pole. This continent, known as Terra Australis Incognita, or "the Unknown Southland," occupies nearly a quarter of the globe. It is as if Antarctica included both Tierra del Fuego and Australia, stretched almost to the Cape of Good Hope, and reached so far into the Indian and Pacific Oceans that it entered the Tropic of Capricorn.

Terra Australis Incognita was one of the great follies of European geography, an idea that made sense in the abstract but for which there was never any actual proof. It was based on a bit of Ptolemaic logic handed down from the ancient Greeks, which held that there must be an equal weight of continental matter in the Northern and Southern Hemispheres, or else the world would topple over and, as the great mapmaker Gerardus Mercator envisioned it, "fall to destruction among the stars." This idea of global symmetry was inherently appealing, but it also made intuitive sense to Europeans, who, coming from a hemisphere crowded with land, found it difficult to imagine that the southern reaches of the planet might be as empty as they really are.

Like many imaginary places, Terra Australis Incognita—or, as it was sometimes more optimistically known, Terra Australis Nondum Cognita, "the Southland *Not Yet* Known"—represented not just what Europeans thought ought to exist in the Pacific but what they wanted to find. It was conflated with a whole range of utopian fantasies: lands of milk and honey, El Dorados, terrestrial paradises. Almost from the beginning, it was linked with the land of Ophir, the source of the biblical King Solomon's wealth, which explains why there are Solomon Islands in the neighborhood of New Guinea. Other rumors connected it with the mythical lands of Beach, Lucach, and Maletur, said to have been discovered by Marco Polo, and with the fabled islands of the Tupac Inca Yupanqui, from which he was said to have brought back slaves, gold, silver, and a copper throne.

For nearly three hundred years, the idea of Terra Australis Incognita drove European exploration in the Pacific, shaping the itineraries and experiences of voyagers, who were convinced that if they just kept looking, they would find a continent somewhere in the southern Pacific Ocean. Of course, there is a continent there—Antarctica—but it is not the kind of continent that Europeans had in mind. They were hoping for something bigger and more temperate, greener and more lush, richer and more hospitable, inhabited by people with fine goods for trade. They were dreaming of another Indies, or, failing that, another New World. But despite the "green drift" reported at 51 degrees south by the Dutch explorer Jacob Le Maire, and the birds he claimed to have seen in the roaring forties, and the mountainous country resembling Norway reported at 64 degrees south by Theodore Gerrards, despite the buccaneer Edward Davis's rumors, and Pedro Fernández de Quirós's claim of a country "as great as all *Europe & Asia*," no continent resembling Terra Australis Incognita ever appeared.

What European navigators found in the Pacific instead was water—vast, unbroken stretches of water extending in every direction as far as the eye could see. For days on end, for weeks, sometimes for months, they sailed on the great circle of the ocean with nothing above them but the vault of the sky and nothing between them and the horizon but "the sea with its labouring waves for ever rising, sinking, and vanishing to rise again." No distant smudges, no piles of clouds, no sea wrack, sometimes not even any birds. And then, just when they had begun to think they might sail onward to the end of eternity, an island would rise up over the rim of the world.

# FIRST CONTACT

## *Mendaña in the Marquesas*

*Breadfruit, after a drawing by Sydney Parkinson, in John Hawkesworth,*
An Account of the Voyages *(London, 1773).*
DEPARTMENT OF RARE BOOKS AND SPECIAL COLLECTIONS,
PRINCETON UNIVERSITY LIBRARY.

**IF WE SET** aside Magellan's two little atolls, both of which were uninhabited at the time, the first Polynesian island to be sighted by
any European was in the Marquesas. This is a group of islands just
south of the equator and about four thousand miles west of Peru, a
location that puts them at the eastern edge of the Polynesian Triangle, in a comparatively empty region of the sea. To the west and
south they have neighbors within a few hundred miles, but you
could sail north or east from the Marquesas along a 180-degree arc
and not meet with anything at all for thousands of miles.

The islands of Polynesia come in different varieties, and the

Marquesas are what are known as "high islands." What this means
to a layperson is that they are mountainous, rising in some cases
thousands of feet from the sea; what it means to a geologist is that
they are volcanic in origin. Some high islands occur in arcs, in places
where one tectonic plate plunges underneath another. But those of
the mid-Pacific are thought to be formed by hot spots, plumes of
molten rock rising directly from the earth's mantle. These islands
typically occur in chains, grouped along a northwest–southeast
axis, with the oldest at the northwest end and the youngest at the
southeast, a pattern explained by the northwesterly movement of
the Pacific plate. The idea is that over the course of millions of
years, islands are formed and carried away as the slab of crust on
which they are sitting drifts, while new islands rise out of the ocean
behind them. The textbook case is the Hawaiian archipelago: the
Big Island of Hawai'i, with its active volcanoes, lies at the southeastern end of a chain of islands that get progressively older and
smaller as they trail away to the northwest, ending in a string of
underwater seamounts. Meanwhile, southeast of the Big Island, a
new volcano is emerging, which will crest the sea sometime in the
next 100,000 years.

The landscape of a high island has a sort of yin and yang about
it. Composed almost entirely of basalt, high islands erode in quite
spectacular ways, exposing great ribs and ramparts and pinna-
cles of rock. On their windward sides, where the mountains wring
moisture from the passing air, they are lush and verdant, while on
their leeward sides, in the rain shadow of these same mountains,
they can be perfectly parched. But perhaps the greatest contrast
is between the dark, heavy loom of the mountains and the bright,
open aspect of the sea. Out from under the shadow of the peaks,
the tangle of trees and vines in the uplands gives way to an air-
ier landscape of grasses, coconut palms, and whispering casuarina.
The ridges flatten to a coastal plain; the mountain cataracts slow
to quiet rivers. At the tide line, the rocks and pools give way, here
and there, to bright crescents of sand. The sea stretches out into the

distance, broken only by a line of white breakers where the reef divides the bright turquoise of the lagoon from the darker water of the open ocean.

In some respects, the Marquesas are typical high islands, with their towering rock buttresses and fantastic spires, their deeply eroded clefts and fertile valleys. But in others they are quite unlike the Polynesian islands pictured in tourist brochures. Lying in proximity to the Humboldt Current, which carries cold water up the South American coast, the Marquesas have never developed a system of coral reefs. They have no lagoons, few sheltered bays, and only a handful of beaches. Their ruggedness extends all the way to the coast, and their shores are largely grim and perpendicular.

The other thing missing in the Marquesas is the coastal plain. This is the part of a high island on which it is easiest and most natural to live. As anyone who has been to the islands of Hawai'i knows, the standard way of navigating a high island is to travel around the coast. And it is easy to see how important this part of the island's topography is—how it enables movement and communication, provides room for gardens, plantations, and housing; how even now the land between the ocean and the mountains is where the human population lives. In the Marquesas, however, there is none of this; the only habitable land lies in the valleys that radiate out from the island's center, enclosed and cut off from one another by the mountains' great arms.

To many Europeans, the Marquesas have seemed indescribably romantic. With their peaks shrouded in mist, their folds buried in greenery, their flanks rising dramatically from the sea, they have a brooding prehistoric beauty. Visiting in 1888, the writer Robert Louis Stevenson found them at once magnificent and forbidding, with their great dark ridges and their towering crags. "At all hours of the day," he wrote, "they strike the eye with some new beauty, and the mind with the same menacing gloom."

It is tempting to imagine that the first Polynesians might have had similarly mixed impressions when they arrived. The discovery of any high island in the Pacific must have been a triumph: here was land, water, safety, sources of food. But archaeological sites in the Marquesas reveal a surprising variety of types of fishhooks from the very earliest settlement period, suggesting, perhaps, a surge of experiment and innovation prompted by the realization that fishing techniques brought from islands with more coral would not work in the deep, rough waters of the Marquesan coast. Still, the animals that were imported thrived (except for, maybe, the dog), the breadfruit trees grew, and the people prospered—so much so that by the time the first Europeans arrived, the Marquesas were "thickly inhabited" by a population that came out to meet the strangers in droves.

THE MARQUESAS WERE discovered in 1595 by the Spaniard Álvaro de Mendaña, who was en route with a shipload of colonists to the Solomon Islands. We say that Mendaña "discovered" the Marquesas, but of course this is not, strictly speaking, true. Indeed, the claim that any European explorer discovered anything in the Pacific—least of all the islands of Polynesia—is obviously problematic. As the Frenchman who later claimed the Marquesas for King Louis XV observed, it is hard to see how anyone could possess an island that is already possessed by the people who live there. And what is true for possession is even more true for discovery: In what sense can a land that is already inhabited be discovered? But what the word "discovered" means in the context of eighteenth-century Frenchmen or sixteenth-century Spaniards is not "discovered for the first time in human history" but something much more like "made known to people outside the region for the first time."

This was Mendaña's second voyage across the Pacific. Nearly thirty years earlier, he had led another expedition in search of Terra Australis Incognita, managing to reach the Solomon Islands before returning, in some disarray, to Peru. Despite the hardships of the journey, cyclones, scurvy, insubordination, shortages of food and water—at one point the daily ration consisted of "half a pint of water, and half of that was crushed cockroaches"—Mendaña was determined to try again. For twenty-six years he pestered the Spanish crown, and in 1595 they finally gave in.

The second expedition was, if possible, even more calamitous than the first. Confused and disorderly from the start, it was plagued by violence and dissension. Mendaña was on a zealot's mission to bring the benighted heathen to God; his wife, an unlovable virago, caused trouble wherever she went; many of his soldiers were self-interested and cruel. Neither the commander nor any of his subordinates seem to have understood just how far away their destination was, despite—at least in Mendaña's case—having been there before. In fact, they never did arrive. The colony, established instead on the island of Santa Cruz, was a disaster, with robberies, murders, ambushes, even a couple of beheadings. Mendaña, ill, broken, and "sunk in a religious stupor," contracted a fever and died like something out of *Aguirre, the Wrath of God*. The rest of the expedition disbanded and sailed for the Philippines.

We have the story from Mendaña's pilot, Pedro Fernández de Quirós, who recorded that just five weeks after setting out from the coast of South America, they sighted their first body of land. Believing this to be the island he was seeking, Mendaña ordered his crew to their knees to chant the *Te Deum laudamus*, giving thanks to God for a voyage so swift and untroubled. This, of course, was ridiculous; the Solomons were still four thousand miles away, at a minimum another five weeks' sailing. But it does illustrate just how poorly these early European navigators understood the size of the Pacific and how easily misled they could be. Eventually, Mendaña realized his mistake and after some consideration concluded that this was, in fact, an entirely new place.

The island, which was known to its inhabitants as Fatu Hiva, was the southernmost of the Marquesas, and as the Spanish approached, a fleet of about seventy canoes pulled out from shore. Quirós noted that these vessels were fitted with outriggers, a novelty he carefully described as a kind of wooden structure attached to the hull that "pressed" on the water to keep the canoe from cap-sizing. This was something many Europeans had not seen, but the development of the outrigger, which can be traced back as far as the second millennium B.C. in the islands of Southeast Asia, was the key innovation that made it possible for long, narrow, compara-tively shallow vessels (i.e., canoes) to sail safely on the open ocean.

Each of the Marquesan canoes carried between three and ten people, and many more islanders were swimming and hanging on to the sides—altogether, thought Quirós, perhaps four hundred souls. They came, he wrote, "with much speed and fury," paddling their canoes and pointing to the land and shouting something that sounded like "*atalut.*" The anthropologist Robert C. Suggs, who did fieldwork in the Marquesas in the 1950s, thinks they were telling Mendaña to bring his ships closer inshore—"a friendly bit of ad-vice," as he puts it, "from one group of navigators to another." Or maybe it was a strategy to get them to a place where they could be more effectively contained.

Quirós wrote that the islanders showed few signs of nervousness, paddling right up to the Spanish ships and offering coconuts, plan-tains, some kind of food rolled up in leaves (probably fermented breadfruit paste), and large joints of bamboo filled with water. "They looked at the ships, the people, and the women who had come out of the galley to see them . . . and laughed at the sight." One of the men was persuaded to come aboard, and Mendaña dressed him in a shirt and hat, which greatly amused the others, who laughed and called out to their friends. After this, about forty more islanders clambered aboard and began to walk about the ship "with great boldness, taking hold of whatever was near them, and many of them tried the arms of the soldiers, touched them in several parts with their fingers, looked at their beards and faces." They appeared confused by the Europeans' clothing until some of the soldiers let down their stockings and tucked up their sleeves to show the color of their skin, after which, Quirós wrote, they "quieted down, and were much pleased."

Mendaña and some of his officers handed out shirts and hats and trinkets, which the Marquesans took and slung round their necks. They continued to sing and call out, and as their confidence increased, so did their boisterousness. This, in turn, annoyed the Spanish, who began gesturing for them to leave, but the islanders had no intention of leaving. Instead they grew bolder, picking up whatever they saw on deck, even using their bamboo knives to cut slices from a slab of the crew's bacon. Finally, Mendaña ordered a gun to be fired, at which the islanders all leapt into the sea—all except one, a young man who remained clinging to the gunwale, refusing, either out of obstinance or terror, to let go until one of the Spaniards cut him with a sword.

At this, the tenor of the encounter changed. An old man with a long beard stood up in his canoe and cried out, casting fierce glances in the direction of the ships. Others sounded their shell trumpets and beat with their paddles on the sides of their canoes. Some picked up their spears and shook them at the Spaniards, or fitted their slings with stones and began hurling them at the ship. The Spaniards aimed their arquebuses at the islanders, but the powder was damp and would not light. "It was a sight to behold," wrote Quirós, "how the natives came on with noise and shouts." At last, the Spanish soldiers managed to fire their guns, hitting a dozen or so of the islanders, including the old man, who was shot through the forehead and killed. When they saw this, the islanders immediately turned and fled back to shore. A little while later, a single canoe carrying three men returned to the ships. One man held out a green branch and addressed the Spaniards at some length; to Quirós he seemed to be seeking peace. The Spanish made no response, and after a little while the islanders departed, leaving some coconuts behind.

**THE ENCOUNTERS BETWEEN** the Marquesans and Mendaña's people were filled with confusion, and many "evil things," wrote Quirós, happened that "might have been avoided if there had been someone to make us understand each other." In this, it was like many early encounters between Europeans and Polynesians: everything that happened made sense to someone, but much of it was baffling, offensive, or even deadly to those on the other side.

In one incident, four "very daring" Marquesans made off with one of the ships' dogs; in another, a Spanish soldier fired into a crowd of canoes, aiming at and killing a man with a small child. On shore, Mendaña ordered a Catholic mass to be held, at which the islanders knelt in imitation of the strangers. Two Marquesans were taught to make the sign of the cross and to say "Jesus, Maria"; maize was sown in the hope that it might take. Mendaña's wife, Doña Isabel, tried to cut a few locks from the head of a woman with especially beautiful hair but was forced to desist when the woman objected—the head, being *tapu*, should not have been touched, as hair was known to be useful for sorcery.

Three islanders were shot and their bodies hung up so that the Marquesans "might know what the Spaniards could do." Mendaña envisioned establishing a colony, leaving behind thirty men along with some of their wives. But the soldiers adamantly refused this mission. Perhaps they understood, no doubt correctly, that it would have been more than their lives were worth, for by the time the Spanish finally departed, they had killed more than two hundred people, many, according to Quirós, for no reason at all.

Quirós was distressed by the cruel and wanton behavior of Mendaña's men. In the islanders, on the other hand, he found much to admire. Indeed, it is through Quirós's eyes that we get our first glimpse of a people who would come to epitomize for many Europeans the pinnacle of human beauty. One later visitor described the Marquesans as "exquisite beyond description" and the "most beautiful people" he had ever seen. Even Cook, a man never given to exaggeration, called them "as fine a race of people as any in this Sea or perhaps any whatever."

The islanders, wrote Quirós, were graceful and well formed, with good legs, long fingers, and beautiful eyes and teeth. Their skin was clear and "almost white," and they wore their hair long and loose "like that of women." Many were naked when he first saw them—they were swimming at the time—and their faces and bodies were decorated with what Quirós at first took to be a kind of blue paint. This, of course, was tattooing, a practice common across Polynesia—the English word "tattoo" is derived from the Polynesian *tatau*—but carried to the peak of perfection in the Marquesas, where every inch of the body, including the eyelids, tongue, palms of the hands, even the insides of the nostrils, might be inscribed. Quirós found the Marquesan women, with their fine eyes, small waists, and beautiful hands, even more lovely "than the ladies of Lima, who are famed for their beauty," and characterized the men as tall, handsome, and strong. Some were so large that they made the Spaniards look diminutive by comparison, and one made a great impression on the visitors by lifting a calf up by the ear.

Ethnographically speaking—remembering that this is the earliest recorded description of any Polynesian society that we have—Quirós's account is slim but interesting. The Marquesans, he wrote, had pigs and chickens ("fowls of Castille"), as well as plantains, coconuts, calabashes, nuts, and something the Europeans had never seen, which they described as a green fruit about the size of a boy's head. This was breadfruit, a plant that would enter Pacific legend two centuries later as the cargo carried by Captain William Bligh of the *Bounty* when his crew mutinied off the island of Tofua. (Bligh was carrying the breadfruit seedlings to the West Indies, where, it was envisioned, they would provide an economical means of feeding African slaves.) They lived in large communal houses with platforms and terraces of neatly fitted stone and worshipped what the Spanish referred to as an "oracle," an enclosure containing carved wooden figures to whom they made offerings of food. Their tools were made of stone and shell; their primary weapons were spears and slings. Their most significant manufactures were canoes, which they made in a variety of sizes: small ones with outriggers for three to ten paddlers, and large ones, "very long and well-made," with room for thirty or more. Of the latter wrote Quirós, "They gave us to understand, when they were asked, that they went in these large canoes to other lands."

What lands these might have been remained a mystery, however. In one curious incident, the Marquesans, seeing a black man on one of the Spanish ships, gestured toward the south, making signs "to say that in that direction there were men like him, and that they went there to fight, and that the others had arrows." This is a baffling remark, and quite typical of the sort of misdirection that is rampant in these early accounts. While it might describe any number of people in the islands far to the west, the bow was never used as a weapon in Polynesia. The only places south of the Marquesas are the Tuamotu Archipelago, and, even farther away, Easter Island—all of whose inhabitants are culturally and physically quite similar to Marquesans. They might well have been perceived as enemies, but they were not archers and they were not black.

But while we have no idea which islands Quirós was referring to, we do know that there were "other islands" in the Marquesans' conceptual universe. Later visitors heard tell of "islands which are supposed by the natives to exist, and which are entirely unknown to us." It was also reported that in times of drought, "canoes went out in search of other islands," which may help explain why, when Cook reached the Marquesas in 1775, the islanders wondered whether he had come from "some country where provisions had failed."

MENDAÑA REMAINED IN the Marquesas for about two weeks, in the course of which he identified and named the four southernmost islands in the archipelago. (A second cluster of islands lay undiscovered to the north.) He called them, after his own fashion, Santa Magdalena, San Pedro, La Dominica, and Santa Cristina, names that have all long been replaced by the original Polynesian names: Fatu Hiva, Motane, Hiva Oa, and Tahuata. The archipelago as a whole he named in honor of his patron, Don García Hurtado de

Mendoza, Marquis of Cañete and viceroy of Peru, and in all the years since 1595 the Marquesas have never been known as anything else. Except, of course, among the islanders themselves, who know their islands collectively as Te Fenua, meaning "the Land," and themselves, the inhabitants of Te Fenua, as Te Enata, meaning simply "the People."

When Mendaña's ships finally sailed away, the Marquesas were lost again to the European world for nearly two hundred years. They had been none too securely plotted to begin with, and their location was further suppressed by the Spanish in order to forestall competition in the search for Terra Australis Incognita. Privately, if the Spanish concluded anything, it was that the Marquesas, with their large, vigorous population of beautiful people, their pigs, their chickens, and their great canoes, *proved* the existence of a southern continent. Lacking "instruments of navigation and vessels of bur- then," Quirós concluded, the inhabitants of these islands could not possibly have made long-distance ocean crossings. This meant that somewhere in the vicinity there must be "other islands which lye in a chain, or a continent running along," since there was no other place "whereby they who inhabit those islands could have entered them, unless by a miracle." Thus the irony of first contact between Polynesia and Europe: that it served to reinforce a hallucinatory belief in the existence of an imaginary continent while obscuring the much more intriguing reality of the Marquesans themselves.

# BARELY AN ISLAND AT ALL

## *Atolls of the Tuamotus*

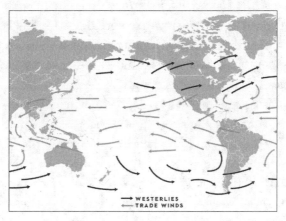

*Winds in the Pacific, based on "Map of the prevailing winds on earth,"*
*in* Het handboek voor de zeiler *by H. C. Herreshoff,*
*adapted by Rachel Ahearn.*
WIKIMEDIA COMMONS.

**MENDAÑA DISCOVERED THE** Marquesas because he sailed west in roughly the right latitude from the port of Paita, in the Spanish viceroyalty of Peru. But those who came after set sail from different ports and followed different routes and, thus, discovered different sets of islands. This was not so much a matter of intention: European explorers in the sixteenth and seventeenth and even eighteenth centuries did not have the freedom to go wherever they wished. On the contrary, for some centuries virtually all their discoveries were determined by the distinctive pattern of the winds and currents in the Pacific Ocean and by the limited points of entry into the region from other parts of the world.

The weather in the Pacific is dominated by two great circles of wind, or gyres, one of which turns clockwise in the Northern Hemisphere, while the other turns counterclockwise in the Southern. Across wide bands from roughly 30 to 60 degrees in both the Northern and Southern Hemispheres, the winds are predominantly westerly, that is, they blow from west to east. In the north, these winds sweep across the continents of Europe, Asia, and North America. But in the Southern Hemisphere, where there are few landmasses to impede them, they can reach fantastic speeds—hence the popular names for the far southern latitudes: the "roaring forties," "furious fifties," and "screaming sixties."

From the equator to about 30 degrees north and south—roughly across the Tropics of Capricorn and Cancer—the winds predominantly blow the opposite way. These are known as the trade winds, a reliable pattern of strong, steady easterlies with a northeasterly slant in the Northern Hemisphere and a southeasterly slant in the Southern. In between, in the vicinity of the equator itself, is an area known as the Intertropical Convergence Zone, or ITCZ, a region of light and variable winds and frequent thunderstorms more commonly known as the Doldrums and greatly feared by early European navigators for its deadly combination of stultifying heat and protracted calms. Anyone who has flown across the equator in the Pacific—say, from Los Angeles to Sydney—may remember a bumpy patch about halfway through the flight; that was the ITCZ.

The major ocean currents in the Pacific follow basically the same pattern, flowing west along the equator and peeling apart at the ocean's edge, turning north in the Northern Hemisphere and south in the Southern and circling back around in two great cells. There is, however, also something called the Equatorial Countercurrent, which flows eastward along the equator in between the main westward-flowing northern and southern currents—just to make things confusing.

What all this meant for ships under sail was that near the equator things could be quite chaotic, and often there would be no wind at all. In the tropics, the winds and currents would, generally speaking, speed a ship on its way west, permit it to sail on a north–south axis, and effectively prevent it from sailing east the vast majority of the time. Thus, if one wanted to proceed eastward across the Pacific, the only sure way to do it was to travel in higher, colder latitudes (that is, farther north or south), where sailors typically encountered the opposite problem: the inability to make any westing at all.

The other major constraint on early Pacific navigation for Europeans was the problem of entry points. In the days before the man-made shortcuts of Panama and Suez, European ships bound for the Pacific were forced to sail to the very bottom of the world and around either Africa or South America in order to reach the Pacific Ocean. The eastern route, by way of Africa, was by far the longest; not only did one have to sail all the way south and around the Cape of Good Hope, but then there was still the whole Indian Ocean to cross, and beyond that the mysterious impediment of Australia. The western route, by way of South America, was shorter and therefore more attractive, but it also presented the greatest danger, in the form of a passage around the dreaded Cape Horn. Here, where the long tail of South America reaches almost to the Antarctic ice, lies one of the most fearsome stretches of ocean in the entire world. It combines furious winds, enormous waves, freezing temperatures, and a shelving, ironbound coast to produce what can only be described as a navigator's nightmare: a maelstrom of wind, rain, sleet, snow, hail, fog, and some of the world's shortest and steepest seas.

Stories of dreadful passages around Cape Horn are legion. Leading a squadron of eight ships around the Horn in the early 1740s, Britain's Commodore George Anson was battered for a biblical forty days and forty nights by a succession of hurricanes so wild they reduced his crew to gibbering terror. Two of the squadron's ships went missing, effectively blown away by the wind, and Anson was ultimately forced to resort to the hideous expediency of "manning the foreshrouds," that is, sending men into the rigging to act as human sails, the wind being too ferocious to permit the carrying of any actual canvas. Needless to say, at least one seaman was blown from his perch. A strong swimmer, he survived for a while in the icy water, but such was the intensity of the storm that his shipmates were forced to watch helplessly as he was swept away by the mountainous seas.

Forty-odd years later, Captain Bligh of the *Bounty* encountered a similar series of storms as he tried to round the Horn on his way to Tahiti, on the voyage that would famously end in mutiny. For a month he battled winds that boxed the compass and was drenched by seas that broke over his ship. At the end of a titanic struggle against "this tempestuous ocean," he finally surrendered. Turning east, he got the wind behind him and bore away for Africa and the Cape of Good Hope, a decision that would add ten thousand miles to his voyage.

There was an alternative to rounding the Horn, and that was to pass through the Strait of Magellan, the route pioneered in 1520 and the earliest known pathway into the Pacific from the Atlantic side. But this narrow, twisting passageway of some 350 miles, which separates the archipelago of Tierra del Fuego from mainland South America, presents navigational challenges of its own. Here the problem is not so much exposure as the complicated nature of the passage itself and unpredictable winds and currents. Magellan himself had been unusually fortunate, making the passage in only thirty-eight days, but the British navigator Samuel Wallis spent more than four months trying to clear the strait in 1767, giving him an effective sailing rate of less than three miles a day.

The Strait of Magellan opens out into the Pacific between 52 and 53 degrees south latitude. Cape Horn lies at approximately 56 degrees south, and navigators who decided to sail around it were routinely obliged to sail into the high fifties; Cook reached as far as 60 degrees south on his first passage round the Horn. But, either way, once they had made it into the Pacific, navigators found it almost impossible to advance. They could make no headway in these latitudes against the ferocious westerly winds. Southward lay the ice and snow—they were nearly to the Antarctic Circle—east was the coast of South America, and the only direction open to them was north.

It is this particular set of circumstances—winds, distances, continental obstacles, and sailing capacity—that explains a curious fact about early European encounters in the Pacific, which is that, even with the whole, wide ocean before them, almost all the early navigators followed variants of the same route. With one or two exceptions, they crossed the South Pacific on a long northwesterly diagonal, or, more properly, a dogleg, sailing north and then turning west once they picked up the trades. They did this not because they thought it was the path most likely to yield important discoveries—as the historian J. C. Beaglehole drily observed, "sailing on some variant of the great north-west line, of necessity a ship made through a vast deal of empty ocean"—but because it was the path dictated by the currents and the winds. As a consequence, many important islands that lie off this route, like Hawai'i, were not encountered for centuries, while others, some of them minuscule, like the tiny atoll of Puka Puka in the Tuamotu Archipelago, were discovered over and over again.

THE TUAMOTUS, ALSO known as the Low or Dangerous Archipelago, feature in almost every early European account of the Pacific, for the simple reason that they lie directly across most variants of the great northwest line. A screen of some seventy-eight "low islands," or atolls, the Tuamotus stretch for eight hundred miles along a northwest–southeast axis about halfway between the Marquesas and Tahiti. Most of these atolls are comparatively small, on average perhaps ten to twenty miles wide, but their key feature, at least from a navigator's point of view, is their height. None of these islands reach an elevation of more than twenty feet; most are barely twelve feet above the tide line at their highest point. They are, as

Stevenson put it, "as flat as a plate upon the sea." What this means for sailors is that they are invisible until one is all but upon them, and later navigators, who knew more about what they were getting into, tended to avoid this maze of reefs and islands that was also sometimes known as the Labyrinth.

From the air, the Tuamotus are a dazzling sight: bright circlets of green and white floating like diadems in a sapphire sea. But, as the early explorers quickly discovered, up close there is not much to an atoll. Barely an island at all, it is really a necklace of islets, or *motu*, to use the Polynesian word, strung along a circle of reef. The *motu* are composed entirely of coral: sand, cobbles, coral blocks, and a kind of conglomerate known as beachrock. Verdant from a distance, they in fact have only the thinnest layer of topsoil and can support just a few salt-tolerant species of shrubs and trees. There are no natural sources of fresh water apart from rain, though there is an interesting phenomenon known as a Ghyben-Herzberg lens. This is a layer of fresh water which floats on top of the seawater that infiltrates the porous coral rock. Under the right conditions—the island cannot be too small, it cannot be in a state of drought, the well cannot be dug too deep—it is possible to extract fresh water from a pit dug into the sand, as a group of seventeenth-century Dutch sailors accidentally discovered on an atoll they named Waterlandt.

It was Charles Darwin who first articulated the theory of how coral atolls are formed. On his way across the Pacific in the *Beagle*, Darwin sailed through the Tuamotu Archipelago, recording his first impression of an atoll as seen from the top of the ship's mast. "A long and brilliantly white beach," he wrote, "is capped by a margin of green vegetation; and the strip, looking either way, rapidly narrows away in the distance, and sinks beneath the horizon. From the mast-head a wide expanse of smooth water can be seen within the ring." It was already understood in Darwin's day that corals were creatures—"animalcules," as one writer put it—and that they could grow only in comparatively shallow water. And yet, here they were in the middle of the ocean, in a place where the water was so deep it could not be measured by any conventional means. (The Dutch named a second atoll Sonder Grondt, i.e., "Bottomless," because they could find no place to anchor.) The obvious question concerned their foundation, or, as Darwin put it, "On what have the reef-building corals based their great structures?"

One theory popular at the time was the idea that atolls grew up on the rims of submerged volcanic craters. There were good reasons for associating them with vulcanism—high islands and low islands are found in close proximity throughout the Pacific. But there were also problems with the crater idea: some large atolls exceed the size of any known volcanic craters; some small atolls exist in clusters that cannot easily be envisioned as craters; and many volcanic islands are closely surrounded by coral reefs, which, if the theory were correct, would make them volcanoes within volcanoes—an explanation that seems unlikely at best.

Darwin's notion, still the most widely accepted view, was that there *is* an association between atolls and volcanic islands, but that atolls begin life not on the rims of extinct craters but in the shallow waters of an island's shores. Like many of Darwin's ideas, his theory of coral atoll formation had the virtue of explaining not just how atolls are formed but how that process is linked to other kinds of coral formations, thus neatly accounting for all instances of what is essentially the same thing. He recognized that fringing reefs (on the shores of islands), barrier reefs (surrounding islands at some distance from the shore), and atolls (rings of coral without any island at all) are, in fact, a series of stages. The key to connecting them was the concept of subsidence—the idea that an island gradually sinks while the coral encircling it continues to grow. Thus, in the course of time, a fringing reef would become a barrier reef, and a barrier reef would eventually become an atoll.

AN ATOLL IS a very natural habitat for anything that swims or flies through the air. Atolls are home to more than a quarter of the world's marine fish species, a mind-boggling array of angelfish, clown fish, batfish, parrotfish, snappers, puffers, emperors, jacks, rays, wrasses, barracudas, and sharks. And that's without even mentioning all the other sea creatures—the turtles, lobsters, porpoises, squid, snails, clams, crabs, urchins, oysters, and the whole exotic understory of the corals themselves. Atolls are also an obvious haven for birds, both those that range over the ocean by day and return to the islands at night and those that migrate thousands of miles, summering in places like Alaska and wintering over in the tropics.

For terrestrial life, however, it is quite a different matter. A typical atoll in the Tuamotus might support thirty indigenous species of plants and trees—as compared with the more than four hundred native plant species that might be found on a high island like Tahiti, or the many thousands that grow on a large continental island like New Zealand—and, among land animals, only lizards and crabs. While there are places on an atoll where one might, for a moment, imagine oneself to be surrounded by land—places where one's line of sight is blocked by trees or shrubs—a few minutes' walk in any direction will quickly dispel the illusion. Strolling the length of even a largish *motu*, you eventually come to a place where you can see water on both sides. At such moments it becomes breathtakingly clear that the ground beneath your feet is not really *land* in the way that most people understand it, but rather the tip of an undersea world that has temporarily emerged from the ocean. The real action, the real landscape, is all of water: the great rollers that boom and crash on the reef, the rush and suck of the tide through the passes, the breathtaking hues of the lagoon.

And yet, when Europeans first reached the Pacific, they found virtually all the larger atolls inhabited. Even those that were clearly too small to support a permanent population often showed signs of human activity. On one tiny, uninhabited atoll, an early explorer found an abandoned canoe and piles of coconuts at the foot of a tree; on another there was the puzzling presence of unaccompanied dogs. Even the pit in which the Dutch sailors found water had almost certainly been dug by someone else. What all this appeared to suggest was that even the most insignificant and isolated specks of land were being visited by people who could come and go.

There are not many good early descriptions of these people. The Tuamotus offered almost none of the things that European sailors needed—namely, food, water, and safe ports—and their complex network of reefs was dangerous to ships. With so little to be gained and so much to be lost, Europeans tended not to linger, and the early eyewitness reports are correspondingly slight. What they did manage to observe about the inhabitants of the Tuamotus was this: they were tall and well proportioned (Quirós referred to them as "corpulent," presumably meaning something like "robust"); their hair, which they wore long and loose, was black; their skin was brown or reddish and, according to the Dutch explorer Le Maire, "all over pictured with snakes and dragons, and such like reptiles," an unusually vivid description of tattooing. Europeans, it is worth noting, had a famously difficult time identifying the color of Polynesian skin; a later Dutch navigator would describe the inhabitants of Easter Island as pale yellow where they were not painted a dark blue.

For food, the inhabitants of the low islands had coconuts, fish, shellfish, and other sea creatures; for animals, it is clear that at least they had dogs. Their knives, tools, and necklaces were made of shell (later investigators would also discover basalt adzes, which could only have been transported from a high island, there being no local sources of volcanic rock). Their principal weapons were spears, with which they armed themselves at the approach of strangers. Many Europeans who sailed past these islands reported seeing the inhabitants standing or running along the beach with their weapons in hand. Some interpreted their shouts and gestures as an invitation to land, others as an exhortation to depart, but, as "both sides were in the dark as to each other's mind," it was difficult to know for sure.

Later observers would describe the "roving migratory habits" of these atoll dwellers, noting that they wandered from place to place, "so that at times an island will appear to be thickly peopled, and at others scarcely an individual is to be found." Census taking proved almost impossible, because some portion of the population was always "away," hunting turtles or collecting birds' eggs or gathering coconuts or visiting in some other corner of the archipelago. All of which raises an interesting question: Since there are almost no trees on an atoll, and certainly none of the larger species that in other parts of the Pacific provided wood for keels and planks and masts, what did the inhabitants of the low islands do for canoes? It being inconceivable that they could ever have lived in this watery world without them.

We have an early description, from 1606, of a fleet of canoes that came out "from within the island," meaning presumably from across the lagoon, on the Tuamotuan atoll of Anaa. The vessels were described as something like a half galley—that is, a boat with both oars and masts—and were fitted with sails made of some kind of matting. Most had room for fourteen or fifteen men, though the largest carried as many as twenty-six. They were made, wrote the observer somewhat enigmatically, "not of one tree-trunk, but very subtly contrived."

There is a picture in A. C. Haddon and James Hornell's *Canoes of Oceania* that sheds some light on this remark. It shows a small canoe from the island of Nukutavake, in the southern Tuamotus, which was brought to England in the 1760s by Captain Samuel Wallis. Now held in the British Museum, it is described as "by far the oldest complete hull of a Polynesian canoe in existence." At just twelve feet long, it is not nearly big enough to carry fourteen or fifteen men and was probably a small fishing boat, to judge by the burn marks on its upper edge, which are thought to have been made by the friction of a running line.

The amazing thing about the Nukutavake canoe is the way it's constructed. It is composed of no fewer than forty-five irregularly shaped pieces of wood ingeniously stitched together with braided sennit, a kind of cordage made from the inner husk of a coconut.

Close up, it looks like nothing so much as a crazy quilt whose seams have been decoratively overstitched with yarn. It is difficult to believe that such neat and painstaking rows of sewing could be made with something as rough as rope; or that what they are holding together could be something as stiff as wooden planks; or that anyone would think of making something as solid and important as a boat using such a method. Everything about it suggests cleverness and thrift and also, plainly, necessity. You can even see where the boards have been patched with little plugs or circles of timber held in place with stitches radiating out like the rays of a sun, and at least one plank shows signs of having been repurposed from another vessel.

It was said, in the eighteenth and nineteenth centuries, that the inhabitants of the Tuamotus were the finest canoe builders in the eastern Pacific, and that when chiefs on the high island of Tahiti wanted to build a great canoe, "they had need of the help of men from the low islands." One eighteenth-century British commander described a double-hulled canoe that he saw in the Tuamotus as having hulls that were thirty feet long. The planks, which were sewn together, he wrote, were "exceedingly well wrought," and over every seam was a strip of tortoiseshell, "very artificially fastened, to keep out the weather." All Polynesians gave proper names to different parts of their canoes, including the thwarts, paddles, bailers, anchors, and steering oars. But in the Tuamotus it is said that even the individual boards were sometimes named, the old timbers serving as "reminders of the courage, endurance, and success" of those who had preceded them upon the sea.

Europeans greatly admired the craftsmanship of these vessels, but they also felt there was something a little startling about the idea of people putting to sea in boats that had been stitched together from scraps of wood. One early-eighteenth-century explorer recalled seeing a man some three miles out to sea in a craft so narrow it could accommodate only one person, sitting with his knees together. It was made, like the Nukutavake canoe, of "many small pieces of wood and held together by some plant," and was so light it could be carried by a single man. Watching the progress of this canoe on the ocean was something of a revelation. "It was for us wonderful," he wrote, "to see that one man alone dared to proceed in so frail a craft so far to sea, having nothing to help him but a paddle." It was the merest inkling that here was a people with a different relationship to the ocean—people who could make their home on an atoll, people who could sail out to sea in a stitched ship—but, having little time or inclination to ponder the matter, the recorder of this interesting little tidbit turned and sailed on.

# OUTER LIMITS

## *New Zealand and Easter Island*

*Murderers' Bay, New Zealand, 1642, from*
Abel Janszoon Tasman's Journal *(Amsterdam, 1898).*
DEPARTMENT OF RARE BOOKS AND SPECIAL COLLECTIONS,
PRINCETON UNIVERSITY LIBRARY.

**ALL THE ISLANDS** in the mid-Pacific are either high or low, volcanic or coralline. But down in the southwest corner, near the ocean's edge, there is a large and important group of islands with an entirely different geologic history. New Zealand is one of the anchoring points of the Polynesian Triangle and a key piece of the Polynesian puzzle, but it differs from other Polynesian islands in several ways. It lies much farther south, in latitudes comparable to the stretch of North America that extends from North Carolina to Maine. It is temperate, not tropical; it can be hot in summer, but in the winter, at least in the south, it snows. New Zealand is also vast by comparison, with plains, lakes, rivers, fjords, mountain ranges, and a land area more than eight times that of all the other islands of Polynesia combined.

The islands of New Zealand are also unique in Polynesia in that they are, geologically speaking, "continental." New Zealand is part of the ancient southern supercontinent of Gondwana, which once included all the Southern Hemispheric landmasses of Africa, South America, Antarctica, and Australia, as well as the Indian subcontinent. About a hundred million years ago, this supercontinent began to break up, and a piece of it drifted off into what is now the Pacific Ocean. Most of this fragment was submerged beneath the sea, but near the junction of the Australian and Pacific Plates, some of it was thrust up by tectonic forces. The result was the landmass we now know as New Zealand, or, to use its modern Polynesian name, Aotearoa. New Zealand still sits on this tectonic boundary, which is why it has earthquakes and active volcanoes.

Because it was part of old Gondwana and because it is insular and was isolated for tens of millions of years, New Zealand has a quirky evolutionary history. There seems to have been no mammalian stock from which to evolve on the Gondwanan fragment, and so, until the arrival of humans, there were no terrestrial mammals, nor were there any of the curious marsupials of nearby Australia— no wombats or koalas or kangaroos, no rodents or ruminants, no wild cats or dogs. The only mammals that could reach New Zealand were those that could swim (like seals) or fly (like bats), and even then there are questions about how the bats got there. Two of New Zealand's three bat species are apparently descended from a South American bat, which, it is imagined, must have been blown across the Pacific in a giant prehistoric storm.

Among New Zealand's indigenous plants and animals are a number of curious relics, including a truly enormous conifer and a lizard-like creature that is the world's only surviving representative of an order so ancient it predates many dinosaurs. But the really odd thing about New Zealand is what happened to the birds. In the absence of predators and competitors, birds evolved to fill all the major ecological niches, becoming the "ecological equivalent of giraffes, kangaroos, sheep, striped possums, long-beaked echidnas and tigers." Many of these birds were flightless, and some were huge. The largest species of moa—a now extinct flightless giant related to the ostrich, the emu, and the rhea—stood nearly twelve feet tall and weighed more than five hundred pounds. The moa was an herbivore, but there were also predators among these prehistoric birds, including a giant eagle with claws like a panther's. There were grass-eating parrots and flightless ducks and birds that grazed like sheep in alpine meadows, as well as a little wren-like bird that scampered about the underbrush like a mouse.

None of these creatures were seen by the first Europeans to reach New Zealand, for two very simple reasons. The first is that many of them were already extinct. Although known to have survived long enough to coexist with humans, all twelve species of moa, the Haast's eagle, two species of adzebills, and many others had vanished by the mid-seventeenth century, when Europeans arrived. The second is that, even if there had still been moas lumbering about the woods, the European discoverers of New Zealand would have missed them because they never actually set foot on shore.

AS WITH THE other islands of Polynesia, the European discovery of New Zealand was essentially a function of geography and winds. The vast majority of early European explorers entered the Pacific from the South American side. But there was another way in, from the west, and in 1642 a captain in the service of the Dutch East India Company sailed this route for the first time.

The Dutch East India Company, which was headquartered in Batavia (now the Indonesian capital of Jakarta), was the great mercantile engine of the seventeenth century, and all the major geographic discoveries in the Pacific during this period were made by Dutch captains in search of new markets and new goods for trade. One of these was a commander named Abel Janszoon Tasman, who, in 1642, set out with a pair of ships bound for the southern Pacific Ocean. Tasman followed what looks, on the face of it, like the most unlikely route imaginable. Departing from the island of Java, he

sailed west across the Indian Ocean to Mauritius, a small island
off the coast of Madagascar, which itself is a large island off the
coast of southeastern Africa. There, he turned south and continued
until he reached the band of powerful westerlies that would sweep
him back eastward, all the way across the Indian Ocean, until he
finally reached the Pacific. Tasman followed this lengthy and unin-
tuitive route—sailing nearly ten thousand miles to reach an ocean
that was less than twenty-five hundred miles from where he had
begun—because the winds and currents in the Indian Ocean oper-
ate the same way they do in the Pacific, circling counterclockwise
in a similar gyre.

The main obstacle between the Indian and Pacific Oceans is
the continent of Australia, and the earliest Dutch discoveries in
the seventeenth century were off Australia's west coast. But Tasman's route took him so far south that he missed the Australian
mainland altogether, and the first body of land he met with after
leaving Mauritius was the island, later named in his honor, of Tasmania. Continuing on to the east, he crossed what is now the Tasman Sea, and about a week later he sighted a *"groot hooch verheven
landt"*—"a large land, uplifted high." It can be difficult to tell how
large a body of land is from the sea—European explorers were constantly mistaking islands for continents—but this time it was unmistakable. The land before them was dark and rugged, with ranks
of serried mountains receding deep into an interior overhung with
clouds. A heavy sea beat upon the rocky coast, "rolling towards it
in huge billows and swells," offering no obvious place to go ashore.
So Tasman turned and followed the land as it stretched away to the
northeast.

For four days they sailed with the wind from the west, keeping
their distance for fear of being driven onto the rocks. From the
sea, the country looked dark and desolate. But at last, on the fourth
day, they came to a long, curving spit bending round to the east, en-
closing a large bay. Here they saw smoke rising in several places—a
sure sign that the country was inhabited. Tasman and his officers

decided that they would go ashore, and by sunset on the following day they had brought the ships to anchor in the bay. From there they could see fires burning on shore and several canoes, two of which came out to meet them in the gloom. When they had come within hailing distance, the islanders called out in "a rough loud voice," but the Dutch could not understand them. They had been equipped at Batavia with a vocabulary, almost surely the word list assembled twenty-five years earlier by the explorers Willem Schouten and Jacob Le Maire, but the language spoken by these people did not seem to match it. The islanders blew on something that sounded to the Dutch like a Moorish trumpet—no doubt a conch shell—and a pair of Dutch trumpeters responded in turn. Then, as darkness was falling, the parley ended, and the islanders paddled back to shore.

Early the next morning, a canoe came out to the ships. Once again, the islanders called out, and this time the Dutch made signs for them to come aboard, showing them white linen and knives. The men in the canoe could not be persuaded, however, and after a little while they returned to shore. Tasman held a second council, at which it was decided to bring the ships closer inshore, "since there was good anchoring-ground and these people (as it seems) are seeking friendship." But before the ink was even dry on this resolution, a fleet of seven canoes set out from shore. Two of these took up positions nearby, and when a small boat ferrying men from one of the Dutch ships to the other passed between them, they attacked it, ramming the boat, boarding it, stabbing and clubbing the men, and throwing the bodies overboard. The attack was fast, furious, and effective; three of the Dutch sailors were killed instantly, one was mortally wounded, and three more were eventually rescued from the sea. The sailors on board the ships fired their guns, but they were too far away or too late or just too inaccurate, and the islanders escaped to safety, taking the body of one of the Dutch sailors with them as they went.

Tasman was shocked by the audacity of this attack and by the steady increase in the number of canoes gathering in the bay—first four, then seven, then eleven, and finally twenty-two—and he ordered his men to set sail as quickly as they could. But the islanders were equally determined not to let their quarry escape, and they pursued them right across the bay, abandoning the chase only when a man standing in one of the leading canoes was shot. Tasman christened the place Murderers Bay and made no further attempts to land in New Zealand. He never grasped that the bay in which he had been attacked (now known as Golden Bay) lay at the opening of the large strait that separates the North and South Islands of New Zealand, or that the "continent" he had discovered was in fact two large islands. Thinking that he might have chanced upon some corner of Terra Australis Incognita, he named it Staten Landt and proposed that it might be connected to the Staten Landt named in 1616 by Schouten and Le Maire. This, however, was unlikely, as Schouten and Le Maire's Staten Landt was an island off the tip of South America, more than five thousand watery miles away.

TASMAN DID AT least get a look at the inhabitants of New Zealand, the people we know today as Māori. He described them as average in height "but rough in voice and bones," with a complexion that was something "between brown and yellow" and long black hair, which they wore tied up on the tops of their heads in the fashion of the Japanese. Their boats were made from two narrow canoes, "over which some planks or other seating was laid, Such that above water one can see through under the vessel." Each carried roughly a dozen men, who handled their craft "very cleverly."

Interestingly, these double-hulled vessels sound a lot like canoes observed by seventeenth-century Europeans in other parts of Polynesia, but by the time the next European reached New Zealand, more than a century later, they were few and far between. What later eighteenth- and nineteenth-century visitors to New Zealand commonly reported were the great *waka taua*: enormous single-hulled war canoes—up to a hundred feet long, with a breadth of five or six feet—which could carry as many as seventy or eighty men. Nowhere else in Polynesia were single-hulled vessels of such prodigious dimensions ever seen, for the simple reason that nowhere else in Polynesia did trees grow to this size. Carved, whenever possible, from a single trunk, they were designed as coastal and river vessels and were never intended for transoceanic travel.

This apparent evolution in canoe design is a salutary reminder that cultures are not static and that there is a logic to their transformations. If the Māori stopped making double-hulled ocean-going canoes, it must have been because they were no longer sailing across the ocean. But Tasman's evidence suggests that as late as the mid-seventeenth century, at least in the South Island, the inhabitants of New Zealand were still using vessels of a type that linked them to the rest of Polynesia and to the tradition of long-distance ocean travel.

Tasman departed New Zealand with little more than a dramatic tale about the "detestable deed" committed by its inhabitants and set his ships on a northeast course, which would bring him, in about two weeks' time, to the islands of Tonga. He was now entering a region of the Pacific with a much higher concentration of islands, a greater population density, and a complex set of relationships among contiguous archipelagoes. Tonga lies a few hundred miles from Samoa, at the western edge of the Polynesian Triangle. Together they constitute the western gateway to Polynesia; here are the oldest Polynesian languages, the longest settlement histories, the deepest Polynesian roots.

Tasman was not the first European to reach this region. The Dutch explorers Schouten and Le Maire had passed through the northern edge of the Tongan archipelago in 1616, stopping at a pair of islands where they traded for coconuts, pigs, bananas, yams, and fish and collected words for their vocabulary. Tasman, coming from the south, made landfall at the southern end of the archipelago, on the island of Tongatapu, where the people he met seemed friendly and eager to trade. He described them as brown-skinned, with long, thick hair, rather taller than average, and "painted Black from the middle to the thighs." They came out to the ships in large numbers, readily climbing aboard, and relations between the two groups were generally amicable. Tasman was glad of the opportunity to get fresh food and water, but he was careful to keep his men armed, since, as his recent experience in New Zealand had taught him, it is difficult to know "what sticks in the heart." The Tongans, however, seemed focused on trade, and much of Tasman's account is given over to detailing the terms: a hen for a nail or chain of beads; a small pig for a fathom of dungaree; ten to twelve coconuts for three to four nails or a double medium nail; two pigs for a knife with a silver band plus eight to nine nails; yams, coconuts, and bark cloth for a pair of trousers, a small mirror, and some beads.

Once again, Tasman tried to use the vocabulary collected by his Dutch predecessors. He reported that he asked specifically about water and pigs—while somewhat confusingly displaying a coconut and a hen—but that the islanders did not seem to understand him. Reading his account, one longs to be able to go back and observe these transactions. Was he using the right part of the vocabulary? How was he pronouncing the words? Did his gestures merely confuse the situation? The story is all the more tantalizing because parts of Schouten and Le Maire's word list had been collected just a few hundred miles away. For "hog" they had recorded the word "Pouacca," a quite respectable rendering of the common Polynesian word *puaka*, meaning "pig." For "water" they suggested "Waij." Adjusting for Dutch spelling and pronunciation, this gives something like the English "vie," which closely resembles a word for "water" in several Polynesian languages. It should have worked, but it didn't, and a connection that might have been made slipped through the cracks.

IT WAS LEFT to the last of the early Pacific explorers to finally put two and two together. Sailing from the Netherlands in 1721, the Dutch navigator Jacob Roggeveen rounded Cape Horn and began making his way up the South American coast. For decades there had been talk of an island, or a chain of islands, or even a high continental coast somewhere in the southeastern Pacific. Many had gone looking for the country known as Davis's Land (after a putative sighting by a seventeenth-century English buccaneer), and Roggeveen was determined to find it. Leaving the coast of South America, he plowed on through seventeen hundred miles of empty ocean, and on Easter Sunday 1722 he caught sight of what would turn out to be the most isolated inhabited island in the world.

Easter Island, or Rapa Nui, to use its modern Polynesian name, lies in the middle of a three-million-square-mile circle of empty sea. Its nearest neighbors, more than a thousand miles to the west, are tiny Henderson Island and even tinier Pitcairn, neither of which was inhabited when Europeans reached the Pacific, though both showed signs of prehistoric occupation. Easter Island is nominally a high island, but it is small, old, heavily weathered, and dry; it has no rivers, uncertain rainfall, and no protective coral reef. Difficult to inhabit and even more difficult to find, it constitutes the southeastern vertex of the Polynesian Triangle and represents the farthest known extension of Polynesian culture to the east.

At first, Roggeveen believed it to be "the precursor of the extended coast of the unknown Southland," but the Dutch were destined to be disappointed on numerous fronts. What looked from a distance like golden dunes turned out to be "withered grass" and "other scorched and burnt vegetation." The fine, multicolored clothes in which the islanders at first appeared to be dressed proved, on closer inspection, to be made of pounded tree bark dyed with earth, while the "silver plates" the Dutch thought they saw in their ears were made from something resembling a parsnip. Roggeveen wrote that he was struck by the "singular poverty and barrenness" of the island. It was not that nothing would grow—the inhabitants seemed well enough supplied with bananas, sugarcane, taro, and sweet potato—but rather that the island was entirely devoid of trees. This was puzzling on many fronts, but especially because it was unclear how, without any kind of strong and heavy wood to use as levers, rollers, or skids, the islanders could have erected their great stone statues—the famous *moai* of Easter Island.

These monolithic sculptures, with their long, sloping, oversize heads, upturned noses, and thin, pouting lips, are by now almost as familiar as the pyramids of Giza and perhaps more challenging to explain. The average *moai* stands about fourteen feet tall and weighs around twelve tons, but some are twenty to thirty feet in height, and the largest, had it been completed, would have stood seventy feet tall and weighed 270 tons. They are made from a kind of solidified ash known as volcanic tuff, and nearly half of the roughly nine hundred known statues still lie in the quarry where they were carved. A third were transported to various locations around the island, where they were erected on stone platforms and topped with stone hats, while the remainder lie scattered about the island, seemingly abandoned en route.

Roggeveen may have been the first, but he was by no means the last person to wonder how these statues had been erected. Indeed, the mystery of the Easter Island *moai*—what they meant, why they were carved, why their production abruptly ceased (there are half-finished *moai* in the quarry that are still attached to the rock), but especially how they were maneuvered into place—has inspired all kinds of speculation. People have tried to show how the statues might have been moved using only locally available materials: rocking them from side to side and walking them forward; sliding them on banana palm rollers; dragging them along on sledges suspended under wooden frames. The main problem, as Roggeveen noted in 1722, is the absence of everything that might have been needed to move a ten- or twenty- or thirty-ton block of stone: wheels, metal, draft animals, cordage, but most obviously timber.

Although Roggeveen found the island essentially barren of trees, modern studies of pollen found in sediment cores and archaeological finds of fossil palm nuts, root molds, and fragments of charcoal show that Easter Island was once home to a variety of tree species. Some twenty-two now vanished species have been identified, including the oceanic rosewood, the Malay apple, and something resembling the Chilean wine palm, which on the South American mainland grows to a height of sixty-five feet. Some of these trees would have produced edible fruit, others would have been good for making fires, at least two are known to have been suitable for making canoes, and still others produce bark that is used for making rope in other parts of Polynesia. Taken together, they would have constituted an entire arboreal foundation for human existence, not to mention a habitat for many now extinct species of birds.

Exactly what happened to all these trees is unknown, and there is a vigorous debate about the cause of what has been described as "the most extreme example of forest destruction in the Pacific, and among the most extreme in the world." One argument points to the island's ecological fragility and its vulnerability to changes brought about by humans. Sediment cores on Easter Island reveal dramatic increases in erosion and charcoal particles around A.D. 1200. This is often taken as a proxy for human activity in the Pacific, where slash-and-burn agriculture was widely practiced, and it has been used to support the argument that Easter Island's ecological collapse began with the arrival of the first Polynesian settlers.

According to this view, the original colonizers began felling trees and clearing land for gardens and plantations as soon as they arrived. On a different island—one that was wetter, warmer, younger, larger, or closer to other landmasses—such activities might have altered the island's ecology without destroying it. But Easter Island is a uniquely precarious environment. The slow-growing trees were not quickly replaced, while the loss of the canopy exposed already poor soils to "heating, drying, wind, and rain." This, in turn, led to erosion, the loss of topsoil, and a general decrease in the island's fertility. Each step in the degradation of the environment led to the next, and once the damage reached a certain level, there was no going back. Others—partly in response to the disturbing image of some desperate and improvident Easter Islander chopping down the last palm tree—have argued that the island's deforestation was caused not by the islanders themselves but by their commensals, in particular the Polynesian rat. It was the rat, they argue, with its taste for nuts, seeds, and bark, its lack of predators, its climbing ability, and its fast rate of reproduction, that spelled doom for the virgin forests on Rapa Nui.

But however it came about, the loss of trees must have reached catastrophically into every aspect of the islanders' lives: no shade, no nuts, no bark for cloth or cordage, no wood for houses or fuel. One of the most disturbing implications is that without wood, the inhabitants of Easter Island would have had no way to make canoes, especially the large, oceangoing kind they would have needed if they ever wanted to leave. For an island off the beaten track, with no near neighbors, this was a potentially ruinous reality. If one consequence of deforestation was that it brought to an end the age of monumental sculpture, an even more poignant implication is that it also spelled isolation from the rest of the world.

FOLLOWING THEIR BRIEF stop at Easter Island, Roggeveen and his men set sail again to the northwest, and May found them wandering among the northern Tuamotus. The hazards of this archipelago were forcefully brought home to them when one of the ships, the *Afrikaansche Galei*, ran aground on the atoll of Takapoto—the very island that, in one of history's little jokes, Schouten and Le Maire had named "Bottomless." Not so bottomless after all, as it turned out. Sailing on, Roggeveen came to the uplifted coral island of Makatea, where he found people who seemed "in all respects similar to those of Paaslant" (a version of the Dutch name for Easter Island), and then to Samoa, at the western edge of the Polynesian Triangle, where he again observed how "like the Paaschlanders in sturdiness and robustness of body, also in painting themselves," the islanders were.

Thus, by 1722, there was finally enough history between Europe and the peoples of the remote Pacific for someone to begin thinking about the big picture. Europeans were still fixated on Terra Australis Incognita, but another poser had at last occurred to them. "To make an end and conclusion of all the islands which we have discovered and found to be peopled," wrote Roggeveen, "there remains merely the presenting of the following speculative question, which seems to me must be placed among those questions which exceed the understanding, and therefore are to be heard, but answered with silence." This question, which is almost completely obscured by Roggeveen's tortured syntax—a sign perhaps of how difficult it was for him even to think—was, in essence: *Who are all these people and how did they end up here?*

Roggeveen appears to have been the first European to note the similarity of one group of Polynesians to another, but what interested him most was the question of how they had gotten to the islands. The problem, as Roggeveen saw it, was one of isolation and distance, something he now understood from hard personal experience—having rounded the Horn in mid-January, he did not reach the far side of the Pacific until the following September. On the grounds that the mysteries of navigation had only recently been unraveled, Roggeveen argued that no one could possibly have sailed such distances in the days before the Spanish and Portuguese. To suggest otherwise, he argued, "would resemble mockery rather than serious thought."

This left only two possibilities. First, that the islanders of the remote Pacific had been brought there by the Spanish and left as colonists, though it was hard to imagine why the Spanish would go to the trouble of setting up "colonies of Indians in these distant regions" when there was nothing obvious to be gained by it. Then, too, the Spanish had always claimed that the islanders were already there when they arrived. That left just one possible solution, in Roggeveen's view: that "the Indians who inhabit these newly discovered islands," the people we now know as Polynesians, had not in fact come from anywhere but had been created in situ by God.

It is probably safe to say that the suggestion that Polynesians

were autochthonous—that is, that they had first sprung into being on the islands on which they lived—was almost as absurd in
1722 as it seems to us today. But it does suggest how perplexing
Europeans found the issue of Polynesian origins. In truth, it was
not yet entirely clear how *very* puzzling a problem this was, since
large swaths of Polynesia had yet to be discovered. Although European explorers had been crisscrossing the ocean for more than two
centuries, long-standing political rivalries meant that knowledge
of the region was still largely piecemeal—the Spanish knew some
things, the Dutch knew others, no one was interested in sharing
information, and everyone remained dazzled by visions of Terra
Australis Incognita. All this, however, was about to change.

*Part II*

# CONNECTING THE DOTS

## (1764–1779)

*In which we travel with Captain Cook to the heart of Polynesia, meet the Tahitian priest and navigator Tupaia, and sail with the two of them to New Zealand, where Tupaia makes an important discovery.*

# TAHITI

## *The Heart of Polynesia*

*"A View taken in the bay of Oaite Peha [Vaitepiha]*
*Otaheite [Tahiti]" by William Hodges, 1776.*
NATIONAL MARITIME MUSEUM,
GREENWICH, LONDON. WIKIMEDIA COMMONS.

BETWEEN MENDAÑA'S VOYAGE of 1595 and the midpoint of the eighteenth century, there were just five European expeditions that intersected in any significant way with the Polynesian world. But beginning in 1764, the number and intensity of these "visitations" increased dramatically, with ships coming thick and fast from England, France, Spain, and Russia—so many that there were sometimes two or three expeditions in the Pacific at one time—and encounters that lasted not days but weeks and months.

The reasons for this were many, but one important factor was the conclusion, in 1763, of the Seven Years' War, a messy international conflict involving all the great European powers and several colonies, from which Britain emerged as a dominant power with the world's most formidable navy. No longer tied up fighting its enemies, the British crown quickly set out to secure new territories and new routes, dispatching Commodore John Byron in 1764 on the first of a series of expeditions to the Pacific. Byron sailed in His Majesty's Ship *Dolphin*, and when he returned in 1766, the *Dolphin* was immediately sent out again under the command of Captain Samuel Wallis. When Wallis returned in 1768, a third expedition was on the verge of departure. The aim of the first two voyages was largely strategic: Byron was to stake a claim to the Falkland Islands, examine the coast of New Albion (California), and look for a Northwest Passage; Wallis was to search for a continent between New Zealand and Cape Horn. But the goal of the third voyage was explicitly scientific: to carry a crew of scientists to a location from which they would be able to observe a celestial event known as the transit of Venus.

A transit of Venus occurs when the planet Venus passes between the earth and the sun. It was of interest to eighteenth-century astronomers because accurate measurements of the event's duration could be used to calculate the size of the solar system, thereby answering one of the burning astronomical questions of the age. Unfortunately, the transit of Venus occurs only infrequently: twice in a period of eight years and then not again for a century or more. It was observed for the first time in 1639 (having passed unnoticed in 1631) and did not occur again in the seventeenth century. Late-eighteenth-century astronomers knew they would have two bites at the cherry—one in 1761 and another in 1769—after which their chances would be over, since it would not come again until 1874. A major international effort to document the transit of 1761 had produced disappointing results, and in the years leading up to 1769, members of the international scientific community, including Britain's Royal Society, mounted a major campaign to ensure that the last opportunity of their lifetimes would not be lost.

An important consideration in all of this is where on the earth the transit can be seen, since it is fully visible only from those places that are in daylight for the duration of the event. In 1761, this had included most of the Eurasian continent, but in 1769 the ideal place from which to observe it was, most inconveniently, the middle of the Pacific Ocean. The only suitable islands known to fall within the "cone of visibility" were, on the eastern end, the Marquesas, last seen in 1595 and none too securely charted, and, in the west, the islands of Tonga, last visited by Abel Tasman in 1642. Between these, so far as anyone knew, there were only low coral atolls with terrible reefs and not a single safe harbor, and no reliable sources of food or water. Still, the Royal Society was committed, and plans were drawn up for an expedition with a final destination *to be determined*.

The man chosen to lead this expedition was a little-known lieutenant with a solid if undistinguished naval career and a reputation for being extremely good at survey work. At forty years of age, James Cook was not young, nor was he a man of rank or birth. He was tall, strong-featured, intelligent, disciplined, and extremely hardworking. Though largely self-taught, he was known as a talented mathematician and admired for his astronomical work, including an observation of a solar eclipse made while he was surveying the coast of Newfoundland. The voyage for which he had been selected was also somewhat out of the ordinary for a Royal Naval expedition. With only one ship (and a small one at that) and a very great distance to be covered, across a vast and largely uncharted sea, there was potential for glory but also significant risk.

The commander appointed, a suitable vessel was selected and rechristened the H.M.S. *Endeavour*, and a complement of sailors, scientists, and supernumeraries were named. These included the lively and observant young gentleman Joseph Banks—"one of the spoilt children of fortune," as his biographer affectionately dubs him—who traveled as a passenger at his own expense, with an entourage consisting of two artists, a secretary, four servants, and a pair of dogs. But with just two and a half months to go before the *Endeavour*'s departure, the expedition still had no clear destination. And then, out of the salt-stained blue, the *Dolphin* returned, bringing news of an unexpected discovery.

• • •

THE *DOLPHIN* HAD been sent out under the command of Captain Wallis to scour the southern reaches of the Pacific Ocean. Wallis's instructions directed him to sail west from Cape Horn for 100 to 120 degrees of longitude (some four to five thousand miles), a course that, had he been able to maintain it, would have brought him all the way to New Zealand. This was plainly impossible, given the strength and direction of the prevailing winds. Emerging into the Pacific from the Strait of Magellan, he was pushed north even as he tried to sail west, and his first sight of anything at all was in the Tuamotus. There was nothing surprising about this—a landfall in the Tuamotu Archipelago was by now to be expected. But Wallis's path intersected the island chain at a point somewhat south of the routes taken by his predecessors, and this put him on the path to one of the most significant landfalls of the eighteenth century: "The island of Tahiti, famous name, the heart of Polynesia."

Tahiti is the largest of a group of high islands known collectively as the Society Islands. They are located in the very center of the Polynesian Triangle and consist of two clusters: a windward group, which includes Tahiti and Moʻorea, and a leeward group, which includes Raʻiatea and Bora Bora. While not objectively large, they are large for islands in this part of the sea; Tahiti itself, though less than forty miles long, is the largest landmass for a thousand miles in any direction. To the modern eye, the Society Islands are perhaps the most striking omission on early maps of the Pacific— the islands it is hardest to believe no one had yet found. In fact, Magellan, Mendaña, Quirós, Schouten and Le Maire, and Byron had all sailed right past them, sometimes at a distance of less than a hundred miles. Roggeveen even caught sight of the peaks of Bora Bora, assumed it was an island discovered by someone else, and inexplicably sailed on.

From the European point of view, the discovery of Tahiti was a dramatic and fortuitous event. Not only had Wallis located an island that was right in the center of the cone of visibility for the 1769 transit of Venus, it was the island of a navigator's dreams. Tahiti is mountainous, like the Marquesas, but, with its habitable coastline, fringing reef, and long stretches of crystalline blue lagoon, its topography is considerably more congenial. Its location, about 2,500 miles due south of Hawai'i, is also meteorologically ideal: not too hot, not too dry, not too wet, not overly subject to hurricanes or typhoons. To the modern visitor it is delightful; to the eighteenth-century voyager it was a paradise on earth.

But, of course, such an island was bound to be inhabited, as indeed it was. When the crew of the *Dolphin* first sighted Tahiti, it appeared to them as a great cloud-covered mountain rising out of the sea. It was still many miles away at that point and, as evening was coming on, Wallis decided to put off his approach until morning. At daybreak he steered again for the island, but when the ship had come within six or seven miles, it was suddenly engulfed in fog. This, wrote the *Dolphin*'s master, George Robertson, "made us all very uneasy," for by now they were close enough to hear the sea breaking and "making a great noice, on some reefs of Rocks." This was nothing, however, next to the shock they received when the fog suddenly lifted to reveal not just a deadly row of breakers between the ship and the land but more than eight hundred men in canoes between the breakers and the ship.

Estimates of the pre-contact populations of Pacific islands vary widely, but in Tahiti at the time of the *Dolphin*'s arrival, there were probably something like 60,000 to 70,000 people, with perhaps 300,000 in the archipelago as a whole. Certainly enough to supply thousands of warriors and hundreds of canoes—Robertson would later describe the ship as being surrounded by more than five hundred canoes, manned, "at a Moderate Computation," by four thousand men. The risks of trying to land on so populous an island were obvious, and there were those who believed—rightly, as it turned out—that "nothing could be hade without blows." At the same time, many of the crew were so debilitated by scurvy that the prospect of sailing on was unthinkable, especially when the tantalizing scent of tropical vegetation wafted out to the ship during the night.

The Tahitians in their canoes paddled round Wallis's ship, holding up plantain branches and making speeches and throwing the fronds into the sea. The British showed trinkets and made friendly signs and tried to entice the islanders on board. The Tahitians seemed cheerful and talked a great deal in a language that sounded to Robertson like that of the Patagonians of Tierra del Fuego (with which it had no relationship whatsoever). More and more canoes continued to arrive, and eventually a "fine brisk young man" scrambled up by the mizzen chains and leapt out of the shrouds onto an awning, where he stood, laughing and looking down on the quarterdeck. Soon more Tahitians were climbing aboard, looking around at everything and snatching whatever they could. After a while—the story is familiar—the Tahitians began to be "a Little surly," the British grew nervous, and the next thing was the firing of a nine-pound gun. At this, the Tahitians all jumped overboard and swam away to their canoes. Wallis ordered his men to make sail, and the islanders returned to shore.

Wallis was not leaving Tahiti, however; he was just circling in search of a safe place to land. As the *Dolphin* sailed round the island, the two sides engaged in a series of tactical maneuvers. At one moment, the Tahitians would be visiting the ship, bringing quantities of pigs, chickens, coconuts, breadfruit, and bananas; at the next they would be hooting and hollering, trying to make off with the ship's anchors, or ambushing its boats. The meaning of all this was obscure to the Europeans, who alternated between trying to make friends with the Tahitians and aggressively fending off what they perceived as attacks.

The Tahitians, meanwhile, were also trying to make sense of what was going on. According to the Reverend James Cover, who lived in Tahiti some three decades later and who talked to descendants of people who had witnessed these events, the Tahitians were astonished by their first sight of a European ship, and "some supposed that it was a floating island," an idea with some basis in Polynesian myth. On closer inspection, they realized that it was, in fact, a vessel, though one unlike any they had ever seen—while the largest Tahitian war canoes were almost as long as the *Dolphin*, they did not have anything like its breadth or height or its huge masts with their elaborate complex of rigging and sails.

How the Tahitians interpreted these events is, as many historians have noted, "by any standard of objective discourse, nothing more than informed guess," since there are no contemporary sources that capture their point of view. But it seems likely that, at least in the beginning, they viewed the *Dolphin* as something come from the realm of the ancestors—a vessel from the mythic homeland of Hawaiki or the netherworld of Te Pō. Some have suggested that—as with Cook's encounter at Kealakekua Bay—the Tahitians may have associated the strangers with an incarnation of the war god 'Oro. The color red, which was prominently displayed on the sides of the ship, on the coats of the marines, and on the pennant that the British planted to symbolize their possession of the island, was linked with this deity, while lightning and thunder (cannon and gun fire) were signs of his terrible power. Then there were the many "wanton tricks" performed by women and girls, who stood on the rocks and in the prows of the canoes exposing their genitals— gestures that were interpreted by the British as "erotic enticement" but that, according to the anthropologist Anne Salmond, were actually a form of ritual behavior that "opened a pathway to Te Po, the realm of the ancestor gods, channelling their power" against the strangers.

When at last the *Dolphin* stopped circling and came to anchor in Matavai Bay, the skirmishing that had marked these first days came to a head. According to those on board the ship, the morning began quite ordinarily. Canoes came out to the ship to trade—nails and "Toys" for hogs, fowls, and fruit—all conducted "very fair." An audience of thousands had gathered on the shore, and the bay was filled with hundreds of canoes. Many of these had a girl in front who "drew all our people upon the Gunwells to see them," and although some of the sailors were worried about the large numbers of stones they could see lying in the bottoms of the canoes, most did not believe that the islanders had "any Bade Intention against us," especially as "all the men seemd as hearty and merry as the Girls."

Then a large double canoe carrying an obviously important figure put off from shore, and, at the same time, a silence fell upon the Tahitian crowd. The dignitary pulled on a red mantle and thrust a staff wrapped in white cloth into the air, and all at once the Tahitians began pelting the *Dolphin* with rocks—so many that in a few seconds "all our Decks was full of Great and small stones, and several of our men cut and Bruisd." The British were slow to react, but when the Tahitians "gave another shout and powerd in the stones lyke hail," they collected their wits and fired the great guns. The effect was dramatic. The explosion of sound, the flash of fire, and the rattle of shot on the canoes struck the Tahitians with "terror and amazement," and they cried, so the Revered Cover tells us, "as with one voice, *Eatooa harremye! Eatooa harremye!* The God is come! The God is come! as they supposed, pouring thunder and lightning upon them."

The battle was fierce but short. The British fired grape and shot into the canoes, hitting even those who had retreated to what the Tahitians clearly believed was a safe distance. The gunners took aim, in particular, at the large ceremonial canoe, hitting it squarely amidships and cutting it in two. At this, the Tahitian armada disbanded—so fast, wrote Wallis, that within half an hour there was not a single canoe left in the bay.

ALTHOUGH THE BATTLE of Matavai Bay mirrored European contact experiences in many parts of Polynesia—New Zealand, Rurutu, and Hawai'i, to name just a few—the story that ultimately made its way back to Europe was not one of attacks and ambushes and fleets of stone-throwing warriors in canoes. It was a tale—familiar to us even now—of beauty and fascination, a story, for the most part, about Polynesian girls.

After the failure of their assault on the *Dolphin*, the Tahitians made no further attempts to attack the British and instead sought to engage and placate them. Wallis struck up a friendship with a powerful local chiefess named Purea, who had a political agenda of her own and who seems to have been interested in co-opting this new and awful form of power. The rest of the crew went from openly fearing the Tahitians to openly consorting with them. On his arrival in Tahiti, Wallis had established an official market for foodstuffs, based on a currency of different-sized nails. But once his sailors had begun to recover from scurvy, what they wanted even more than fruit and vegetables was sex, and by the end of their second week in Tahiti a black market had emerged. The currency of choice was nails, inflation quickly set in, and within a matter of weeks the whole thing was so out of hand that every cleat in the *Dolphin* had been drawn, two-thirds of the men were sleeping on the deck (having traded away the nails used to sling their hammocks), and the carpenter was saying to anyone who would listen that he feared for the integrity of the ship.

It is possible that, had Wallis been the only European to return with stories of Tahiti, the narrative might have been somewhat more nuanced: a story of light and dark, of amity and aggression, of both love and war. But the era of Polynesian isolation was over: just eight months after Wallis's appearance, a second group of ships arrived, this time from France. They were commanded by Louis-Antoine de Bougainville, whose name lingers on in the beautiful bougainvillea, and although they remained in Tahiti for just nine days, it was long enough to form a vivid impression. The Tahitians, now experienced in the ways of Europeans, did not even try to attack the French ships but instead moved quickly to engage the strangers, and the French experience was largely one of hospitality.

Everything about Tahiti enchanted the elegant, erudite Bougainville: "The mildness of the climate, the beauty of the scenery, the fertility of the soil everywhere watered by rivers and cascades." "I thought," he wrote, "I was transported into the garden of Eden." He saw the landscape in terms of the picturesque—"nature in that beautiful disorder which it was never in the power of art to imitate"—and the inhabitants as children of nature. The islanders, he wrote, "seemed to live in an enviable happiness," and the worst consequence—for the French—of shipwreck in these parts "would have been to pass the remainder of our days on an isle adorned with all the gifts of nature, and to exchange the sweets of the mother-country, for a peaceable life, exempted from cares." Writing for an audience of cosmopolitan Parisians, Bougainville cast the Polynesian inhabitants of Tahiti as innocent sensualists. Wallis had taken possession of Tahiti on behalf of the British, dutifully, if unimaginatively, naming it King George the Third's Island. In the first shimmer of what would come to be known as *le mirage tahitien*— that constellation of images of indolence and hedonism that still cluster about Polynesia today—Bougainville rechristened the island New Cythera, after the place at which the goddess Aphrodite had risen from the sea.

# A MAN OF KNOWLEDGE
## *Cook Meets Tupaia*

*"Review of the war galleys at Tahiti" by William Hodges, 1776.*
NATIONAL MARITIME MUSEUM, GREENWICH, LONDON.

**WALLIS ARRIVED BACK** in England in May 1768, and Cook sailed for Tahiti in August. The end of January found him off the coast of Tierra del Fuego, on the Pacific side of Cape Horn. From then until the end of March, when the first unmistakable signs of land began to appear, the *Endeavour* was abroad on the great ocean. They were making anywhere from twenty-five to one hundred forty miles a day, keeping to a general northwesterly direction, though periodically the wind would force them round to the southwest. Cook logged the distance and direction traveled, the speed and strength of the wind, the latitude and longitude of their position. But as January bled into February, and February gave way to March, there was little else to report. Mile upon mile of ocean slipped by; masses of cloud swept in and were torn away by the wind; the sea rose, whipped to a froth, and then fell to a smooth, flat calm. There were creatures of the deep—porpoises and bonitos—and of the air: red- and white-tailed tropic birds replacing the high-latitude shearwaters and petrels as the *Endeavour* plowed steadily northward, enclosed in the great circle of sea and sky.

Inside the great cabin, Cook plotted their progress, aware that oceans were known for their deceits. Others passing this way had written of cloud banks looming in the distance like high land, and one of the maps he consulted—Alexander Dalrymple's "Chart of the South Pacifick Ocean, Pointing Out the Discoveries Made Therein Previous to 1764"—showed numerous "signs of continent" in this quadrant of the sea. This chart, and the history in which it appeared, had been drafted in support of Dalrymple's fervid belief in the existence of Terra Australis Incognita and thrust into Joseph Banks's hands on the eve of their departure. It detailed all the known landfalls of the previous two centuries, as well as all the unsubstantiated rumors, but Cook encountered none of these. Keeping his ship's head pointed for Tahiti, he tracked steadily through the emptiness of the southeastern Pacific, making a long, clean, northwesterly run of more than four thousand miles.

The atmosphere on board the *Endeavour* was increasingly one of anticipation as each day brought them closer to the island they had all heard so much about. At 39 degrees south latitude, Banks reported that the weather had begun to feel "soft and comfortable like the spring in England." The next day the ship was surrounded by killer whales. On March 1, Banks wrote that he had begun the new month "by pulling off an under waistcoat," and the next day he "began to hope that we were now so near the peacefull part of the Pacifick ocean that we may almost cease to fear any more gales." Soon, however, they discovered a new kind of discomfort: the weather turned hot and damp, and everything began to mold. When, a few days later, the wind increased, they thought briefly they had picked up the trades. But there was more troublesome weather ahead: heavy squalls of rain and hot, damp air and days of frustratingly light wind.

Toward the end of March, Cook reported some egg birds, a kind of tern seen only in the vicinity of land, as well as some man-of-war (i.e., frigate) birds, which were never known to rest at sea. "All the birds we saw this Day went a way to the NW at Night," observed the master's mate. A few days later, a log of wood floated past the ship. The next day someone spotted a piece of seaweed—all noteworthy events after fifty-eight days of blue-water sailing. About this time, a disturbing incident occurred: a young marine named William Greenslade threw himself overboard. Caught in a minor act of thieving while on duty, he had been hounded by his fellow marines and, according to Banks, was so demoralized that, on being called to account, he slipped over the side instead. Poor Greenslade—just nine days later their first Pacific island hove into view.

It was an atoll about four miles long, with an oval lagoon, a handful of small islets, and long stretches of barren beach and reef. At one end there was a clump of trees, and near the middle a pair of tall coconut palms, which, with their fronds flying before the easterly wind, reminded Cook of a flag. It was inhabited by men who "March'd along the shore abreast of the Ship with long clubs in their hands as tho they meant to oppose our landing." Cook sounded but found no bottom, and in the absence of an anchorage, he ordered the ship to sail on. He named this, his first Pacific atoll, Lagoon Island—a lot of them would have lagoons, as it turned out. Historians have concluded that it was Vahitahi, an island at the southeastern end of the Tuamotu Archipelago.

As he picked his way through the reefs and islands over the next few days, Cook sighted several of the Tuamotus, naming them mostly according to shape: Bow Island, Chain Island, Two Groups. Some were inhabited, and on a couple of occasions he slowed the ship and waited to see if the islanders would come off in their canoes—they did not. From a distance, he admired the palms and the reef-enclosed bodies of water, which, with a kind of persistent Englishness, he described as "lakes" and "ponds." But there was nowhere to stop, and in any case he was not particularly interested in stopping, for they were now getting close to their destination. Then, on the morning of April 11, they sighted Tahiti, rising dark and rugged from the sea, a dramatically different vision from the flat, bright rings of coral in their wake.

Cook quickly established himself in the same bay that Wallis had occupied, setting up camp on a point of land that he named Point Venus—not for the reasons that had inspired Bougainville but in honor of the event they had come to observe. No one would have missed the double entendre, however; even before the ship had come to anchor, Cook implemented a prohibition against the giving of "any thing that is made of Iron . . . in exchange for any thing but provisions." The Tahitians showed no signs of aggression, welcoming Cook and his officers and leading them on a pleasant ramble through the woods. The shade, wrote Banks, was deep and delicious among "groves of Cocoa nut and bread fruit trees loaded with a profusion of fruit." Houses were scattered picturesquely here and there. It was, he wrote, "the truest picture of an arcadia . . . that the imagination can form."

And yet, something was amiss. Four of the *Endeavour*'s men had been to Tahiti with Wallis, and it was clear to them that something had happened in the intervening years. Several of the large houses and canoe sheds that had formerly lined the bay were gone, and many of the people they had expected to see were nowhere to be found. One of these was Purea, the chiefess whose star had been in the ascendant in 1767. She had since been defeated by a rival and forced to flee to another part of the island, but once word got around of the *Endeavour*'s arrival, she put in an appearance, accompanied by her counselor Tupaia.

And here steps onto the stage one of the most intriguing figures in this story. Tupaia, who is variously described as Purea's right-hand man, her chief priest, and her lover, was a tall, impressive man of about forty, with the bearing and tattoos of a member of the chiefly class. He belonged to an elite society of priests and per-formers known as the *'arioi* and was an expert in the arts of poli-tics, oratory, and navigation. Banks considered him "a most proper man, well born," and "skilld in the mysteries of their religion."

Cook admired him but was inclined to think him proud. Georg Forster, who sailed with Cook on his second voyage and knew of Tupaia only secondhand, described him as "an extraordinary genius." Richard Thomson, a missionary writing some seventy years later, observed that he was "reputed by the people themselves . . . to have been one of the cleverest men of the islands."

Although he is generally referred to as a "priest," a better term, as Banks suggested, might be "Man of Knowledge." The Tahitian word is *tahu'a* (*tohunga* in Māori, *kahuna* in Hawaiian), and its core meaning is something like "an adept," that is, a master, expert, or authority. The idea can be narrowly associated with a particular craft or specialization, like canoe building or oratory, but when used in a general sense it implies a remarkable constellation of different types of knowledge. A man like Tupaia might be responsible for maintaining not only the history and genealogy of the ruling family to which he was attached, including their sacred rituals and rites, but all the esoteric knowledge of the people in general—"the names and ranks of the different . . . divinities, the origin of the universe and all its parts," as well as the "Practise of Physick and the knowledge of Navigation and Astronomy." His fields, if one can refer to them as such, included cosmology, politics, history, medicine, geography, astronomy, meteorology, and navigation, all of which, in a world with no clear division between natural and supernatural, were inextricably entangled with religion. But Tupaia was not just a repository of information; he clearly had a deep and inquiring mind. The anthropologist Nicholas Thomas describes him as an "indigenous intellectual with experimental inclinations"—a phrase that seems to capture something of both the man and the age in which he lived.

WALLIS'S FIVE-WEEK SOJOURN in Tahiti had been long by comparison with those of other European explorers, but Cook's was of another order altogether. The *Endeavour* remained in the Society Islands for a full four months, arriving in April, in good time to observe

June's transit of Venus, and not leaving until the beginning of August. This meant that there was ample time for the visitors to learn about Tahitian ways, and Banks, with no official duties, was at leisure to explore. In the end, he compiled a substantial account of Tahitian manners and customs, based both on what he himself had observed and what Tupaia and others told him. As with much ethnography, it is heavily weighted in favor of the observable—how to make fishing nets and breadfruit paste, the distribution of houses, procedures for tattooing, varieties of tools, weapons, and musical instruments, the dimensions of various structures, and so on.

Many of Banks's observations are fascinating for their novelty, like his claims that "a S[outh]-Sea dog was next to an English lamb" in tenderness and flavor, that Tahitians bathed three times a day, and that both men and women plucked "every hair from under their armpits" and looked upon it "as a great mark of uncleanliness in us that we did not do the same." He observed that while Tahitians were often ribald in gesture and conversation—one of the most popular entertainments for young girls was a dance that mimicked copulation—they observed the strictest of food taboos, expressing "much disgust" when told that in England men and women ate together and shared the same food. But he also made a number of valuable technical observations, including remarks on the size, shape, and seaworthiness of different types of canoes.

Banks described both the regular *va'a*—a single-hulled canoe with an outrigger, used for fishing and shorter trips—and the larger *pahi*, a double-hulled vessel with V-shaped hulls, a large platform, and one or two masts, which was used both for fighting and long voyages. *Pahi*, wrote Banks, ranged in length from thirty to sixty feet, but the midsize ones were said to be the best and least prone to accidents in stormy weather. "In these," he adds, "if we may credit the reports of the inhabitants[,] they make very long voyages, often remaining out from home several months, visiting in that time many different Islands of which they repeated to us the names of near a hundred."

Much of this information came from Tupaia, who gave lists of islands to both Cook and the *Endeavour*'s master, Robert Molyneux, along with information about whether the islands were high or low, whether they were inhabited and, if so, by whom, whether they had reefs or harbors, and how many days' sail they were from Tahiti. As evidence of Tahitian geographic knowledge, these lists are un-paralleled—no other European in the first two-hundred-odd years obtained anything of the kind—but they are not without complications. To begin with, there is no single authoritative version: Cook's list contains seventy-two island names, Molyneux's fifty-five, and the two lists share thirty-nine names between them. Cook reported that Tupaia had at one time given him an account of nearly one hundred thirty names and that he had collected some seventy-odd from other sources, but that all of these accounts differed in both the number of islands and their names.

Then there is the problem of transcription. Both Cook and Moly-neux wrote the names phonetically, but English is a terrible language in which to try to represent sounds—think of the number of sounds represented by the letters *ough*—*uff, oh, ow, oo,* and so on. The result of Cook's and Molyneux's efforts is a list of words that is quite mystifying at first glance. The name Fenua Ura, for example, appears as "Whennuaouda"; the island of Tikehau is rendered as "Teeoheow"; the island of Rangiroa as "Oryroa." The British also frequently made the mistake of attaching the grammatical prefix "O" to the beginnings of proper nouns. Thus, "O Tahiti," meaning something like "the Tahiti" or "this is Tahiti," was heard as "Ota-heite," Cook's standard name for the island. A third complication arises from the fact that Tahitian is short on audible consonants; a name like Kaukura might be rendered in some dialects as "'Au'ura," where the *k*'s have been replaced by glottal stops and then written down by an eighteenth-century Englishman as "Ooura." One of the islands on Cook's list is actually spelled "Ooouow."

Some of the islands on these lists might not even be specific locations. They might be islands with no cartographic equivalent—

"non-geographic" or "ghost" islands, mythological locations, or names taken from stories of ancestor gods. Some of the names begin with a prefix meaning "border" or "horizon," while others include terms meaning "leaning inward" or "leaning away," suggesting that perhaps these are concepts or ideas rather than actual locations. Still others may belong to an earlier era, for even within the historical period the names of many Polynesian islands have changed.

But even when you set aside all of the islands on the list that, for one reason or another, cannot be identified, quite a number remain. Fifty of the names on these lists can be correlated with islands that we can identify today. The implication is striking: Tupaia and his fellow Tahitians appear to have had knowledge of islands stretching east–west from the Marquesas to Samoa, a distance of more than two thousand miles, and south some five hundred miles to the Australs. Tupaia did not claim to have visited all of the islands whose names he knew; he told Cook that he himself had firsthand knowledge of only twelve. But he had second- or thirdhand knowledge of several more; he spoke at one point of islands that were visited by his father. The rest may have been islands that no one in living memory had seen but that were known to have been visited at some point in the past. They may, in other words, have belonged to a body of geographical knowledge that was handed down by word of mouth from generation to generation.

Cook's reaction to Tupaia's list of islands was composed, in almost equal parts, of admiration and skepticism, and here it helps to know a little something about Cook. In the years before he was picked for the *Endeavour* command, he had been engaged in a detailed survey of the coast of Newfoundland. This was one of Cook's areas of expertise; his biographer, J. C. Beaglehole, wrote that "nothing he ever did later exceeded in accomplishment" his surveys of the Canadian coast, which is saying something, given his achievements. And so, when Cook looked at the Pacific, it was not, as Keats would later have it, with "a wild surmise," but with the eyes of a surveyor.

Everywhere he went, he examined the coastlines, often going beyond the call of duty and far beyond what any of his predecessors
had done. Seen from this perspective, Tupaia's information was tantalizing but awkward. Cook felt that it was "vague and uncertain,"
lacking as it did any fixed coordinates or objective measures of distance, and he was not sure how far it could be trusted. At the same
time, it was clear to him that Tupaia knew "more of the Geography
of the Islands situated in these seas . . . then any one we had met."

Tupaia, for his part, also appears to have taken an interest in the
ways in which these strangers conceived and represented the physical world. A striking example of this, which has only fairly recently
come to light, is a series of watercolors depicting various subjects
in Tahiti, New Zealand, and Australia. For two centuries it was assumed that these sketches had been painted by Joseph Banks, since
they were found among his papers. But in 1997, a letter surfaced in
which Banks made it clear that "Tupia the Indian who came with
me from Otaheite" was the artist. This information was oddly startling; seeing the work of Tupaia's own hand brings him close in a
way that secondhand accounts of his actions have never been able to
do. But the watercolors are also interesting from an anthropological
perspective. Polynesia is famous for its decorative arts, but there
was no naturalistic tradition of illustration in the islands. Tupaia's
paintings, while stylistically naive, are closely observed and seem
to confirm what was so often said about him: that he was a man of
boundless curiosity and a natural experimenter.

Nothing proves this point so conclusively, though, as the fact
that when Cook decided it was time for the British to leave Tahiti,
Tupaia announced that he would like to go with them. He was not
the first Polynesian to sail away on a European ship; a Tahitian
named Ahutoru had joined the French expedition under Bougainville and was, at that very moment, being feted in France. And there
would be others—both of Cook's ships on his second voyage carried
Tahitian passengers part of the way, and on his third voyage he gave
passage to a pair of Māori boys. But the insouciance with which

Polynesians, including Tupaia, sailed away from their islands in the eighteenth century is quite stunning. No doubt it seems more so to us than it did to them—they were seagoing people, and the idea of sailing off to a new place may not have struck them as exceptionally adventurous. In truth, though, it was hideously dangerous—especially for them. Of the first three Tahitians to join European expeditions, only one returned. Beyond the rigors of the voyages themselves, which could last years and which exposed the islanders to a whole range of unfamiliar hardships, including extreme cold, unfamiliar and often undigestible food, loneliness, and social isolation, there was the very real danger of contact with diseases to which they had no immunity.

One wonders whether they understood how far they were going, how long it would take, what kinds of risks they were running. It is hard to see how they could have, and yet they certainly knew they were going farther than they had ever been, to places that until recently they had never heard of, with people they had only just met. This speaks to the daring of men like Tupaia, but it also says something about the cultures of Polynesia. Within a very few decades, Polynesians of all stripes would be crisscrossing the ocean—Tahitians, Marquesans, Hawaiians, Māori—signing on as deckhands on ships out of Sydney, San Francisco, Nantucket, Honolulu. Described by one European traveler as "cosmopolites by natural feeling," with "a disposition for enterprise and bold adventure," they quickly became ubiquitous in sea stories of the nineteenth century. One has only to think of Richard Henry Dana's Hawaiians camped out on the California coast, or Melville's Queequeg the harpooner.

Cook was not, at first, very interested in the idea of taking on a passenger. He had no need of extra hands, and he worried about what would happen when they got back to England. He himself was not a man of means, and he did not think the government would thank him for bringing back someone it would be obliged to support. Banks, however, had other ideas. "Thank heaven," he wrote, "I have a sufficiency and I do not know why I may not keep him . . . the amusement I shall have in his future conversation, and the benefit he will be of to this ship . . . will I think fully repay me." With this aspect of the problem solved, Cook relented, acknowledging that, of all the Tahitians they had met, Tupaia "was the likeliest person to answer our purpose."

That purpose was to lay down as much geography as possible, and the first order of business after leaving Tahiti was a survey of the "islands under the wind," the Leeward Society Islands. This was Tupaia's home territory; originally from Ra'iatea, he had been forced to flee when his island was overrun by warriors from neighboring Bora Bora. On the voyage there, Tupaia proved himself an excellent navigator, each of the islands appearing precisely when and where he said it would. He further impressed Cook when, on their arrival at Huahine, he instructed a man to dive down and measure the *Endeavour*'s keel to make sure it would clear the passage into the lagoon. He was useful in all kinds of ways: piloting the ship, mediating with the chiefs, instructing the British on how to behave. There is a suggestion that he may have had his own motives, that perhaps he was hoping Cook would help him exact vengeance on the Bora Borans who were still in control of his ancestral lands. But Cook would not be drawn into local politics. He had other objects in mind, and on the tenth of August, under cloudy skies, he bade adieu to the Society Islands and, as Banks put it with characteristic brio, "Launchd out into the Ocean in search of what chance and Tupia might direct us to."

# TUPAIA'S CHART

## *Two Ways of Seeing*

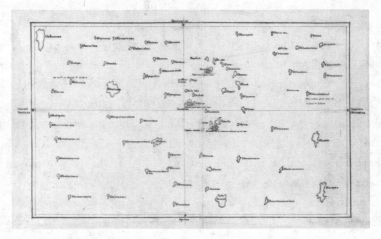

*Chart of the Society Islands by Captain James Cook,*
*after a drawing by Tupaia, 1769.*
THE GRANGER COLLECTION, BRITISH LIBRARY, LONDON.

**COOK HAD BEEN** provided with a second set of "secret" instructions, which directed him, once the transit of Venus had been observed, to sail south from the Society Islands in search of Terra Australis Incognita. They were "secret" in the sense that they were not officially acknowledged, but anyone who thought about it would have known that the Admiralty would hardly send a ship all the way to the South Pacific without undertaking a little reconnaissance, and the Unknown Southland was still the object of greatest interest back at home. What this meant was that the *Endeavour* was now headed to a part of the Pacific where no European vessel had ever been. All the cross-oceanic traffic thus far had fallen within a narrow belt of twenty to twenty-five degrees on either side of the equator, and nobody knew what lay farther south (or north) in the middle of this vast sea.

A day or so out of Ra'iatea, Tupaia explained that if they steered for a point on their weather bow—that is, southeast—they would come to an island called Mannua on the morning of the third day. Cook, however, ignored this advice, keeping his ship's head pointed south, and when on the third day no island was in sight, Tupaia told Banks that it was "*etopa*," meaning it had "fallen behind." He then told them that the next day, or the day after, they would come to an island called Oheteroa, and at 2 P.M. on the following day an island duly appeared. This island, which now goes by the name Rurutu, is one of a widely spaced chain of islands now known as the Australs.

All this time, Tupaia was eager for Cook to steer the ship west, telling him that if he would only go in that direction he would meet with plenty of islands. He was right about that: the vast majority of islands in the Pacific do lie west of Tahiti, though even the closest of them are five to six hundred miles away. Cook had very little information about what lay in this direction, and much of it was erroneous, but he believed that Tupaia might be referring to the islands discovered by Schouten and Le Maire in the northern Tongan archipelago. Tupaia gave him to understand that it would take ten to twelve days to reach these islands from Tahiti and thirty or more to return, which accorded well with Cook's understanding of the prevailing winds, the distance, and the sailing ability of Tahitian vessels. Interestingly, Cook seems not to have considered a sailing rate of 120 miles a day overly optimistic for a Tahitian *pahi*, noting that these large canoes could sail much faster than a European ship.

It was all academic, though, because Cook had no intention of turning west, however many islands there might be. Instead he pressed Tupaia for information about what lay to the south. Tupaia replied that he knew of only one other island in that direction, that it was another two days' sail, and that, although his father had told him of others, he could not say for certain where they were. In fact, there are just three islands south of where Cook was at that moment: Tubuai, Raivavae, and tiny, isolated Rapa; south of that there is nothing but ocean and ice. None of these was what Cook was looking for, and although he continued to query Tupaia, "we cannot find," he wrote, "that he either knows or ever heard of a continent."

And so, on they sailed, past the last island, standing south for the great unknown. Almost immediately Cook observed a large, steady swell from the southwest, suggesting strongly that there was nothing but ocean in that direction. They were making about fifty miles a day on average, and gradually the weather and the birdlife began to change—the wind picking up, the temperature dropping, the albatrosses and shearwaters reappearing. They now had strong gales with thunder and lightning, squalls of rain, and a waterspout "the breadth of a Rain Bow" that descended from the clouds. A comet appeared in the sky and remained there, foreshadowing, so Tupaia told them, an attack on the Ra'iateans by the Bora Bora men. The pigs and chickens they had brought from Tahiti began to die about twelve days out, possibly from the cold, which was steadily increasing, or perhaps because the food they were accustomed to eating had run out and they seemed unable to adapt to a shipboard diet. Tupaia, too, was feeling both the cold and the ill effects of the change in diet; he was eating almost nothing and complained of a pain in his gut.

All this time they were searching for signs of land. One day a cloud bank appeared that looked so persuasively like an island that Tupaia named it, and then found himself obliged to recant. Clumps of weed and chunks of wood floated past the ship, but when they were hauled aboard, they showed signs of having been in the water a long time. Sometimes a change in the color of the ocean encouraged Cook to sound, but there was never any bottom, and the types of birds that sailed by on the wind argued strongly against the presence of a continent, for "All these kind of birds," wrote Cook, "are generally seen at a great distance from land." Strong, variable winds and a large sea kept them busy—all except the boatswain's mate, who, having been given a bottle of rum, drank the whole thing off at one go and was found dead in his hammock the next morning.

By the second of September they had reached the 40th parallel. They had "not the least visible sign of land," and with the weather "so very tempestuous," Cook decided to stand north again for the sake of his sails and rigging. Or, more precisely, northward—the line, he found, between bad and better weather seemed to lie at about 37 degrees south—but also west, for there was nothing to be gained by going back the way they had come. This set the *Endeavour* on a long, zigzagging course, first northwest, then southwest, then due west, as the days of September ticked by. "Now do I wish," wrote Banks in his journal, "that our freinds in England could by the assistance of some magical spying glass take a peep at our situation: Dr. Solander [the expedition's naturalist] setts at the Cabbin table describing, myself at my Bureau Journalizing, between us hangs a large bunch of sea weed, upon the table lays the wood and barnacles" that had recently been pulled from the sea. Tupaia was there as well, though Banks did not mention him, for one of the many projects on which the gentlemen of the *Endeavour* were engaged during this long, rather uneventful segment of the voyage was a chart of all the islands Tupaia knew.

UNLIKE HIS DRAWINGS, this extraordinary document has been credited to Tupaia from the start. Cook referred in his journal to "a Chart of the Islands Drawn by Tupaia's own hands," and Johann Forster, Cook's naturalist on the second voyage, mentioned two different copies: one given to him by an officer from the *Endeavour* and one in the possession of Joseph Banks. Forster himself created yet another version, which he "caused to be engraved as a monument of the ingenuity and geographical knowledge of the people in the Society Isles, and of Tupaya in particular," and included in his own book. The original of all of these—the chart actually drawn by Tupaia himself—has been lost, but a copy drawn, signed, and dated by Cook was preserved among Banks's papers.

It is a truly remarkable artifact: a translation of Tahitian geographical knowledge into European cartographic terms at the very first moment in history when such a thing might have been possible; a collaboration between two brilliant navigators coming from geographical traditions with essentially no overlap; a fusion of completely different sets of ideas. There was no precedent for it; it has no known equal; and, with the benefit of hindsight, it looks like something of a miracle that it was ever created at all.

Tupaia's chart can be understood only as the product of a complex collaboration. Whether it was initiated by Tupaia or by Cook is impossible to say, though both seem to have been interested in the project. Tupaia, for his part, was clearly taken with the problem of graphical representation. Even before they left Tahiti, he had begun to dabble in mapmaking, drawing a chart of Ra'iatea that showed reefs and passages, islets and mountains, with place names that appear to have been added by Banks. Cook, on the other hand, was a gifted and indefatigable chart maker and was profoundly interested in anything that would help him navigate this inadequately mapped sea.

Unfortunately for Cook—though interestingly for us—Tupaia's chart is "opaque with trans-cultural confusion." It depicts seventy-four islands, ranged in concentric circles around the Society Islands, with Tupaia's home of Ra'iatea in the center. Some of these—for example, the islands in the northeast quadrant of the map—lie in what we would consider the correct orientation vis-à-vis Tahiti. These include many of the Tuamotus and some of the Marquesas, both of which are northeast of the Society Islands, at distances of two to eight hundred miles. But many of the islands on the chart, including some that would appear from their names to belong to the Samoan, Tongan, Cook, and Austral archipelagoes, are wrongly positioned—north when they should be south, southwest when they should be northwest, or, most confusingly, split between north and south when they should be together in one place or the other.

Over the years, there have been many attempts to make sense of this muddle. One of the earliest and most intriguing analyses was that made by Horatio Hale, the philologist attached to the United States Exploring Expedition, which surveyed much of the Pacific in the 1830s and '40s. Hale was extremely impressed by the amount of information contained in Tupaia's chart. He noted that every important island group in Polynesia, with the exception of New Zealand and Hawai'i, was represented, "though not accurately, yet with a certain attention to bearings and distances, which enables us to identify them." But, he added, "much confusion has been made in the chart by a mistake of those for whom Tupaia drew it."

This mistake had to do with the chart's orientation. It is marked with the directions N, S, E, and W as well as with Tahitian directions: OPATOEROW on the north, OPATOA on the south, TATAHIETA OHETOOTTERA on the east, and TEREATI TOOTTERA on the west. The key terms here—a little hard to decipher behind the veil of Cook's orthography—are *to'erau* (*tokerau* in Māori, *ko'olau* in Hawaiian), a widespread Polynesian word signifying a northerly wind, and *to'a* (or, more familiarly, *tonga*), a term for winds from a southerly direction.

Hale believed that Cook and the other Europeans had fundamentally misunderstood what was meant by the designations "Apa-to'erau" and "Apa-to'a" on the north and south sides of the chart. Knowing that *to'erau* signified the north wind and *to'a* the south, "they concluded naturally that *apatoerau* and *apatoa* were names applied to the corresponding points of the compass; whereas," Hale wrote, "*apatoerau* signifies, in fact, the point towards which the north wind blows,—i.e. the south, and *apatoa*, for the same reason, the north." Thus, taken as cardinal directions, "Apa-to'erau" and "Apa-to'a" meant exactly the opposite of what they purported to indicate on the map: north was south and south was north, and the map, Hale argued, was, "in fact, printed upside down."

But even assuming that this argument is correct, it still fails to explain the full complexities of Tupaia's chart. Hale made the further ingenious suggestion that Cook might have meddled in the arrangement of the islands, looking over Tupaia's shoulder as he drew and encouraging the "correct" placement of islands that he himself was familiar with. He noted that it was precisely those islands that Cook already knew—the Marquesas, Tuamotus, some of the Australs—that were oriented correctly, while those he had never seen or heard of were most likely to be located on the wrong part of the map. It was a creative solution to a tricky problem, but whether it is true or not is impossible to say.

FOR MANY YEARS, the emphasis among those seeking to explicate this document was on rationalizing Tupaia's knowledge, that is, finding a way to make it correspond to the realities of geography as we understand them. This meant that Tupaia's chart was always being viewed in terms of what was "right" and "wrong" about it, which aspects of it were "accurate" and which were "incorrect." But this is to miss what is most interesting about the diagram, which is that it represents a fusion of two completely different knowledge systems, both of which placed the very highest value on information about the physical world but constructed and deployed that information in entirely different ways.

For the eighteenth-century Briton, the world of oceans and islands was understood in terms of mostly quantitative descriptive systems: latitudes and longitudes for location; distances in nautical miles; calendrical time (months, days, hours, minutes); winds measured on what would come to be known as the Beaufort scale. These systems were defined by their objectivity; they did not depend upon the perspective of the observer, and the phenomena they described were understood to exist outside of human experience and independent of any sort of supernatural force.

For an eighteenth-century Tahitian, on the other hand, there was no separation between the natural and supernatural worlds.

One of Tupaia's navigational techniques involved invocations to the god Tane for a favorable wind—an action that was cynically derided by Banks, who could not believe that Tupaia himself believed in the efficacy of what he was doing. But in the Tahitian worldview, the wind, the god Tane, and Tupaia himself were interconnected, and it was not just possible but obligatory for the navigator to attempt to influence the elements by calling upon his relationship with the god. For a Tahitian, the physical world was less like a set of discrete, objective phenomena and more like a web of connections in which gods, ancestors, humans, fish, birds, insects, rocks, clouds, winds, and stars were linked to one another genealogically.

European charts, such as those that Tupaia was introduced to by Cook, depicted the world in terms of conceptual systems that were entirely alien to Tahitians. Position, distance, and direction were defined in terms of a mathematical scheme of measurement based on the size and shape of the earth. The perspective was not that of a participant on the ground but of an observer high in the sky, the so-called bird's-eye view. What such charts most emphatically do not capture is the way we actually experience geography—the perspective, for example, of someone standing on the deck of a boat. (It is worth noting that European navigators also drew coastal profiles in order to show what a coastline actually looked like to someone approaching it from the sea.)

In Tahiti, by contrast, there were few if any systems of absolute measurement. Distances were measured in time, and even then it was not in terms of a universal standard but time as experienced by a subject under certain conditions—as in Tupaia's assertion that the western islands were ten days going (with the wind) and thirty coming back (against it). Positions were likewise relative rather than absolute. An island was not in some particular location—17°35' S, 149°48' W—but so many days' sail from one place and so many days' sail from someplace else. Although Tahitians did use a fixed directional system at sea, based on sun, stars, and winds, on land they employed a relative system based on the speaker's position. On many islands in Polynesia, one does not travel east or west or north or south, but along axes determined by the local topography. In Hawai'i, for example, you go *mauka*, toward the mountain, or *makai*, toward the sea—directions that can point north, south, east, or west, depending upon where you are standing.

This kind of subject-centered understanding was central to Tahitian thinking, and, at one level, it is possible to envision Tupaia's chart simply as a translation of his ego-centered frame of reference into the objective terms of a European chart. For a contemporary example of how this might work, consider the famous *New Yorker* cover by Saul Steinberg, "View of the World from 9th Avenue," which depicts the world receding logarithmically from Manhattan across the Hudson River to New Jersey, Kansas City, Nebraska, the Pacific, and finally Japan. While not consciously ironic in the same way, Tupaia's chart seems similarly subjective: dense and informed at the center (around his home island of Ra'iatea) and increasingly metaphorical as it goes out.

BUT SUPPOSE THAT instead of thinking about geography, which is inherently static, we think in terms of navigation, which, while it depends upon a comparable body of knowledge, is essentially an *action*. Tupaia was not just a repository of geographical information; he was a navigator, a man who knew how to use the information he had and who only had it in order to put it into practice. One very interesting argument that follows this line of thinking suggests that Tupaia's chart is not so much a map as a mosaic of sailing directions or bearings. That is, it is not a description of *where* certain places are, but an account of *what it would take to reach them*, a "navigator's attempt to teach Cook and his officers the directions to surrounding islands."

All known early seafaring traditions employed some kind of compass or scheme for "segmenting the circle of the horizon with invariant directional axes." We know, from several different sources, that Polynesian navigators used the stars, in addition to winds, currents, cloud formations, sea marks, birdlife, and other indicators, to help them find their way across the ocean. Unfortunately, no early observer managed to get much in the way of detail about how this actually worked, but it is widely believed that they used a mental construct known as a "star compass." The way a star compass works is this: You begin by envisioning the horizon as a circle marking the meeting point of the earth and the sky—which, of course, is exactly how it looks from a boat on the ocean or the high point of a small island. In the mind of an experienced navigator, this circle is dotted with points marking the rising and setting positions of particular stars. When the navigator imagines himself at the center of this circle and his destination as a point on the horizon, the star compass becomes a plotting diagram, giving the bearing of his target island in terms of the rising and setting points of particular stars. A "star path" is a course defined by the series of stars that rise over the course of a night in a particular direction.

Using a model of this kind, some thirty-three of the islands on Tupaia's chart, including several that had remained obscure, can be identified in terms of plotting diagrams using five different islands of departure. Like Hale's, this is an ingenious solution, and, as with Hale's, it is impossible to say whether it is actually correct. But it does have the merit of asking whether there is knowledge encoded in Tupaia's chart that might be difficult for us to see because it is based on unfamiliar assumptions about how information is most usefully organized. For us, the islands are most easily conceptualized in terms of a mathematical grid of latitude and longitude. But Tupaia might have conceived of them *strategically*, as clusters of islands that could be reached from a variety of starting points, given certain sets of bearings.

Everyone who has ever looked hard at Tupaia's chart has found it tantalizing in the extreme. On the one hand, it is a unique and irrefutable testament to the breadth of Tahitian geographic knowledge at the end of the eighteenth century. On the other hand, many aspects of it remain stubbornly mysterious. Everyone who has ever thought about it has no doubt wished he or she could go back and shake Cook, Banks, and the others and demand that they try harder to extract what Tupaia knew, that they ask more questions, take better notes, pay more attention to the possibility—which they never denied—that there was knowledge here worth documenting, so that we, in the future, could more fully understand what the world looked like from Tupaia's point of view.

What we can conclude, based on what we have, is that Tahitian geographic knowledge extended well beyond the Society Islands, encompassing the major island groups of central and eastern Polynesia. This does not necessarily mean that eighteenth-century Tahitians were routinely traveling to all these places—though they were certainly routinely traveling to some—but it does suggest that they knew these various islands existed and that this knowledge was culturally important enough to be handed down. But Tupaia's chart also suggests—though, again, it does not prove—the limitations of Tahitian geographic understanding. There are three places in Polynesia that are not included on this chart. These are, not surprisingly, the islands and archipelagoes at the limits of Polynesian reach, the places it would have been the hardest to get to, the ones separated by the greatest and emptiest expanses of water. They are, of course, the three points of the Polynesian Triangle: Hawai'i, Easter Island, and New Zealand—the last of which Cook and Tupaia were now on course to intercept.

*"A war canoe of New Zealand" by Sydney Parkinson,*
*in John Hawkesworth,* An Account of the Voyages *(London, 1773).*
HOUGHTON LIBRARY, HARVARD UNIVERSITY.

ALL THROUGH THE month of September and into early October, the
*Endeavour* plowed westward through an utterly empty region of the
sea. There was little to remark apart from the birdlife, and Banks,
normally a lively reporter, was reduced to keeping track of the albatrosses and petrels. Toward the end of the month, there was a clear
escalation in signs pointing to the proximity of land. Large clumps
of seaweed drifted by, "some in heaps as much together as would fill
a large wheelbarrow." Groups of whales and seals were sighted, and
a shoal of porpoises ruffled the waves, leaping over one another like
"a pack of hounds." The ship was hit by a short, violent squall, which
was taken as a sign of land, since such squalls were rarely met with
on the open ocean. A Port Egmont hen—a kind of skua—was spotted, another good indication. The color of the water seemed lighter,
and Cook cautiously began to sound. Sure enough, at the end of the
first week in October, a boy at the masthead called out "Land."

They had traveled some 3,500 miles since leaving Tahiti, crossing more than twenty degrees of latitude, and they were now back at 38 degrees south. The sea was colder, the sky was paler, and the land before them was high and rugged, with cliffs along the foreshore and hills rising to a great chain of mountains inland. There was nothing in the geography of New Zealand to suggest that the people who lived there might have anything in common with the people in the tropical islands they had left behind; indeed, Banks and many of the others were firmly of the opinion that they had come to the Unknown Southland at last.

Cook, however, was fairly sure that they were approaching the land discovered by Abel Tasman in 1642. As the *Endeavour* drew closer, they could see "many great smoaks" rising from points along the coastline. Cook was eager to make contact with the inhabitants, and as soon as he could, he brought the ship to anchor in a bay. Seeing some people on the shore, he directed his rowers to land near them, but as soon as the islanders spotted the boats, they vanished into the trees. Cook and his party landed and set off down the beach. But as soon as they vanished round a bend, the islanders reemerged from the forest and made as if to attack one of the boats, which had been left in the care of four boys. At this, a marine in the second boat opened fire, hitting one of the islanders, who fell instantly to the ground. The man's companions dragged him about a hundred yards up the beach and then fled when they saw Cook's party, which had been alerted by the shots, racing back to the scene.

The Māori, who had been shot through the heart, was dead, and Banks took some time to scrutinize the corpse. He described him as a midsize man, brown-skinned and tattooed on one cheek with a perfect spiral. He was dressed in a fine kind of cloth that the English had not seen before. It was tied, Banks noted, exactly as shown in the engraving from Tasman's account of New Zealand.

The following day, Cook tried again, this time taking two additional precautions. First, he landed with a party of marines, and, second, he took Tupaia with him. Cook wrote that he had tried to speak to the people of New Zealand in "the George Island Language," meaning what he knew of Tahitian, but that they had answered him by flourishing their weapons and breaking into a war dance. This—the famous Māori *haka*—was vividly described by Lieutenant John Gore:

> About an hundred of the Natives all Arm'd . . . drew themselves up in lines. Then with a Regular Jump from Left to Right and the Reverse, They brandish'd Their Weapons, distort'd their Mouths, Lolling out their Tongues and Turn'd up the Whites of their Eyes Accompanied with a strong hoarse song.

Cook responded to this intimidating display by drawing up his marines and marching them up the beach with the Union Jack paraded before them. The stage was set for a confrontation—and then something unexpected occurred. Tupaia stepped forward and addressed the warriors in fluent Tahitian and, to the surprise of everyone present, he was immediately understood.

The significance of this moment was monumental, both in terms of what it meant for the successful prosecution of the voyage and from a larger, theoretical point of view. Cook later acknowledged what a "prodigious advantage" it had been to have Tupaia on board during the six months they spent circumnavigating New Zealand. His knowledge of the language and his negotiating skills were indispensable in helping the British obtain geographical information, procure supplies, and, above all, avoid conflict with the Māori. Locally, Tupaia became something of a celebrity. He was often seen "preaching" to crowds or discoursing from the stern of the ship to canoe-loads of people who had paddled out to hear him. Years later, when Cook returned to New Zealand, one of the first questions he was asked was "Where is Tupaia?"

Tupaia, it is worth noting, did not exactly identify with the inhabitants of New Zealand. That is, he did not place his clear but distant kinship with them above his more immediate alliance with the British. On the contrary, he often observed that the Māori were great liars, and he warned the British to be on their guard in their dealings with them. This was similar to the approach he had taken at Rurutu, in the Australs, where he also told the British that the islanders were not to be trusted. At the same time, he plainly acknowledged a common heritage with the inhabitants of New Zealand. According to Banks, the subject of Tupaia's long conversations with the Māori priests was "their antiquity and Legends of their ancestors," which, while they no doubt differed in many details, would have exhibited significant similarities. One old man told Tupaia that "he knew of no other great land than that we had been upon," but that his ancestors had come "originaly from *Heawye* . . . which lay to the Northward where were many lands." This was a reference to Hawaiki, the mythic ancestral homeland recognized by islanders throughout the eastern Pacific.

To the Europeans, the resemblance between Tahitians and Māori was unmistakable, though there were contrasts as well. Some months later, as he was leaving New Zealand, Banks summed up the comparison: the Māori, he thought, were more active and less inclined to fat than the Tahitians; they were more modest in their carriage but less clean; they were better paddlers but worse sailors; they were less given to stealing but were cannibalistic, a practice the Tahitians claimed to abhor. On balance, however, it was clear to Banks that the similarities far outweighed the differences. "There remains," he wrote, "little doubt that they came originaly from the same source: but where that Source is future experience may teach us."

This question of whether the inhabitants of the many different islands across the Pacific were related to one another and the associated issue of where they might have come from were problems that Cook would return to repeatedly over the next few years. In the course of his second voyage to the Pacific—a long, complex expedition in the years 1772–1775, involving three passes along the edge of the southern ice and two tropical island sweeps—he visited several more Polynesian islands, including the Marquesas, Niue,

Tonga, and Easter Island, in addition to returning to both Tahiti and New Zealand. On his third and final voyage (1776–1779), he returned again to Tonga, Tahiti, and New Zealand, visited some of the southern Cook Islands, and reached the as-yet-undiscovered islands of Hawai'i, where he was killed. By 1778 he had effectively seen it all—the entire Polynesian Triangle—and had fully grasped the scope of the Polynesian diaspora.

Writing in 1774 of the inhabitants of Easter Island, the most easterly island in Polynesia, Cook was so struck by their affinity to the inhabitants of the far western isles that he was moved almost to lyricism. "It is extraordinary," he wrote, "that the same Nation should have spread themselves over all the isles in this Vast Ocean . . . which is almost a fourth part of the circumference of the Globe." It *was* astonishing, even in the abstract. But to one who had actually covered this distance himself, the idea must have had special resonance. When he wrote these words, Cook had just completed an eight-thousand-mile passage across the southern Pacific Ocean, steering a zigzagging course from New Zealand to Easter Island. If anyone understood just how far apart these islands were, it was him.

It is interesting to follow Cook's logic regarding the relatedness of all these different islanders. A methodical thinker, he considered three different types of evidence in turn. First, there was the way the islanders looked. Brown-skinned, black-haired, often tall and physically robust, they were not only extremely similar to one another in appearance; they were also markedly different from the inhabitants of islands to the west, in Papua New Guinea, the Solomons, and Vanuatu, who were both more varied in appearance and typically darker-skinned.

Then there was the islanders' material culture, the things they made and used: their fishhooks and clothing, their houses and canoes. Here, the broad outlines of an underlying resemblance were also apparent. Foods were similar, tools were similar, methods of cooking were widely the same. Canoes, while exhibiting interesting variations, showed broad similarities in design; the arrangement of houses and ceremonial spaces was often analogous. Though it was not always easy to tell—Cook spent months in both the Society Islands and New Zealand, but his visits to some of the other island groups were measured only in days—there seemed to be parallels even in some of the more recondite aspects of the islanders' culture. In many places, for example, Cook noticed altars piled with offerings of food, and ceremonial gestures were often repeated, like the waving of palm fronds or other greenery at the meeting of two groups.

But what really persuaded Cook that the inhabitants of all these islands belonged, as he put it, to "the same race of People" was the similarity of their languages to one another. Tupaia's unexpected ability to communicate with the Māori was the most dramatic illustration of this, but even before they reached New Zealand, Tupaia had given Cook to understand that "the same language was spoken in all the isles." This was later confirmed on Cook's second voyage, when a different pair of Tahitians traveled with him to Tonga, New Zealand, Easter Island, and the Marquesas. Although neither was a match for Tupaia in knowledge and linguistic ability, they were able to make themselves understood in all the islands except Tonga. No one at the time would have known it, but this actually makes good linguistic sense, as Tongan is both the earliest branch of the Polynesian language family and one of the most conservative, linguistically speaking.

COOK'S VOYAGES TO the Pacific coincided with a great leap in understanding about the nature of languages in general and their relationships to one another. In 1786, a British philologist named Sir William Jones, who had made a study of Indian languages and culture, suggested that the "affinity" of Sanskrit to Latin and Greek was too strong to have been the result of chance. It occurred to him that all three of these languages might have sprung from some common source—a different language altogether, one that perhaps might not even still exist. Jones went on to argue that several other languages, including Gothic (an extinct Germanic language), Celtic, and even Old Persian, might also be derived from this same original language. This insight led ultimately to the recognition of what is known as the Indo-European language family, a group of hundreds of historically related languages, both living and dead, covering a geographic range that stretches from the Indian subcontinent to Iceland.

It had, of course, long been understood that there were relationships among languages. Latin and Greek show many similarities; the Romance languages are obviously a group; Dutch, German, and the Scandinavian languages are all clearly related. But the idea that linguistic relationships might go far beyond this and include languages that seem, on the surface, to have no family resemblance whatsoever—Bengali, Manx, and Armenian, for example—was truly electrifying, as was the idea of a single protolanguage from which this great diversity might have sprung. In Europe, this hypothetical ancestral language, known as Proto-Indo-European, was reconstructed during a period of intense linguistic activity in the nineteenth century by scholars in England, Denmark, France, and Germany (among the field's early pioneers was one of the fairy-tale-collecting Brothers Grimm), using a methodology that is still practiced today.

In its basic outlines, the comparative method is deceptively simple. The first step is to identify what are known as cognate sets, that is, groups of words in different languages that appear to resemble one another in both meaning and sound. The next question is whether the differences between these words are regular and systematic. It is a curious fact of linguistics that when languages change, they do so systematically. If, under certain conditions (like at the beginning of a word or before a certain kind of vowel), a sound in one language changes to a different sound in a related language, then it should always do so under those conditions. Between Latin and English, for example, there are certain predictable shifts, like the change from an initial *p* to *f*, as in *pater/father* and *ped-/foot*, or from *d* to *t*, as in *decem/ten* and *dent-/tooth*. This principle of regularity was the great discovery of nineteenth-century philology; without it there would be no meaningful way to compare languages or to illustrate their relationships over time.

Sometimes, though, similarities between languages are just accidental. The Greek word *theós*, meaning "god," and the Aztec *teotl*, meaning "sacred," have nothing to do with one another; they just happen to resemble each other in both meaning and sound. In other cases, a similarity can be so widespread as to constitute a language universal; common examples of this are baby-talk words, like the English *ma* and the Mandarin *mā*, both of which mean "mother." Another source of confusion comes from onomatopoeic words, that is, words that sound like the thing they are describing. The Greek stem *pneu-*, meaning "breathe," is remarkably similar to the Klamath (Native American) word for "breathe," *pniw-*, but there is no relationship between them beyond the possibility that they may both reflect the sound of blowing or breathing out.

Finally, there is the problem of borrowing. English is a great borrower of words from other languages—*goulash* from Hungarian, *veranda* from Tamil, *caribou* from Micmac, *gecko* from Javanese, and the list goes on—but all languages borrow from one another. Borrowed words come into a language through contact between speakers of different languages, often to express a concept for which the host language has no word; they are not words that occur in both languages because they have descended from a shared ancestral root. So if two languages exhibit regular similarities of meaning, grammar, and sound, and if words that appear to be cognate are not onomatopoeic, universal, or borrowed, chances are good that the languages have a "genetic" relationship, meaning that they are derived from a common linguistic ancestor.

None of this would have been of terribly much interest to Cook, who was a man of action. But it was precisely the sort of thing that engaged the attention of Joseph Banks, who later in life actually corresponded with Jones and who was already thinking along these lines even before Tupaia first revealed the mutual intelligibility of Māori and Tahitian. During the long weeks at sea between Tahiti and New Zealand, when there was little to do but read and write, Banks devoted himself to recording his observations of the Society Islands. Among the topics he covered was the Tahitian language, which he described as "very soft and tuneable," abounding in vowels and easy to pronounce. (Tahitian is sometimes difficult to read for this same reason; see, for example, a name like Faa'a—or, as it is sometimes written, Fa'a'a—the district that has given its name to Tahiti's international airport.)

Banks lists about a hundred Tahitian words for things like head, hair, dog, shark, sun, moon, rope, net, house, cloud, and bone, as well as a few important verbs—to eat, to drink, to steal, to be angry. His orthography is idiosyncratic, but it is roughly possible to work out what he heard. Two words on his list have since been borrowed into English—*mahimahi*, a popular type of fish, and *moa*, which Banks glosses as "a fowl," though we know it as the name of an extinct flightless bird.

Making word lists was a conventional thing for explorers and their scientific companions to do in the seventeenth and eighteenth centuries. Like drawing charts and coastal profiles or pictures of new animals and plants, it was part of the great European project of describing newly encountered portions of the world. Navigators also compiled and shared vocabularies, in the hope that they might come in handy, and one often reads of an explorer—like Tasman, for example—trying out some word list on a group of islanders, usually to no avail. But Banks, with time on his hands and a good library at his disposal, took the idea one step further. Using word lists from two different books—the vocabulary compiled in 1616 by Schouten and Le Maire and a word list from a collection of voyages by the Dutch East India Company—he made a chart comparing the Tahitian words for the numbers one to ten with the words for these numbers in three other languages: those of the Cocos Islands, New Guinea, and Madagascar.

Numbers, as it happens, are one of the very best tests for relatedness among different languages. Like words for body parts or essential actions, they have a kind of durability, in part because they tend not to be borrowed. The number two, for example, shows remarkable consistency across a wide range of languages in the Indo-European family: Greek *dúō*, Vedic *dvá(u)*, Latin *duo*, Welsh *dau*, Old Church Slavonic *dŭva*, and so on. Banks's chart is similarly persuasive: two is given as *rua* in Tahitian, *loua* in the language of the Cocos Islands, *roa* in New Guinea, *rove* in Madagascar. Seven is *hetu* in Tahitian, *fitou* in the Cocos, *fita* in New Guinea, *fruto* in Madagascar. Even allowing for errors, the overall effect is to suggest strongly that the languages in Banks's set are related.

It is not entirely clear exactly which languages Banks was actually comparing, but we can make an educated guess. What Schouten and Le Maire called the "Cocos Islands" are almost certainly a pair of small islands in the northern reaches of what is now the Kingdom of Tonga. Today Tongan is spoken on these islands; in 1616 it was likely a language closer to Samoan, but either way, it was undoubtedly a Polynesian language. What was meant by "New Guinea" is less certain, but it seems probable that it was New Ireland, an island off the northeast coast of New Guinea, far to the west of the Polynesian Triangle. Here the linguistic picture is much more complicated, but some of the languages spoken in this region do belong, if more distantly, to the large language family that also includes the languages of Polynesia.

From Tahiti to the islands of northern Tonga is a distance of about sixteen hundred miles; from Tahiti to New Ireland is more than four thousand miles. So we are already looking at a startling geographic range. But what made the whole thing almost too hard to credit was the idea that a version of this same language might also be spoken on the island of Madagascar. Madagascar is not even in the Pacific Ocean. It is an island off the southeastern coast of Africa in the Indian Ocean, nearly ten thousand miles from Tahiti by the shortest possible sea route. Banks himself was astonished by these results. "That the people who inhabit this numerous range of Isles should have originaly come from one and the same place and brought with the[m] the same numbers and Language," he wrote, "is in my opinion not at all past beleif, but that the Numbers of the Island of Madagascar should be the same as all these is almost if not quite incredible."

Incredible maybe, but also, as it happens, true. Banks had stumbled upon one of the most remarkable facts about the peopling of the Pacific, which is that all the languages of Polynesia, Micronesia, Fiji, New Caledonia, Vanuatu, and the Philippines, as well as almost all the languages of Indonesia and the Solomon Islands and some of the languages of Malaysia, New Guinea, Madagascar, and Taiwan, belong to a single language family known as Austronesian. Today there are believed to be more than a thousand languages in the Austronesian family, with more than three hundred million speakers worldwide, making it one of the largest language families on the planet. Banks, writing in 1769, could not possibly know this—it would be well into the twentieth century before the full picture emerged—but he had glimpsed one of the key pieces of the Polynesian puzzle.

CARTOGRAPHERS SOMETIMES JOKE that early maps of the Pacific can be placed into one of two categories: B.C. or A.C., meaning Before or After Cook. This is an acknowledgment of Cook's unequaled contribution to geographic understanding, but it is also broadly true of the region's history. Before Cook, the world of the Pacific belonged to the islanders who inhabited it; Europeans were infrequent and often incompetent visitors; outside understanding of the region was essentially nil. After Cook—and partly, though not entirely, because of him—the outlines of the Pacific and its islands came into sharper focus; the region became much more accessible; and outsiders began arriving, first in a trickle and then in a flood. After Cook, the remote Pacific—a world that had been changing gradually for centuries—was abruptly and in some ways cataclysmically transformed.

Cook himself did not live to see any of this, having met his death in Hawai'i in 1779. Nor, sadly, did his collaborator and informant Tupaia. Tupaia left New Zealand in the *Endeavour* with Cook and sailed across the Tasman Sea to Australia—a country he certainly knew nothing about—where he painted a group of Aborigines spearing fish from their bark canoes. He then sailed to the Dutch East Indies, where, during a stop to refit for the long voyage back to England, he died of dysentery and fever, along with about half the *Endeavour*'s crew.

Although Cook's voyages are celebrated primarily as spectacular feats of navigation, they produced much more than just knowledge of where the reefs and coastlines lay. In terms of our understanding of Polynesian history, they constitute a sort of opening gambit, the first serious attempt on the part of Europeans to examine Polynesian experience and knowledge, and the first significant interaction between European and Polynesian ideas. They are, of course, less satisfactory than one would wish. While it is fascinating to learn that no matter how far Tupaia got from Tahiti, he always knew exactly where it lay, it is frustrating to find that no one ever seems to have asked him how he knew this. And while it is useful to learn from Banks that on their "longer Voyages" the Tahitians steered "in the day by the Sun and in the night by the Stars," it is disappointing to discover that no one ever got any details about how this was actually done.

Still, what did emerge from these voyages was significant: first, the realization that all the islanders of the remote Pacific formed a single, identifiable cultural group and, second, the suggestion that they could be linked, linguistically at least, with people far to the west of them. Here, then, were the bones of a theory about who the Polynesians were. It was based on eyewitness observation and firsthand Polynesian accounts, along with a bit of clever thinking about linguistics, and it was a pretty solid piece of deduction—certainly much better than the notion that Polynesians had been created in their islands by God. But it was not by any stretch of the imagination complete. Over the course of the next hundred-odd years, all kinds of people would attempt to fill in the gaps, coming up with an array of hypothetical Polynesian histories—some clever, some not so clever, some downright wacky—even as Polynesia itself morphed under the pressure of contact with the outside world.

# Part III

# WHY NOT JUST

# ASK THEM?

# (1779–1920)

*In which we look at some of the stories that
Polynesians told about themselves and consider the
difficulty nineteenth-century Europeans had trying to
make sense of them.*

# DROWNED CONTINENTS
# AND OTHER THEORIES
## *The Nineteenth-Century Pacific*

*"Dupetit Thouars taking over Tahiti on*
*September 9th, 1842" by Louis Le Breton, 1850.*
MUSÉE NATIONALE DE LA MARINE, PARIS. WIKIMEDIA COMMONS.

**IN THE REMOTE** Pacific, the nineteenth century was the century when everything changed. With Cook's death in Hawai'i in 1779, the era of European discovery effectively drew to a close. The big geographic questions—the size of the ocean, the existence (or not) of a southern continent, the locations of the major archipelagoes—had all been answered, and this, along with improvements in maritime technology (notably the development of the chronometer, which finally enabled European navigators to find their way about the ocean with some precision), made the Pacific much more accessible to outsiders. The result was an influx of missionaries, whalers, traders, government officials, and settlers.

The first mission ship bound for Polynesia set out from England in 1796, carrying thirty evangelical men and women. The initial ventures—to be distributed among three fledgling missions in Tonga, Tahiti, and the Marquesas—were not a success. Three of those sent to Tonga were killed in an outbreak of tribal war; all but one of the group stationed in Tahiti abandoned their posts; and of the two men sent to the Marquesas, one could not even be persuaded to go ashore. But the process of Christianization had begun, and within a matter of decades armies of Anglican, Wesleyan, Presbyterian, Congregationalist, Catholic, and Mormon missionaries were fanning out across the region, catechisms in hand. It was also only a matter of time, once the geography of the great ocean was known and a few safe harbors identified, before the lure of trade would begin attracting commercial adventurers. The dream of Terra Australis Incognita, with its imagined hoard of silk, spices, and gold, was gone, but the Pacific offered a broad range of exploitable products: fur seals, sandalwood, flax, timber, pearl and turtle shell, bêche-de-mer, and, of course, that most lucrative and alluring of all the ocean's resources: whales.

The first whaling ships arrived in the Pacific hard on the heels of Captain Cook, and each year the numbers increased, so that by the mid-1840s as many as six or seven hundred vessels could be found cruising the Pacific at any time. Whalers carried crews of about thirty men and remained at sea for an average of three and a half years. Their routes, not so different from those of the early explorers, typically brought them into the Pacific by way of Cape Horn, where, during the southern summer months, they trolled the southeastern reaches of the ocean. At the end of the season they shifted north, and in between they called at islands in search of water, food, women, and supplies. At the height of the boom, in the 1830s and '40s, this meant tens of thousands of men from all over the world—lascars, Spaniards, Native Americans, Brits, Balts, Russians, Scandinavians, Chinese—pouring into island ports in Polynesia. The major stops were Hawai'i, the Marquesas, and New Zealand, but there were so many whalers in the Pacific during these decades that even small islands like Wallis and Rotuma had firsthand experience of their crews.

All these people needed food, clothing, and entertainment, and they often had money in their pockets to spend. The result was a whole host of secondary industries—bakeries, blacksmiths, brothels, laundries, boardinghouses, grog sellers—which sprang up to cater to those passing through the major ports. These, in turn, became famously unruly places, and as the size and complexity of these settlements grew, the need for order became increasingly urgent. Before long there were signs of nascent government—consuls, harbormasters, jails—and by the middle of the nineteenth century several of the more populous Polynesian islands had come under some form of colonial control.

The impact of all this on the islanders was dramatic, particularly in the places where foreigners were concentrated. Societies that had been shielded for centuries by distance and isolation were suddenly inundated with new influences. There were new trade goods like scissors, knives, and mirrors, new animals like horses, rabbits, and cats. There were new foods like flour, cabbage, and onions, new weeds like sow thistle, dandelion, and gorse. Stone adzes and clubs were replaced by guns and hatchets, digging sticks by shovels and hoes, clothing of plaited flax and beaten tapa by woolen blankets, jackets, trousers, and cotton frocks. There were new laws, new languages, and new religions, as well as new vices, like tobacco and drink. Polynesians became literate and, in some cases, well traveled and were exposed in large numbers to Old World pathogens for the first time.

Meanwhile, back in Europe, the idea of Polynesia began surfacing in the popular culture. There had long been an armchair fascination with voyages: explorers' accounts were a major seventeenth- and eighteenth-century genre, even spawning a new branch of literature—both *Robinson Crusoe* (1719) and *Gulliver's Travels* (1726) were fictional extrapolations of the genre of factual travel writing. At the same time, a new zeitgeist was emerging in Europe, one that privileged nature over culture, the past over the present, the far over the near. Folklore, previously of no real interest, suddenly became fascinating; foreign and archaic subjects assumed a new prestige, as did the histories of peoples outside the classical lineages of Greece and Rome.

A list of literary touchstones from the period gives some indication of where things were going. In 1762, the poet James Macpherson published a fraudulent but wildly successful poem cycle purportedly based upon Scottish Gaelic folktales. In 1770, extracts of the Prose Edda—one of the primary sources of Norse mythology—appeared in English for the first time. In 1797, Samuel Taylor Coleridge wrote "Kubla Khan," a poem set in the summer palace of the Mongol emperor. In 1805, Walter Scott published the first of many historical romances set among the Scottish border clans. In 1812, the first collection of German fairy tales was published by the Brothers Grimm. In 1826, James Fenimore Cooper wrote *The Last of the Mohicans*, a novel set at the edge of the American frontier.

With the rise of Romanticism—which is the name we give to this cultural moment—Europeans seized on the Pacific as a fit setting, like the Orient or the colonial frontier, for quests and adventures. Poets like Keats and Coleridge incorporated references to the Pacific into their work; adventure stories began featuring cannibals and volcanoes; minor (and even major) characters in European novels lit out for the Pacific to make their fortunes or were sent there as punishment for their sins. The market for travelogues continued to flourish, but now, in addition to the journals of explorers like Cook, there were narratives by missionaries, traders, and colonial officials, who passed through the Pacific and wrote up their impressions for the benefit of curious readers back home.

A handful of these writers would ultimately settle in the islands, learn Polynesian languages, and make what could be fairly called a study of Polynesian ideas. They would collect and translate Polynesian histories, interpret Polynesian myths, compare Polynesian names and languages, and, out of all this, produce influential theories about the origins and history of the Polynesian people. But even those with no more than a cursory understanding of the region took up the vexed question of where Polynesians had come from. And so, in the nineteenth century, we see a proliferation of theories—which both helped to define the problem of Polynesian origins and, at the same time, introduced a number of wayward ideas.

COOK AND HIS companions had arrived, toward the end of the eighteenth century, at what we might call a "baseline" explanation. On the strength of what they had been able to observe, as well as what had been told to them by islanders, they concluded that the inhabitants of the remote Pacific had probably island-hopped their way across the ocean, starting somewhere in Southeast Asia. Cook, true to his calling, had arrived at this position by considering the possibilities conceived as a series of cardinal points. He did not believe that the inhabitants of Polynesia had come from the east (that is, the Americas), and, as to the north and south, experience had taught him that there was no undiscovered continent or hidden homeland in either the far northern or southern reaches of the ocean. West, however, seemed like a good possibility, especially given what he had learned from Tupaia. "For," he wrote, "if the inhabitants of [the Society Islands] have been at Islands laying 2 or 300 Leagues to the westward of them," as Tupaia had reported, "it cannot be doubted but that the inhabitants of those western Islands may have been at others as far to the westward of them and so we may trace them from Island to Island quite to the East Indies."

It was a well-reasoned argument, but it left a number of important questions unanswered, foremost among them the problem of the prevailing winds. The same winds that had swept European navigators westward across the middle of the Pacific Ocean on "some variant of the great north-west line" presented a seemingly insurmountable obstacle to the idea of Polynesian voyagers traveling the opposite way. In order to reach the islands of Polynesia, voyagers from the East Indies would have had to sail straight into the teeth of the easterly trades—something no sailing vessel, then or now, is able to do. This led some nineteenth-century theorists to conclude that the inhabitants of Polynesia must have crossed the Pacific in the other direction, starting out in the Americas and traveling west. As one Spanish missionary put it, given the strength and regularity of the prevailing winds, it would have been much "easier to populate all these islands from South America than from any other part of the globe."

But while an American point of origin solved the problem of the prevailing winds, it was contradicted by other bodies of evidence. As early as 1775, Cook's naturalist, Forster, a prodigious linguist, had concluded that there was no connection between the languages of Polynesia and those spoken along the coast of South America, in Chile and Peru. Other observers, coming along a bit later, also noted that the native inhabitants of the Americas were not skilled mariners, and that pigs, dogs, and chickens, all ubiquitous in the Pacific, were unknown in South America, all of which diminished the likelihood of an American starting point.

Neither the west-to-east nor the east-to-west migration route was thus without its difficulties, leading an English missionary by the name of William Ellis to devise a theory that satisfied the demands of *both* an Asiatic point of origin *and* a sea route in keeping with the prevailing winds. According to what we might term the "Beringian solution," the progenitors of the Polynesian people had begun their migrations on the Asian mainland. From there they had traveled north to the Aleutian Islands, across the Bering Strait, and down along the coasts of California and Mexico before turning back into the Pacific, "under the favouring influence" of the trades. It was a huge circuit of the northern Pacific Rim, tens of thousands of additional miles—hardly the most parsimonious explanation.

Still another way to think about the great Polynesian diaspora was to account for it not in terms of the movement of *people*—east to west, west to east, around in a great circle—but in terms of the movement of *land*. Proponents of this view argued that the islands of the Pacific were the peaks of a drowned continent and that the islanders were the remnants of a population that had survived by clinging to the mountaintops. There was no real evidence for this, though one writer, pointing to the ubiquitous traces of vulcanism—the scoriae, basalt, pumice, and blocks of black glass—that could be found throughout the islands, concluded that the Pacific, that watery waste, must at some earlier time have been an "abode of fire." Others, however, were less sanguine. As one nineteenth-century skeptic put it, even "supposing a remnant to have escaped, it is scarcely possible that life could be sustained, as usually there is nothing to eat on these lofty mountains, to say nothing of the difficulty of obtaining water."

Sunken continents and lost civilizations were popular nineteenth-century solutions to apparently insoluble mysteries (hence "Lemuria," a lost continent proposed to explain the presence of lemurs on the island of Madagascar). They combined current scientific and philosophical debates about geology and the history of the world (whether change was slow and incremental or proceeded "catastrophically" by fits and starts) with flood myths, echoes of Atlantis and Terra Australis Incognita, and a Romantic enthusiasm for forgotten worlds. But while there have undoubtedly been eruptions, tempests, typhoons, tsunamis, and changes in the level of the sea, there has never been any scientific evidence for the existence of an inhabited lost continent in the mid-Pacific—a fact that has made little or no difference to the enduring popularity of the idea.

AMONG THE MORE enthusiastic proponents of the drowned-continent theory was a Belgian "merchant adventurer" named Jacques-Antoine Moerenhout, who spent a decade or more in Tahiti as a trader and government official in the early nineteenth century. Moerenhout was deeply interested in the Polynesian puzzle. He accepted that the linguistic evidence pointed in the direction of the East Indies, but, like many, he was troubled by the winds. He also rejected the competing American solution, however, on the grounds that there were no linguistic or cultural connections. This left him with only one alternative: Polynesians must have come from where they already were, and since that was in some sense inconceivable, something else must have been there that was now gone: a great continent that had been "suddenly destroyed by the waters of the sea."

Central to Moerenhout's thinking on this subject was his view that Polynesian culture exhibited signs of great antiquity, traces of beauty and sophistication that could be explained only as the echoes of some long-lost civilization. Moerenhout marshaled various bits of evidence in support of this idea—the presence of colossal statues on Easter Island, some obscure but tantalizing fragments of astronomical lore—but his primary proof was a Tahitian cosmogony, or story of the origin of the world, that he himself had collected during a strange and vivid encounter in 1831.

At the time, Moerenhout was living in a place called Papara, on the south coast of Tahiti. He was friendly with a chief there from whom he had learned something of Tahitian customs. There were things, however, that the chief did not know, and Moerenhout was anxious to find someone who could fill in the gaps in his knowledge. He had been told about an old priest who was said to know all the ancient traditions, but he had been unable to persuade this man to speak with him or to divulge any of his esoteric lore.

Then, one night, there was a knock on his door and a voice called out, "Mr. Moerenhout come now!" Opening the door, Moerenhout found a Tahitian messenger, who pulled from beneath his tapa cloth a large banana leaf on which was written a communication from the old priest. It read, "Taaroa was his name; he kept in the void. No land, no sky, no sea, no men. Taaroa called; but nothing responded to him; and existing alone, he was changing in the universe." Moerenhout described himself as having been "dazzled by this astonishing discovery." All of a sudden, he wrote, he could see "the veil being raised before my eyes which up to then had hidden the past." Despite the fact that it was past nine o'clock and pitch dark, he ordered a canoe and set out immediately to visit the old priest.

It was a wild and exhilarating journey. Because of the location of the old priest's village, the voyage could not be conducted within the safety of the reef, and the canoe was forced out onto the open ocean. The Tahitians paddled close to the breakers—so near that Moerenhout felt sure the canoe would be dashed to bits on the reef—but the wind was light and the paddlers expert, and the canoe skimmed along through the night. Suddenly, as they came around a bend, the moon rose from behind a peninsula. The peaks of the mountains were drenched in pale silver, the fronds of the coconut palms shivered in the night breeze. Overcome by the vision before him, Moerenhout gave vent to his feelings:

> In the state of mind which I then was, what I was about to learn
> of the traditions of these islanders, the object of this nocturnal
> excursion, the spectacle which was surrounding me, this so very
> tranquil night, this so beautiful place, so singular, these Indians
> isolated in the middle of the most vast seas; so many diverse ob-
> jects presented themselves at the same time to my mind, and the
> confusion of my thoughts making me forget where I was I cried
> out with force: "Ah! If I am going to learn finally where all this
> owes its origin!"

Moerenhout also reported good-humoredly that his Tahitian paddlers, at first struck dumb with astonishment at this outburst, had exploded into fits of laughter.

At length, the traveling party reached the village where the old priest lived. After sleep and a meal, the two men sat down to a recording session, with the priest recounting what he knew and Moerenhout taking dictation. The process was laborious: the old priest, who spoke from memory, "could only recite consecutively while declaiming" as Moerenhout struggled to write everything down. Although he had a fair command of Tahitian, there was much that Moerenhout failed to understand. The very first song the old priest recited was completely lost on him, and even with the chants he did comprehend, he was obliged to make the old man say them over and over, for "it was only by dint of some repetitions that I succeeded in getting on to paper the details." All of this was tiring for the old priest, whose memory sometimes betrayed him, and it took several sessions for Moerenhout to compile a coherent, if still partial, account.

At the heart of the priest's narration was the creation myth, the first lines of which had been sent to Moerenhout on the banana leaf:

He was (or there was); Taaroa was his name;
He stood in the void (or the immensity);
no land, no sky
no sea, no men;
Taaroa called, but nothing replied to him;
And alone existing he changed himself into the universe;
His pivots, axes or orbits, that is Taaroa;
the rocks, the bases, that is he;
Taaroa is the sand, the atoms or elements.
That is how he himself is called.

At first, Moerenhout wrote, he was puzzled by this chant, not because of its inherent obscurity but because he felt that its "extreme elevation" was not consistent with the state of Tahitian society as he himself had experienced it. The old priest's cosmogony was too elegant, too abstract, too metaphysical, he felt, to be the work of a "primitive" people like the Polynesians. Some of the concepts expressed—a beginning in darkness, a deity who is both cause and effect, "at the same time the matter and the mover of all matter"—called to mind the language of a Zoroaster, a Pythagoras, and compared "advantageously" with "the most sublime" creation stories of other nations. It could only be the work, he concluded, of some ancient civilization, a fragment of something from remotest antiquity that "had crossed the centuries of barbarism," only to be rediscovered like a potsherd or a flake of sharpened stone. Who these ancient people were was unknowable, however, since all their glories—their science and their cities, their writing and their art— had been destroyed by the waters of a great primeval flood.

HERE, THEN, WE have a glimpse of the next great chapter in the quest to decode the origins of the Polynesians. Moerenhout's logic was, of course, flawed—the islanders were not a remnant of some ancient civilization that had been washed away in a great deluge—but his approach represents a whole new way of thinking about who they might be. Cook and Banks had observed in the 1770s that it was almost impossible to understand anything of what was told to them about Polynesian arcana. But by the 1820s or '30s, this was no longer the case. As more and more outsiders began to settle in the region, Polynesians and Europeans gradually became fluent enough in one another's languages to converse on difficult, even esoteric, subjects. Polynesians could begin to communicate something of what they believed, including their own ideas about where they had come from. And Europeans, newly taken with the idea of origins in general and fascinated by this window into Polynesian thought, could begin to get answers to the questions they most wanted to ask. If, for sixteenth-, seventeenth-, and eighteenth-century Europeans, the Pacific had presented itself as a great geographical puzzle, for those in the nineteenth century the enigma lay in trying to make sense of what Polynesians said.

# A WORLD WITHOUT WRITING

*Polynesian Oral Traditions*

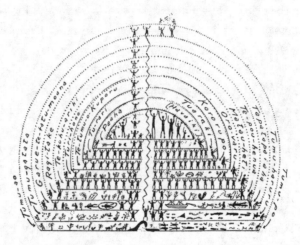

*Tuamotuan chart of the origin of the world,*
*from "The Tuamotuan creation charts by Paiore"*
*by Kenneth P. Emory,* Journal of the Polynesian Society *(1939).*
THE POLYNESIAN SOCIETY, UNIVERSITY OF AUCKLAND, NEW ZEALAND.

**IT SOMETIMES SEEMS,** on the face of it, as though it should have been easy for Europeans to get answers to their questions once they were able to converse with the inhabitants of Polynesia. Why not, after all, *just ask them* who they were? But the answers that Polynesians gave were confusing to Europeans: they were not framed with the right sort of knowledge, and did not address the right points or provide the sort of information that Europeans were after. It is easy to forget just how different people once were from one another. But at a fundamental level, these were cultures with very dissimilar ways of thinking, and, at least in the beginning, every piece of information that passed between them had to be traded across this epistemological gap.

One important difference was that, until the nineteenth century, everything Polynesians knew—or, indeed, had ever known—
had to be transmitted by word of mouth. This was true not only of
practical knowledge, like sailing directions or boat-building techniques or the uses of various plants and animals, but of family and
tribal histories, genealogies, legends, folktales, and myths, all of
which were stored in the memories of individuals whose responsi-
bility it was to maintain this knowledge and who handed it down
from generation to generation.

It is almost impossible to imagine such a world today: one without books or calendars or accounts, never mind the Internet, one in
which nothing has ever been documented and all the information
that can be possessed is held in the minds of a few. But literacy has
emerged only in the past five or six thousand years, and for most of
human history this was how knowledge was stored and communi-
cated. The advent of writing is often seen as one of the watershed
developments in human history, and it can be argued that the presence or absence of writing shapes cultures in fundamental ways—
some would even say it shapes consciousness itself. But even if that
is too great a claim, it is certainly true that the ability to document
what is known changes the way knowledge is constructed, including the kinds of information that can be transmitted and the shape
that information takes.

In an oral culture, the single most important consideration is
the conservation of essential knowledge, and many of the most distinctive characteristics of oral traditions are qualities that make
them easier to remember. Oral traditions are often chanted or sung
and exhibit distinctive rhythmical or rhetorical qualities that make
them easier to retain. They often contain formulaic elements; the
Homeric epithets—wily Odysseus, the wine-dark sea—are classic
examples. They are frequently marked by a high degree of redun-
dancy and repetition, particularly around significant concepts and
ritual behavior—which is why in Homer there is so much pouring
of water and wine and burning of thighbones wrapped in fat. By

the same token, anything that becomes culturally unimportant can easily disappear. Although oral traditions often seem focused on the past, they are actually quite present-centered. In an oral culture, only what matters to the living is retained.

Historically, when people from literate cultures came into contact with people from oral ones, the former were often astonished by how much the latter could recall. This was certainly true in the nineteenth-century Pacific, where Europeans reported prodigious feats of memory on the part of Polynesians. One Māori man from New Zealand was reported as having dictated eleven volumes of traditional material entirely from memory, "and that at a very advanced age"; another was able to recite the genealogical descent of every member of his tribe going back thirty-four generations; a third dictated a genealogy consisting of nearly two thousand names. Still, there is an upper limit to what any single person can remember, and modern studies of nonliterate cultures have shown that even the most remarkable feats of memorization are not exact. Unlike writing, which fixes words in a given sequence, oral traditions can never be said to be "archival." They are fluid and mutable and change over time, both accidentally—in the way that anything repeated over and over again changes—and strategically, in response to people's evolving experience and needs.

This means that there are no canonical versions, no truest or most correct account of the creation of the universe, or the origin of fire, or the snaring and slowing of the sun. Instead there exist a multitude of variants, which differ not only from archipelago to archipelago but from island to island, tribe to tribe, even priest to priest. Efforts to document these traditions, such as those undertaken by Europeans in the nineteenth-century Pacific, can therefore never capture more than a slice or cross section of the whole. A written account—compiled at a particular moment in a particular place from a particular person or group of people—is by definition neither definitive nor complete. And one consequence of reducing oral traditions to written texts is the fixing of particular versions, which then tend to become canonical with the passage of time—a point that many Polynesian chiefs and priests appreciated.

AS THE NUMBER of oral cultures in the world has diminished, interest in them has grown, and one of the most intriguing questions is whether there might be such a thing as an *oral way of seeing*, a worldview common to oral peoples that might be different in some generalizable way from the worldview of people in cultures with writing. One idea that seems intuitively correct is that knowledge in an oral culture remains "close to the living human lifeworld," that is, embodied in the world of experience and things.

In a famous study from the 1930s that seems to support this idea, nonliterate subjects from remote regions of Uzbekistan and Kyrgyzstan were asked to identify a series of geometric figures. Instead of using abstract terms like "circle" or "square," they referred to familiar objects: "A circle would be called a plate, sieve, bucket, watch, or moon; a square would be called a mirror, door, house, apricot-drying board." In another experiment, informants were asked to group four objects, three of which belonged to a single category. They consistently analyzed the objects not in terms of the categories that the researchers had in mind but in terms of practical situations—how one might actually use the objects in the real world. Presented with pictures of a hammer, saw, log, and hatchet, one informant said, "They're all alike. The saw will saw the log and the hatchet will chop it into small pieces. If one of these has to go, I'd throw out the hatchet. It doesn't do as good a job as a saw." When it was suggested that the hammer, saw, and hatchet belonged together because they were all tools and that the log belonged to a different category, the informant replied, "Yes, but even if we have the tools, we still need wood—otherwise we can't build anything." Not only is the knowledge organized in terms of real-life situations, but the situations themselves imply action, and so the whole cluster of ideas is embedded in a kind of story. The wood and the tools are not just *things*; they are things that someone is going to *use*. They matter because they are part of a human drama about building something that someone actually needs.

Of course, many people, reading this, will immediately think of some practically minded person they know who would have responded exactly like the Uzbek carpenter. (I myself am married to such a person.) But the point is not that such thought patterns disappeared with the advent of writing. On the contrary, many of the characteristics we associate with oral narratives—dramatic storytelling, situational thinking, concrete detail—are central to the way people communicate in literate societies (and essential to good writing, as any creative writing teacher will tell you). But there are other things we take for granted that did not and could not have existed in a world without writing, ways of organizing information that involve too many sequential stages to be held entirely in the mind.

In a world without writing, there are no inventories or statistics; in fact, writing, so far as anyone knows, was invented in order to make accurate lists of commodities like she-goats and oxen and amphorae of wine. There is no "abstractly sequential, classificatory, explanatory examination of phenomena," no definitions or comprehensive descriptions, no abstract categorization or stated truths. Whole bodies of thought, like geometry, rhetoric, algebra, symbolic logic—indeed, higher mathematics generally—and most of what we call science are impossible in a world without writing. This is not to say that oral peoples do not possess technical knowledge or think abstractly, or that they do not employ "science-like elements of empiricism" in order to solve complex problems. But simply that, by enabling the abstraction of information from its context—distancing the knower from the known—writing may create the conditions for a worldview that privileges objectivity.

Edward S. C. Handy, an anthropologist who spent time in the Marquesas in the 1920s, argued that what he called "subjective and objective reactions"—visions, dreams, divinations, as well as a knowledge of what we would call "verifiable facts"—were "unified" in the minds of the Marquesans, and that from their point of view, no useful distinction could be drawn between them. It is of course possible that Handy was reading into the situation some sense of what he believed Marquesans *ought* to be like. But there is an interesting story, recorded in New Zealand in 1897 by the linguist and scholar Edward Tregear, that seems to corroborate Handy's observation.

Tregear was an Englishman who immigrated to New Zealand in the 1860s and found work as a surveyor on the colonial frontier, a circumstance that brought him into contact with many Māori people. He had had a good early education: as a child he had learned both Latin and Greek, and he soon became conversationally fluent in Māori. He eventually went on to become something of a European authority on Polynesian languages, publishing the massive *Maori-Polynesian Comparative Dictionary* in 1891 and co-founding the Polynesian Society, the preeminent scholarly society for the study of Polynesian cultures in the twentieth century.

One day, wrote Tregear, he was walking along the banks of the Waikato River with a Māori acquaintance when the man volunteered to show him something that "no white man has ever yet seen." The Māori, whose name was not recorded, guided Tregear away from the riverbank and up a narrow valley until they reached a large conical stone about thirty feet tall. "That is my ancestor, Raukawa," he said. "He was a giant; he leapt across the Waikato River at the place where Cambridge now stands."

Tregear recorded that he wanted to understand exactly what his friend meant. "Do you want me to know that this stone was set up in memory of your ancestor and made sacred for him?" he asked. "No," said the Māori, "this is my ancestor himself." But Tregear was not satisfied with this answer. "You must know that you are talking nonsense," he said. "You mean that the stone has been named for Raukawa, or else, perhaps, that your giant forefather was turned into stone by the gods and the petrified hero stands in this spot." "No," said the Māori. "That is Raukawa and the red

mark"—a patch of red ocher about twenty feet up—"is the place
where he was mortally wounded." Tregear described himself as
having been unable to follow the logic of his friend's thought, but
he also felt sure that the man was telling him the truth and that he
appeared to believe "in some queer idea of personality in the stone."

There are many examples in Polynesian traditions of thinking that seems to flow along similar lines—stories, for example,
in which an island is described as a fish, or a fish is also a type of
stone. Europeans have generally understood such statements to be
metaphorical, but Polynesians have often insisted that they were
true. Such claims presented a problem for Europeans, whose idea of
truth precluded the possibility of a stone being a man or an island
being a fish. But Polynesians had their own problems with European categories and with the kinds of stories that Europeans told.

One early missionary report from Tahiti recounted the islanders' reaction to a dialogue that one of the missionaries had composed. The story, which had been written as an instructional text,
involved two imaginary Tahitians, Oomera and Taro, one of whom
had just returned from a visit to England with much to relate about
his experiences there. Tahitian readers were interested in this,
though they were critical of the way the characters interacted, inquiring after the details of each other's domestic affairs in a manner that was considered unbecoming. In general, however, they
accepted the story of Oomera and Taro—until it was revealed to be
*a work of fiction.* At this point, wrote the missionary, "the enquiry
became general—Who was Oomera and who was Taro? where did
they live?" When the Tahitians were told that the dialogue was invented, that it was "an allegory constructed as a vehicle for truth,"
they were disgusted. "It is a lying book," they said.

Missionary attempts to translate *The Pilgrim's Progress* into
Tahitian were similarly confounded. The Tahitians described it as
"a very dark book," not because of its emphasis on the wages of sin
but because it "did not relate to any person but was entirely a 'parau
faau,' figurative account. That is, a tale without foundation." To

the missionaries, the problem was the Tahitians' failure to grasp the allegory's message. "They appear destitute of such doubts and fears," wrote one. "They cannot view sin in its true light, nor feel its burden." But the Tahitians were focused on something else entirely; in their contempt for the very idea of fiction, they could not see the point of allegory as a form.

Europeans and Polynesians, it would seem, had very different ideas about the purpose of narratives and the relative meanings of "falsehood" and "truth." For Polynesians, stories that were "made up" were both immoral, as lies, and useless from a practical point of view, containing no trustworthy information. Europeans, on the other hand, considered many Polynesian stories to be either false or incomprehensible because they were inconsistent with the laws of nature and the physical world. The "truth" of what Tregear's Māori friend told him—that the man, his ancestor Raukawa, and the rock were all part of the same living continuum—could not be squared with the kind of "truth" that Tregear—who saw the Māori as alive, the ancestor as dead, and the rock as inanimate—could accept or understand.

POLYNESIAN ORAL TRADITIONS could be many things, from prayers and dedications to love songs and taunts. Tahitian traditions recorded in the early nineteenth century included enigmas, romances, political speeches, night invocations (to be taught in the dark), war songs, lullabies, directions for travel, instructions on how to reveal thieves and cast out disorders, disenchantments from witchcraft, and prayers for rain. But the starting point for most Europeans was the cosmogonies, or accounts of how the world first came into being, which were widely understood as clues in the quest to discover who Polynesians were.

Creation myths were recorded throughout Polynesia in the nineteenth century: there are cosmogonies from Tahiti and the Society Islands, Hawai'i, New Zealand, the Chatham Islands, Tonga, Samoa, the Tuamotus, the Marquesas, Easter Island, and Mangaia.

The words written on a banana leaf and delivered to Moerenhout by an emissary of the old Tahitian priest were part of a Society Islands cosmogony, several versions of which were recorded. These myths are by no means identical: some tell of a creator god who sleeps in a shell at the beginning of time, others of a female primordial deity who plucks the first generation of gods from her body, still others of gods born from the union of rocks. But while there is no single, definitive version, it is possible to speak broadly of a Polynesian cosmogonic vision, which is characterized by two closely related themes.

The first is that the relationships among all forms of matter are ones of kinship; everything that exists is, in a fairly literal sense, related to everything else. The stone that is the ancestor Raukawa is also, *in its own right*, an ancestor, being part of the same continuum of creation as the man and the ancestral hero. The second is that the mechanism of creation for everything in the world—not just humans, animals, and gods but even things that we would describe as inorganic, like sand and stones—is a form of sexual reproduction. Creation in traditional Polynesian myths is, fundamentally, a matter of procreation.

According to many Polynesian creation stories, the origin of the universe begins in something known as Te Pō. Typically described as a period of chaos or darkness or a kind of night, Te Pō is what existed before any gods, sky, land, sea, plants, animals, or humans had come into being. It is associated not just with the dim beginnings of the world but with the time before birth, the time after death, and the mysteries of the spirit world. In the dualistic philosophy of the Polynesians, it is opposed to Te Ao, the world of light and ordinary human endeavor. We live in Te Ao, but it is from Te Pō that we come, and to it that we ultimately return. The New Zealand ethnologist Elsdon Best described Te Pō as a time or place of metaphorical darkness. He tells the story of a Māori acquaintance who, when asked about a particular series of events, replied, "I do not know any of those matters, for at that time I was still in the Po," by which he meant that he had not yet been born.

References to Te Pō occur in myths and chants throughout Polynesia, including one of the most famous of all, a two-thousand-line Hawaiian creation chant known as the Kumulipo, meaning "Beginning in deep darkness." Composed at the beginning of the eighteenth century to mark the birth of the high chief Lonoika-makahiki, it begins, in Queen Lili'uokalani's translation:

> At the time that turned the heat of the earth
> At the time when the heavens turned and changed
> At the time when the light of the sun was subdued
> To cause light to break forth
> At the time of the night of Makalii [winter]
> Then began the slime which established the earth,
> The source of deepest darkness
> Of the depth of darkness, of the depth of darkness,
> Of the darkness of the sun, in the depth of night,
> It is night,
> So night was born.

Similar chants collected in nineteenth-century New Zealand describe the many phases of Te Pō, iterating, in long incantatory sequences, a series of nights—or perhaps one long night—in terms that strongly suggest a period of gestation and labor:

| | |
|---|---|
| *Te Po-nui* | The great night |
| *Te Po-roa* | The long night |
| *Te Po-uriuri* | The deep night |
| *Te Po-kerekere* | The intense night |
| *Te Po-tiwhatiwha* | The dark night |
| *Te Po-te-kitea* | The night in which nothing is seen |
| *Te Po-tangotango* | The intensely dark night |
| *Te Po-whawha* | The night of feeling |
| *Te Po-namunamu-ki-taiao* | The night of seeking passage to the world |

| *Te Po-tahuri-atu* | The night of restless turning |
| *Te Po-tahuri-mai-ki-taiao* | The night of turning towards the revealed world |

Thus, the world is born quite literally from darkness.

In some traditions, Te Pō is associated with Te Kore, a word that in common speech expresses simple negation but here is elevated to mean something like "Nothingness" or "the Void." Like Te Pō, Te Kore can be qualified—Kore-nui (the Vast Void); Kore-roa (the Far-Extending Void); Kore-para (the Parched Void); Kore-rawea (the Void in Which Nothing Is Felt)—suggesting that it is less a matter of true absence or emptiness and more a kind of liminal space between being and nonbeing—a "realm of potential being," as one early missionary put it. Both of these concepts—Te Kore and Te Pō—can seem highly abstract, and much of the language used to translate them reinforces this impression. But this is probably a misapprehension. As one modern scholar puts it, "Ideas of infinity and eternity denote limitlessness in space and time, which does not seem to me to be a category of ancient Māori thought; instead, the abundance of multitude is always stressed, and this is characteristic of the concreteness of Māori thinking."

"Abundance of multitude" is a good way of describing what happens next, as the cosmogonic darkness gives way to creation, and through the union of opposing elements everything in the world is brought into being. In chants from Tahiti and Bora Bora, the "first generation of growth" arises from the conjunction of different types of rock:

Rock from the cliffs and ocean rock may meet and unite, there is affinity between them.
Slate rock and clay rock may meet and unite, there is affinity between them.
Pebbles and crumbling rock may meet and unite, there is affinity between them.

Black rock and white rock may meet and unite, there is affinity
between them.

In Hawai'i, night gives birth to the coral polyp, which is followed, in turn, by the birth of the grub, the earthworm, the starfish,
the sea cucumber, the sea urchin, the barnacle, the mother-of-pearl,
the mussel, the limpet, the cowrie, the conch. In a chant from Easter Island,

Grove by copulating with Trunk produced the ashwood tree.
Dragon fly by copulating with Bug-that-flies-on-fresh-water
produced the dragonfly.
Stinging-fly by copulating with Swam-of-flies produced the
fly. . . .

The central principle here is of generation through the pairing of male and female elements: gods, concepts, personifications of
nature, even curious abstractions like "Growth-of-comeliness" and
"All-rushing-land." Each pair gives rise to new elements, which in
turn unite and produce still more, so that through a series of "be-
gats" the entire universe is created: rock and sand, salt water and
fresh water, rivers and mountains, forests and reefs, moss and trees,
swimming things and crawling things, gods and men. The result
is a kind of cosmic genealogy, or family tree, in which any given
individual can trace his or her descent not just back to a pair of
founding ancestors but to the rocks and trees and corals and fish, all
the way back through the physical matter of the world to the very
fiber of the universe itself.

NINETEENTH-CENTURY EUROPEANS were fascinated by this mythology, which they viewed as a kind of direct testimony, the simplest,
truest, most authentic source of information about Polynesian history: *what Polynesians themselves had to say about their own past.*
They envisioned scenarios like Moerenhout's encounter with the

old Tahitian priest, in which learned members of these societies would divulge what they knew and the shrouds obscuring the islanders' origins would fall away. In practice, however, it was all a lot more complicated than that. Collecting, transcribing, and translating were time-consuming and difficult; Polynesians were often reluctant to share what they knew. There were mixed motives on the part of both collectors and informants: Europeans often suppressed bits that confused or offended them; Polynesians sometimes altered information with which, for tribal or other reasons, they disagreed. In some cases informants were paid for their knowledge—a standard ethnographic practice, but one with obvious potential for warping the results. For Europeans, the primary problem was interpretation: how to extract from these fragments a map and a history; how to make Polynesian mythology tell them what they wanted to know. For help with this, they turned to the nascent fields of comparative linguistics and mythology, disciplines that in the nineteenth century seemed to be opening up the history of the world. When it came to the history of Polynesia, however, this foray into folklore and philology proved not quite so illuminating. In fact, for the next several decades, it led everyone astray.

# THE ARYAN MĀORI

## *An Unlikely Idea*

*Cover of* The Aryan Maori *by Edward Tregear (Wellington, 1885).*
REED GALLERY, DUNEDIN PUBLIC LIBRARY, NEW ZEALAND.

**IF WE WERE** to look at Polynesian mythology today, we would probably be struck by what is unusual or distinctive about it. We would likely be most curious about those aspects of the traditions that appear to reflect something unique about the Polynesian world. But nineteenth-century Europeans took a very different approach to this material. They did not see a collection of strange and esoteric narratives about dragonflies and earthworms and copulating stones, but rather a series of familiar motifs. They noted, for instance, the elemental pairing of earth and sky that occurs in many Polynesian mythologies, a good example of which can be found in the New Zealand story of Rangi (Sky) and Papa (Earth). According to this popular Māori myth, at the dawn of time Rangi and Papa are clasped together in a tight embrace with their children, the gods of wind, war, sea, and so on, trapped in the darkness between them. After a time, the children grow weary of their close confinement and plot to push their parents apart. Each one tries and fails until, finally, Tane, god of forests and trees, rests his back on Papa, his mother, and, using his feet, thrusts his father, Rangi, up into the sky. In a related myth from the Society Islands, the god Tane uses great logs as pillars to separate the earth from the sky, while in a chant from the Tuamotus it is the first generations of men who raise "the layer above them with their arms, mounting upon each other's shoulders . . . until the highest trees could stand upright."

To Europeans, this idea of a tree, prop, pillar, or man holding up the sky was perfectly recognizable, instantly conjuring the Greek Titan Atlas, whose shoulders (in Homer's telling) "lift on high / the colossal pillars thrusting earth and sky apart." They were also entirely familiar with the idea of a Sky Father and an Earth Mother, versions of which appear in many European traditions, including the ancient Greek myth of Zeus and Demeter. In fact, the expressions "Father Heaven" (Dyaus Pitā in Sanskrit, Zeus Pater in Greek, Jupiter in Latin) and "Earth Mother" are so common in Indo-European languages that terms for them can be reconstructed going back more than five thousand years.

Another concept that rang a bell for nineteenth-century scholars was Te Pō, that deep Polynesian darkness at the beginning of time. This notion of something emerging from nothing—of presence from absence, order from chaos—was instantly legible to Europeans as an echo of the book of Genesis: "And the earth was without form, and void; and darkness was upon the face of the deep." For those with a classical education, it further called to mind Ovid's *Metamorphoses*:

> Before the ocean and the earth appeared—
> Before the skies had overspread them all—
> The face of Nature in a vast expanse
> Was naught but Chaos uniformly waste.

Other scholars would see links with Hesiod's *Theogony*, the Sanskrit Rigveda, and even the Norse sagas, where the world is said to have sprung from the great abyss Ginungagap, which, like Te Pō, is without form and void.

Even now, it is not easy to know what to make of such resemblances. Modern suggestions include the idea that themes of this kind are archetypal, a reflection of some psychological condition that all human beings share. Another intriguing proposition is that such similarities are evidence of a truly ancient mythological substrate, a "Laurasian" mythology, spanning the cultures of Eurasia, North Africa, Oceania, and the Americas and going back far beyond the traceable beginnings of either Polynesian or Indo-European culture, as far back perhaps as twenty thousand years. Alternatively, one might argue that there is, in fact, no connection, that such apparent resemblances are simply the artifact of a process that selects for similarity: Europeans find dragon and flood myths in Polynesia because they are interested in dragons and floods. Nineteenth-century folklorists, however, concluded none of these things. What they thought they were looking at was evidence of a *genealogical connection*.

Faced with what looked to them like traces of their own most ancient traditions, nineteenth-century Europeans concluded that Polynesian and European mythologies had sprung from the same roots and that the ancestors of the Polynesians and their own forebears must therefore be related. It was not immediately obvious just where in history—or geography—this connection was to be found. Some argued that Polynesian origins could be traced to the ancient Greeks, others that they were to be found somewhere in Egypt, among the pharaohs and their tombs. An idea popular among the early missionaries was that the inhabitants of Polynesia were descended from a lost tribe of Jews. The Reverend Samuel Marsden, founder of the first Christian mission in New Zealand and an early proponent of this idea, found evidence for the Māori's Semitic origin in what he described as their "great natural turn for traffic," for, as he put it, "they will buy and sell anything they have got." Rather more romantically, the Reverend Richard Taylor envisioned Polynesians as a tribe of wandering nomads who had made their way from the eastern Mediterranean, across what is today Iraq, Iran, Pakistan, India, Bangladesh, Myanmar, Thailand, and Malaysia, "until in the lapse of ages they reached the sea, and thence, still preserving their wandering character, from island to island driven by winds and currents, and various causes, they finally reached New Zealand." But the idea that ultimately gained traction among nineteenth-century Europeans was that Polynesians were neither Semites, Egyptians, nor ancient Greeks, but that they were *Aryans*.

**IT IS IMPORTANT** to recognize that the term "Aryan" did not mean in the mid-nineteenth century what it means to us today. It had nothing to do with Teutons or fair-haired Nordic types but referred first and foremost to a group of Sanskrit-speaking herders and horsemen who are thought to have migrated from the Iranian Plateau into what is now northern India in the second millennium B.C. These people, who referred to themselves using the Sanskrit word *ārya* (meaning "noble") were known to nineteenth-century Europeans as "Indo-Aryans," or just plain "Aryans." At the time, Sanskrit was the oldest known language in the Indo-European family (older languages have since been discovered), and the Sanskrit-speaking Aryans were presumed to be the people from whom all the other Indo-Europeans—Greeks, Romans, Celts, Slavs, and so on—had sprung. Thus, "Aryan," originally a fairly narrow designation of a particular Indic tribe, became synonymous in the nineteenth century with "the mother of modern civilization."

The later appropriation of this term by the Nazis—which arose from the mistaken claim that the homeland of these early Indo-Europeans was located somewhere in Northern Europe—has distorted its meaning so severely that it is difficult to re-create its nineteenth-century sense. But at the time, it was linked with a feeling of excitement about discoveries in the field of comparative linguistics and the implications these had for the study of human history as a whole. To nineteenth-century scholars, the idea of a chain of related languages reaching back thousands of years, well beyond the bounds of recorded history, beyond Homer and the Bible, was nothing short of revelatory. It offered a glimpse of their most ancient forebears, people who had lived centuries before Greece and Rome and who, up until that point, had been essentially unimaginable. As philologists began to piece together this story, working out the relationships among more and more languages (and thus more and more peoples), it gradually became possible to envision a hypothetical mother tongue, an even more ancient language, perhaps five or six thousand years old, of which not only Greek and Latin but Sanskrit itself was merely an offshoot, and from this reconstruction to deduce something about the common ancestor of the vastly disparate peoples who had spread across the world from Iran to Iceland.

It could be inferred from this protolanguage, for instance, that the technology of these people included the wheel. They had words for axles, yokes, and some kind of cart or wheeled conveyance, as well as a verb that meant "to plow." They had a word for field and another that meant "to lead away cattle," which did double duty as a word for marriage, as in "leading away" the bride. They had words not only for cows, oxen, bulls, and steers but for sheep, goats, dogs, pigs, and, especially, horses. They distinguished between movable and immovable wealth and, in the former category, between four-footed chattels (livestock) and two-footed chattels (slaves). They were polytheistic, and the name for their most securely reconstructible deity relates to the word for "sky." Their word for human, on the other hand, was derived from their word for "earth" or "land." Their poetry revolved around themes of fertility, reciprocity, immortality, and heroic deeds; a single famous phrase, best known to us from the Homeric epics, is glossed as "imperishable fame."

There are still debates about where, exactly, these ancient Aryans lived, but again something can be deduced from their vocabulary.

They had words for mountain, river, lake, and marsh, and for animals associated with forests: bear, wolf, fox, beaver, otter, and elk. In several of the daughter languages, the word for wolf has undergone what is known as "taboo deformation" (which is what happens when people replace a word like "damn," which is blasphemous, with the inoffensive "darn"), suggesting that the creature was highly feared. They seem to have had words for only two kinds of fish—trout and salmon—but for many types of birds, including raven, eagle, falcon, crane, thrush, crow, sparrow, pheasant, owl, and stork. They had words for honeybees and leeches, words for hornets, mice, and fleas. They had a word for snow and a word for berry. They had a story about the slaying of a dragon and a myth about the theft of fire.

Quite unexpectedly, what was in essence a highly technical field—philology is a matter of rigorous phonological and morphological comparison—had opened up a whole new historical vista, giving Europeans a vivid and romantic new sense of who they were. It also offered a new way of thinking about their relationship to other peoples in a vision of kinship that extended across half the world. "To learn," wrote one enthusiast, "that many nations, separated by distance, by ages of strife and bloodshed, by differing religious creeds, and by ancient customs, yet had a common source of birth, that their forefathers spoke the same tongue, and sat in one council-hall, was as delightful to the man of pure intellect, as it was valuable to the student of history."

THE DEVELOPMENT OF the comparative method of linguistics has been described as one of the great intellectual achievements of the nineteenth century, contributing enormously to our understanding of world history. But it also resulted in a number of inanities, one of which pertains directly to the problem of Polynesian origins. Advances in Indo-European philology were achieved by adding more and more languages for the purpose of comparison, but outside of Eurasia, most of the world's languages were poorly documented. (In some regions of the world, including much of Melanesia, this is still the case.) Polynesia was one of the exceptions. So much linguistic data had been collected by explorers during the seventeenth and eighteenth centuries that by the mid-nineteenth it was possible to establish with some certainty that there was an identifiable Oceanic language family, which came to be known as Malayo-Polynesian.

Then, in 1841, the celebrated German philologist Franz Bopp, a pioneer of Indo-European studies, made the further startling suggestion that there was a direct link between the Indo-European and Malayo-Polynesian language families. Specifically, Bopp argued that Malayo-Polynesian was a decayed form of Sanskrit. A second, even more radical suggestion followed: that Malayo-Polynesian actually *predated* Sanskrit and that all the languages of the Indo-European family were in fact descended from an earlier incarnation of the languages of the South Seas. According to this theory, Polynesians were the "remnants of a race once extensively dominating in Asia," who had colonized the Pacific in *"very very remote antiquity."*

This suggestion was taken up in some very influential quarters, including by Max Müller, Oxford University's famous Sanskritist and translator of the Vedas. "Strange as it may sound," he wrote, "to hear the language of Homer . . . spoken as an offshoot of the Sandwich Islands, it was not very long ago that all the Greek and Latin scholars of Europe shook their heads at the idea of tracing the roots of the classical languages back to Sanskrit." No one could demonstrate decisively which way it went—whether Malayo-Polynesian was a form of Sanskrit, or Sanskrit a form of Malayo-Polynesian—but by the end of the nineteenth century the most influential scholars writing about Polynesia were convinced that, one way or another, the languages of Europe and those of the remote Pacific shared a common root.

In fact, this was incorrect. But in the second half of the nineteenth century, vast quantities of ink were spilt in attempts to prove the validity of the thesis. One of those who embarked on this project was the New Zealander Edward Tregear. Tregear was both a student of Polynesian languages and a devotee of Müller's, and in 1885 he set out his claims in a little volume entitled *The Aryan Maori*. In it he argued that the Māori were descendants "of a pastoral people, afterwards warlike and migratory," and that this could be proven using nothing more than Māori language and myth. The Māori language, Tregear wrote, had preserved, "in an almost inconceivable purity," a memory of various aspects of Aryan life—"animals, implements, etc."—which had been "lost to the Maori for centuries."

Tregear's goal was to demonstrate the existence of what are known as linguistic "survivals," echoes of lost knowledge or forgotten experience that remain obscurely encoded in modern words. (An English example is the word "footman," which in common parlance means a male household servant but which once referred to a servant who literally ran *on foot* beside his master's carriage.) Noting that the ancient Aryans had been herders and that most if not all Indo-European languages have words for animals like cow, horse, and sheep, Tregear argued that traces of terms for these important beasts ought to be discoverable in Māori. He was aware, of course, that no cow, horse, goat, sheep, or pig had ever set foot in New Zealand before they were brought in European ships, but this only reinforced the argument. "Knowing that the Maoris were strangers to the sight of certain animals," he wrote, "I resolved to try to find if there was any proof in the verbal composition by which I could trace if they had once been familiar with them."

Combing the Māori lexicon for traces of the Latin *equus* (horse), the Greek *ois* (sheep), and especially the Sanskrit *gaus* (cow), Tregear found what he believed to be many instances. "I found *kaupare*, to turn in a different direction," he wrote, "and was struck by its resemblance to [Sanskrit] *go-pala*, a herdsman." He looked at *kahu*, meaning "surface," and the expression *kahu o te rangi* (sometimes translated as "cloak of heaven") and recognized "'cow of heaven,' a sentence to be met with in every work concerning the Aryans." In the Māori word *kahurangi*, meaning "wandering" or "unsettled," he discovered "sky-cow," an Aryan metaphor for clouds. In *kahu-papa*, meaning "bridge," he found "flat cow," on which the ancient Aryans crossed their streams. In *kauruki*, meaning "smoke," he saw "cow-dung," used for fuel by pastoralists the world over. In *kauhoa*, meaning a "litter" or "stretcher," he discovered "cow-friend"; and in *mata-kautete*, meaning "sharp teeth of flint lashed to a piece of wood," he astonished the reader by deciphering "cow-titty," a reference, presumably, to the implement's shape.

One doesn't have to be a linguist to recognize that *The Aryan Maori* exhibits some pretty fanciful etymological reasoning. It was the subject of a wicked satire in the *Transactions and Proceedings of the New Zealand Institute* by a "crotchety but highly intelligent" lawyer who was conversant in both the principles of comparative linguistics and the Māori language, and who parodied Tregear's method with his own pseudo-derivation of the phrase "a cock-and-bull story." (This involved an absurd tale about a group of Aryans who visit New Zealand and discover a "large grunting ground parrot" known as a *kakapo*. When they return to their homeland, their account of this creature is "received by their stay-at-home Aryan countrymen with 'incredulity and ridicule,' hence the first 'cock and bull story.'")

Stung by this criticism, Tregear nevertheless refused to concede that there was anything wrong with his methodology. But the truth is he was not doing it right. The comparative method of linguistics works, but only if it is performed according to the strictest conventions. In order to prove that words in different languages are related, correspondences between them must be consistent and predictable. If *p* in one language becomes *f* in another under certain circumstances, it must do so in all comparable cases. This principle of regularity of sound change is considered the foundation of the method and the one unbreakable rule. Tregear, who was entirely self-taught, did not fully grasp this, but he was not alone. Even many people who should have known better were swept away in the latter half of the nineteenth century by a "mania" for tracing everyone—Brits, Balts, Celts, Greeks, Romans, Persians, *and* Polynesians—back to the "cradle in Central Asia."

**TODAY IT IS** quite difficult to see how anyone could ever have supposed that the oceangoing peoples of the remote Pacific, with their outriggers and their fishhooks and their mother-of-pearl, could have been descended from the ancient herders and horsemen of the Eurasian Steppe, those wolf-fearing, bride-leading, milk-drinking tribes, with their axles and chattels and their imperishable fame. But the Aryan theory of Polynesian origins made sense to nineteenth-century Europeans in ways that it could never make sense to us. It dovetailed with their passion for folklore and history, which new methodologies in comparative linguists were expanding in fascinating new ways. And it fit the Romantic zeitgeist of the period, with its love of foreign and exotic subjects and its fascination with anything ancient, primitive, or remote.

For writers and thinkers in Europe, the Aryan theory of Polynesian origins was part of a much larger thesis about language and history, a small but intriguing piece of a vast intellectual puzzle. For that subset of Europeans who sought a home for themselves in the remote islands of the Pacific, it may also, as the historian K. R. Howe has argued, have represented a means of taming these strange new worlds. Once brought into the Indo-European fold, Polynesians were no longer "primitive aliens," but people with a history, mythology, and culture that Europeans "could understand, relate to and willingly embrace." One can see this as an act of usurpation: the annexation of Polynesian history by Europeans and "a feat of intellectual occupation, possession and control." But it was also an assertion of kinship. In tracing the source of Polynesian culture to one of the oldest branches—if not, indeed, the very trunk—of the Indo-European family tree, the Aryan theory reflected a nineteenth-century desire for a shared point of origin—a sort of folkloric equivalent of Darwin's *Descent of Man*—that would unite the various peoples of the world in a kind of grand universal genealogy. Europeans and Polynesians, as Tregear liked to think of them, were just two branches of one great family—the Aryans of the East and the Aryans of the West, met again in the wide Pacific, to which they had both come as voyagers and colonists, "seeking new homes beneath strange stars."

# A VIKING IN HAWAI'I

## *Abraham Fornander*

*Abraham Fornander, ca. 1878.*
NATIONAL LIBRARY OF SWEDEN, STOCKHOLM.
WIKIMEDIA COMMONS.

**THE ARYAN THEORY** of Polynesian origins can look like little more than a crackpot detour in the history of debates about who the islanders of the remote Pacific were. But its fiercest proponents were also some of the best nineteenth-century scholars of Polynesian languages, the most committed recorders of Polynesian traditions, and the staunchest defenders and champions of a heroic narrative in which Polynesians star as the greatest seafarers in human history. The man who was primarily responsible for this story line was a Swede named Abraham Fornander, who cast up on the islands of Hawai'i in the mid-nineteenth century and died one of the foremost collectors of Hawaiian lore.

Fornander was typical of a certain kind of European who could be found roaming the Pacific in this period. Born in 1812 into a middle-class family on an island off the coast of Sweden, he was sent to university at sixteen. There he fell under the spell of Sweden's Romantic poets, whose popular historical ballads depicted the ancient Scandinavians (newly christened "the Vikings") as a rugged and daring tribe of adventurers with a restless love of the sea. In 1831, for reasons that may have had to do with a failed love affair, Fornander abandoned his university studies and ran away to sea. For the next decade he lived the life of a wanderer, making his living as a sailor out of ports in Europe, North America, and the West Indies. He sailed to the Azores, Saint Helena, the Cape of Good Hope, and up and down the coast of South America. He doubled Cape Horn three times and crossed the Pacific from California to Kamchatka. Of this period of his life he later wrote, "I will say nothing of the hardships, the escapes from danger, the vicissitudes of life which I experienced . . . I have stood beneath the portals of death several times, ashore and on the sea."

In 1841, at the age of twenty-nine, Fornander signed on with the *Ann Alexander*, a whaler out of New Bedford, Massachusetts. The ship was bound for the South Seas fishery by way of Cape Horn, and he joined as a harpooner. In whaling stories of the nineteenth century, the harpooner is a man of unusual strength and daring who is often depicted as an outsider, set apart from the rest of the crew by the danger and difficulty of his job. The four pagan harpooners in *Moby-Dick* are good examples of the type: Daggoo the giant African, Tashtego the Indian from Gay Head, Fedallah the Zoroastrian, and, of course, Queequeg the tattooed South Sea Islander. Fornander, who was tall and broad-chested, could almost have been a character in one of Melville's books, as the two men actually crossed paths in the spring of 1843, the one shipping out of the port of Lahaina just as the other arrived.

When Fornander jumped ship in Honolulu after more than a decade at sea, he had found the home from which he would never depart. In 1847, he took the unusual step of swearing an oath of allegiance to the then-reigning monarch, King Kamehameha III, and becoming a naturalized citizen of the Kingdom of Hawai'i. This was something few Europeans of the period bothered to do; barely a third of the foreign-born residents of Honolulu were citizens. But naturalization was required of anyone who wanted to work for the government or marry a Hawaiian, and Fornander, who was then thirty-five, was in love with a twenty-three-year-old Hawaiian named Alanakapu Kauapinao.

Pinao, as she was familiarly known, was the daughter of a former governor of the island of Moloka'i. She had a distinguished genealogy, with chiefly ancestors on both sides and strong connections to the ruling Kamehameha dynasty. She was Fornander's first teacher of Hawaiian, and the first chants and genealogies he learned were those of her family. But Pinao's influence extended beyond the historical and linguistic knowledge she was able to impart. Fornander's politics were consistently pro-Polynesian and anti-Evangelical. Like Melville, he disliked the humorless brand of Calvinism imported to Hawai'i by missionaries from New England, and he was a strong supporter of the Hawaiian monarchy. Culturally and temperamentally predisposed to side with the Hawaiian elite, he was also influenced by his attachment to Pinao. "I have a native wife and family," he wrote, "thus the native interest is my interest."

In 1849, the Fornanders' first child, a daughter named Catherine Kaonohiulaokalani, was born. In 1851, a second daughter, Johanna Margaretha Naokalani Kalanipo'o, was born, but died before her second birthday. In 1853, a third daughter, Anna Martha Alaikauokoko, was stillborn. In 1855, a son, Abraham Kawelolani Kanipahu, was also stillborn, probably prematurely. In 1857, two months before her tenth wedding anniversary, Pinao gave birth to her fifth child, a boy named Charles Theodore Kalililani Kalanimanuia. Four days later, she died from complications of childbirth, and a week and a half later the baby also died. Fornander, who was only in his midforties, was shattered. Though he lived to be almost seventy-five, he never remarried and would write that his "holiest memory lies in a Hawaiian grave." Of the five children born to him, the only one to survive was Catherine, a solemn-looking child who inherited her mother's dark hair and dark eyes.

Such a shocking succession of infant and maternal deaths was by no means unheard of in the nineteenth century, but it is important to see these events in the Hawaiian context. Inhabitants of isolated or remote regions where there has been little or no contact with the outside world are often described as "epidemiologically naive." What this means is that they have limited immunity to diseases like influenza and measles that are endemic in other parts of the world, and when exposed to them they often suffer high rates of death. One of the best-known examples comes from the pandemic of 1918, in which certain populations, notably indigenous Alaskans and Pacific Islanders, died at rates that were four, five, and in some cases even ten times those of other populations. The pandemic is thought to have killed between 3 and 6 percent of the global population; in Western Samoa, 20 percent of the population died.

In the nineteenth-century Pacific, this scenario played itself out over and over. As early as the 1830s, missionaries in the Society Islands were already beginning to speak of depopulation. There were major epidemics in Tahiti of smallpox in 1841, dysentery in 1843, scarlet fever in 1847, measles in 1854. Much the same story can be told of Hawai'i, which was also subject to wave after wave of imported disease. In 1848 and 1849, when Pinao was pregnant with her first child, a series of devastating epidemics struck the Hawaiian Islands. Measles, arriving from Mexico on an American frigate, and whooping cough, on a ship from California, hit at the same time, killing an estimated ten thousand people. Whole villages were prostrate, wrote one observer, "there not being persons enough in health to prepare food for the sick," while "a large portion of the infants born in the Islands in 1848, even as large a proportion as nine-tenths in some parts, are supposed to be already in their graves." No doubt there were other diseases in the mix as well; mumps, which had been in the islands some years earlier, was reported again, as were "pleurisy," "bilious fever," and something that was probably dysentery. The combined assault was especially hard upon the very young and the very old. "The aged," wrote one observer, "have almost all disappeared from among us."

Although the absolute size of pre-contact populations in the islands of Polynesia is often debated, the overall trajectory is not. From a high of something like 250,000 at the beginning of the nineteenth century, the population of the Hawaiian Islands had been reduced to less than 40,000 by the century's end. In New Zealand, the Māori population declined by nearly two-thirds over the same period. And in the Marquesas, where estimates put the number of inhabitants before contact with Europeans at approximately 50,000, the population crashed so completely that by 1926 there were just 2,225 Marquesans left. Robert Louis Stevenson, visiting the Marquesas toward the end of the nineteenth century, remarked gloomily that songs and dances could no longer be performed, because there was no one left who knew the words and movements, and that coffins, newly arrived in the islands, had become objects of prestige.

IT WAS AGAINST this backdrop of population collapse—of "death coming in like a tide," as Stevenson put it—that Fornander began his great oeuvre: *An Account of the Polynesian Race: Its Origins and Migrations and the Ancient History of the Hawaiian People to the Times of Kamehameha I.* He dedicated it to his surviving daughter, Catherine, "as a reminder of her mother's ancestors and as a token of her father's love." Fornander had by then been living in Hawai'i for decades, working first as a plantation manager, then as a journalist and public servant, and finally as a judge. For years, in his capacity as inspector general of schools, he had made an annual round of the archipelago, traveling to the remotest corners of the islands, accompanied by two or three Hawaiians. Everywhere they went, they collected stories, chants, prayers, and genealogies—anything, as Fornander put it, with a "bearing upon the ancient history, culte, and customs of the people." These he assembled and translated, conferring with Hawaiian scholars like Samuel Kamakau, Kepelino, and King Kalakaua. It was all part of the great work of his life: "to unravel the snarled threads" of Polynesian history.

Hawaiians, Fornander observed, were often reluctant to share what they knew, especially when it came to the more esoteric traditions. The old people, he wrote, "maintain the greatest reserve on such subjects, even to their own countrymen; and to a foreigner, unless most intimately and favourably known, any such revelation is almost impossible." This was also true in other parts of Polynesia. In New Zealand, it was said that some kinds of knowledge were considered too *tapu*—too sacred and dangerous—to be shared with outsiders. One Māori *tohunga* who was persuaded to share a creation myth with a European collector agreed to do so only under the cover of darkness and with the understanding that his family was never to know. Another, who provided a European collector with details of priestly ceremonies and the sacred purposes of certain shrubs, was charged by his grandfather with having given secrets "to a 'common man.'" When both this informant and his son died a short time later, their deaths were widely attributed to this betrayal.

Clans and tribes had always jealously guarded their more powerful and secret kinds of lore, but the prospect of handing it over to Europeans raised a whole new set of concerns. Why, exactly, were Europeans recording these traditions? With whom would they share them? What would it do to the potency of the knowledge to write it down, to print it, to make it public? There was fear that the process would lead to sacrilege. As one Māori elder put it, "in olden times the house was closed by *karakia* [prayers or incantations] to men outside and to those who desecrate the house; now, because the talks were to be written, the house was open forever."

At the same time, it was clear that the threats to Polynesia's traditional knowledge base were multiplying: the flood of foreigners and their imported ideas; the disruption of local political structures and the ensuing wars, feuds, and annexations; widespread conversion to Christianity and the overturning of every settled idea; above all, the recurrent plagues of sickness and the rising tide of death. Faced with the possible extinction of a whole body of thought—one European collector wrote of the need to "embalm" native traditions before it was too late—both Europeans and Polynesians felt the urgent need to "rescue" Polynesian knowledge from what Fornander described as "the isolation and oblivion which were fast closing over it."

NO EUROPEAN HAD ever attempted anything like Fornander's history of the Polynesian people, which spans more than two thousand years and was based on an analysis of genealogies, customs, legends, place names, numerals, and mythological traditions from Hawai'i, the Society Islands, the Marquesas, Tonga, Samoa, Fiji, and New Zealand. Fornander was committed to the Aryan thesis, and he dedicated a great deal of energy to proving that the ancestors of the Polynesians were "a chip of the same block from which the Hindu, the Iranian, and the Indo-European families were fashioned." He trotted out evidence of ancient Zabaism (sun worship) in Polynesian legends and found links to Latin, Welsh, and Old Babylonian deities in the names of Polynesian gods. He saw elements of serpent worship (a "peculiarly Cushite outgrowth of religious ideas") in stories about lizards and identified signs of a Shiva cult in the ritual use of stones. But this was only part of the larger project: a sweeping history of the Hawaiian people from their most ancient roots to the unification of the Hawaiian Islands under Kamehameha I, in 1795.

Fornander's history is worth summarizing because it represents the first really systematic attempt to lay out the migrations of the Polynesian people from beginning to end. It starts in India centuries before the birth of Christ. How long the ancestors of the Polynesians resided in the foothills of the Hindu Kush, or what "the manner or the occasion of their leaving," Fornander was unable to say. But at some point they began their migrations eastward toward the Asiatic archipelago, ultimately settling in the islands of what we now know as Indonesia and the Philippines. Then, around the first or second century A.D., they began a second migration out into the Pacific, reaching as far as the islands of Fiji, where again they paused. "After several generations of *séjour*," they continued onward, settling the increasingly distant islands of Tonga, Samoa, the Society Islands, and the Marquesas and reaching remote Hawai'i around the fifth or sixth century A.D.

For some hundreds of years after this, according to Fornander, Polynesian traditions were strangely silent. But suddenly, around A.D. 1000, there is an efflorescence in the lore. "Polynesian folklore in all the principal groups becomes replete with the legends and songs of a number of remarkable men, of bold expeditions, stirring adventures, and voyages undertaken to far-off lands. An era of national unrest and of tribal commotion seems to have set in, from causes not now known, nor mentioned in the legends." For the next three or four hundred years (roughly A.D. 1000 to 1400), Fornander argued, a great "migratory wave swept the island world of the Pacific." This was a period not just of out-migration but of repeated return voyaging among the archipelagoes. Fornander believed that the Hawaiian Islands, for example, had been "visited by expeditions from the Samoan, Society, and Marquesas groups, and that Hawaiian expeditions visited them in return."

The reasons for this explosion of activity, Fornander thought, were probably overpopulation and natural disasters, including volcanic eruptions and the subsidence of coasts. (One of Fornander's pet theories was that there used to be more islands in the Pacific than there are now, a kind of echo of the drowned-continent theory.) But this great era of unrest and exploration lasted only a few centuries, coming to an end in the 1300s or 1400s, when the last great wave of Polynesian settlers reached New Zealand. From this point onward, Fornander argued, the major Polynesian archipelagoes were isolated from one another until they were once again reconnected by the arrival of European ships.

It was a remarkably seamless story, and one that would ultimately prove both spectacularly right in some places and spectacularly wrong in others. A big part of the problem lay in the inherent
difficulty of translation—not just from one language to another
or one culture to another, but from one way of thinking to another. There is a huge difference—in style, tone, logic, everything,
really—between the type of sequential historical narration that
Fornander was aiming for and the "almost impenetrable jungle of
traditions, legends, genealogies, and chants" from which he tried to
extract it. History, as Fornander understood it, required "sequence,
precision, and clarity," none of which was particularly characteristic of Polynesian oral traditions, which were densely poetic, ellip-
tical, evocative, and occasionally obscure even to those who could
recite them. Translating the one into the other involved a good deal
of interpretation, and one of the first difficulties confronting Fornander was the absence of a clear chronology.

Fornander's history demanded dates, but there are no dates in
Polynesian traditions. There is no absolute system of time beginning at some specified moment and proceeding at regular intervals.
There are cyclical calendars tied to the seasons and the phases of
the moon, but there is nothing like the term "1850" or any kind of
conceptual system that might generate such a term. But Fornander
had an ingenious solution for this, which was to count generations
in the long and detailed genealogies that were such an important
part of Polynesian lore. He was not the first person to think of this,
but his use of genealogies to establish a timeline for Polynesian
events attempted to reach much further back into the past.

Later, in the mid-twentieth century, when a scientific method
for dating using radiocarbon isotopes was developed, this method of
genealogical dating would come to be seen as irredeemably quaint.
But Polynesians cared enormously about their lineages and scru-
pulously maintained information about who was descended from
whom, making their genealogies extremely valuable as historical
sources. The only problem was that, as they went back in time,

Polynesian genealogies moved seamlessly from what we might consider the "historical" through the "legendary" to the "mythological." Some of the genealogies Fornander used ran to as many as ninety-nine generations, which meant a span of nearly three thousand years. Even the much more common twenty- or thirty-generation genealogies that were routinely used to date Polynesian events span periods of six hundred to nine hundred years—three or four times the conventionally accepted time frame for accurate transmission of oral information.

While they undoubtedly served to mark the passage of time, Polynesian genealogies were never designed to establish accurate chronologies. Their purpose was social, political, even metaphysical, connecting an individual back through his ancestors "to the rocks, trees, streams, even the stars in the sky." An important genealogy might start with the story of the creation of the world and continue on down through the ages, with the pairing of gods, the emergence of men, the division of lands, and so on, culminating finally in the immediate descent line of the individual in question. Thus, while the modern end of a genealogy might be highly accurate, the beginning "in deep darkness" was by definition mythic, and the question for Europeans was where the boundary between the two lay.

Fornander was not unaware of this problem. But he was simultaneously wedded to a Polynesian view of the traditions' absolute veracity *and* to a European conception of historical fact. The result was a strangely tortured theory, in which we find him asserting, for example, that a chief named Wakea (an ancient Polynesian name for the primordial Sky Father) and Papa, his wife (the Earth Mother), were living on the island of Gilolo, in the Moluccas, in the first century A.D. But while this extreme literalness introduced certain absurdities into Fornander's history, it also reflects an important dimension of his view.

For reasons that were both personal and intellectual—having to do with his Hawaiian wife and daughter as well as the Romantic antiquarianism of his youth—Fornander was strongly pro-Polynesian.

Unlike many Europeans both before and after him, he took it entirely for granted that the ancestors of the Polynesians had explored and colonized the entire Pacific, that they had made voyages over the open ocean of hundreds, if not thousands, of miles, and that, for at least three or four hundred years, they had traveled back and forth among the archipelagoes on voyages "undertaken purposely and accomplished safely both in going and returning." He believed they had possessed everything they needed to accomplish these great journeys: vessels "sewn or stitched together," with holds "sufficient to contain men, animals, and stores"; knowledge of the stars, "their rising and setting at all times of the year, both in the Southern and Northern Hemisphere"; the strength to endure long voyages; the ability to recognize "the approach of land, by flight of birds and other signs"; above all, the requisite personal traits, "courage, hardihood, and perseverance that never failed them at critical moments."

For Fornander, there was no doubt about any of this; it was a matter of record. If "the Icelandic folklore which tells of exploits and voyages to far distant lands" was to be believed, he asked, why not "the Polynesian folklore which tells of voyages between the different groups?" It was a perfectly straightforward question, and the answer, he thought, was equally clear. To know the story of the Polynesian peoples' origin and migrations, one had only to look at their sagas. But as the efforts of both Fornander and his successors revealed, translating the stories of Polynesia's voyaging heroes into chronological historical accounts was a matter less of science than of art.

## VOYAGING STORIES
### *History and Myth*

*"Departure of the Six Canoes from Rarotonga for New Zealand"*
*by Kennett Watkins, 1906.*
AUCKLAND ART GALLERY, NEW ZEALAND.

**EVERY BRANCH OF** Polynesian mythology has voyaging stories—
tales of heroes and heroines who set out on journeys to discover
new lands or revisit old homelands, or to seek adventure or procure valuable goods—and in the wake of Fornander's great oeuvre,
these moved to the center of the debate about the history of the
Polynesian migrations. These tales, the sea stories of a sea people,
run the gamut from the obviously fabulous to the plausibly historical. At one end of the spectrum are cosmogonic navigator-gods;
at the other, discoverers, settlers, and founders of lineages that are
still claimed by people today. Virtually all have what might be described as both a "texture of history" and a "texture of myth."

The characters in these stories are often described as making
use of magic objects to aid them in their travels: magic boats,
bones, paddles, fishhooks, nets, baskets, gourds. They might hold
the winds in a magic bag and or be guided by meteors or talking

stars. Sometimes they are assisted by uncanny creatures—sailfish who swim to windward to protect them from waves, or sharks who rescue castaways or drag overturned canoes to land. Or they may be beset by monsters from the deep: enormous octopuses, murderous billfish, giant tridacnas. The ocean itself is a place of supernatural hazards, in the form of whirlpools, waterspouts, fogs, storms, waves, and hidden reefs. Even the islands themselves are occasionally mysterious, wandering off or floating away or vanishing into thin air.

At the same time, even the most marvelous of these stories contain oddly specific details: what tools to use for building a suitable vessel; what kinds of provisions to take and how to store them; what to do to prevent a canoe from sinking; how to make a cooking place from sand on the deck. They are filled with practical advice about how voyages should be conducted: "first procure choice food" for the canoe builders; select the "bravest and most experienced warriors who would of their own accord volunteer"; "let the course be to the right of the setting sun, or moon, or Venus in the month of February." They also contain rationales and motives—something that is hard for historians to see. Voyages are made to fetch valuable objects—birds' eggs, feathers, tortoiseshell or pearl shell, special kinds of rock—or to seek lost family members or procure desirable brides. Sometimes they are explicit about the need for new territory: often a younger male figure sets out after quarreling with an older relative or committing some kind of transgression, like stealing someone else's wife. Occasionally there is famine or some other kind of trouble, but usually it is a matter of chiefly ambition or pride. All of this rings true—or, at least, plausible—and so, while they are in no sense documentary, it is impossible to avoid the impression that there is lived experience behind these tales.

Even cosmogonic myths are interwoven with knowledge that can only have come from actual voyages. Take the story of Ru, a Tahitian deity, who, with his sister, Hina, sets out in a canoe named *The Hull* to discover and name all the islands of the world. "The

Canoe Song of Ru" is an origin story and also, plainly, a lesson in geography. Before they depart, Ru looks about him and names the directions: "The east he called Te-hitia-o-te-ra (The-rising-of-the-sun), the west Te-tooa-o-te-ra (The-setting-of-the-sun), the south he named Apato'a, and the north Apatoerau"—terms we have encountered before, in the margins of Tupaia's chart. Then, sailing from the west toward the Society Islands, Ru and Hina draw their canoe to each of the islands in turn, naming them in their proper geographic order: first Maupiti, then Bora Bora, then Taha'a, then Ra'iatea. A similar sequence occurs in the well-known Hawaiian story of the volcano goddess Pele, who sets out from her home in Kahiki in a canoe belonging to her brother Whirlwind, with Tide and Current as paddlers. Approaching the Hawaiian Islands from the northwest, she reaches first Ni'ihau, then Kaua'i, then O'ahu, then each of the others in turn—following the correct geographic sequence—until, finally, she settles in a crater on the island of Hawai'i.

Stories of Rata, one of the greatest wayfinders in the Polynesian pantheon and a hero whose name is known throughout the triangle, catalog the right rituals for building and launching a voyaging canoe, as well as some of the hazards that might be encountered on a long journey. Embarking on a voyage to avenge his father's death, Rata faces a series of oceanic dangers, each of which—in an interesting detail—he at first mistakes for land: a giant school of fish that threatens to swamp his canoe; a swordfish that tries to pierce the hull; a powerful, predatory giant cavalla; a monstrous clam that tries to suck the canoe in through its terrible valves. In other versions, Rata's challenges include whales, rogue waves, and unexpected reefs.

Most of these voyaging stories detail successful journeys (though some are undertaken to search for someone else who has been lost). But the human cost of voyaging is memorialized in an interesting tale from the Marquesas, in which the hero, Aka, decides to sail to Aotona to get valuable red feathers (known throughout much of Polynesia as *kula*). Aka does not know how to get to Aotona, so he sends his sons-in-law to ask their father. "We have come for the story of the *kula*," they say, only to be told, "You two cannot reach it. Much food is necessary; a great quantity of cooked *ma* [fermented breadfruit], raw *ma*, coconuts, raw taro, cooked taro, raw *kape* [another kind of taro], and cooked *kape*. You have to go far out in the sea, there is no more food and it is a long time before land is found." Still, they decide to try. They build two boats, which they tie together, collect sail mats and food, and look for "seven times twenty" men to join the crew.

In one version, the voyage is recounted, as in the stories of Pele and Ru, as a series of island stops within the Marquesan archipelago. But in another it is described as a series of legs, each defined by the appearance of a star in the sky who challenges the voyagers with a question about their identity. Only when they give the correct answer—"We are Pepeu and Utunui, Mahaitivi's boys, like the wind, like the wind we glide behind the sky, our hair darts into the air, we go to Aotona"—does the star permit them to move on. This idea of sailing under a series of stars perfectly matches the concept of a star path—a sequence of stars rising at roughly the same point on the horizon, each of which is used, in turn, to maintain a constant heading—one of the presumed techniques of ancient Polynesian navigation.

But it is a long way to Aotona. The food runs out, the water runs out, and the men begin to die. "Twenty died. Two times twenty died, three times twenty died, four times twenty died, five times twenty died. Twice twenty men remained with Aka." At length they reach their destination, fill their baskets with red feathers, and set off home. But the voyage back is just as arduous, and they are "at sea for as long as a large bread fruit harvest." When they finally reach home, the women, who have been awaiting the canoe's return, look down from the cliffs on the returning voyagers. Of the "seven times twenty" men who sailed to Aotona, fewer than a third have returned alive.

. . .

**VOYAGING STORIES WERE** a staple of late-nineteenth- and early-twentieth-century attempts to place the Polynesian migrations on a firm historical footing. After Fornander's death, in 1887, the locus of this kind of work shifted to New Zealand, where a man named S. Percy Smith picked up the trail. Like Tregear, with whom he later collaborated, Smith first came into sustained contact with Māori people while working as a surveyor in the New Zealand backcountry in the 1850s and '60s. By the age of twenty he was fluent enough in Māori to be employed as an interpreter, and he soon began to collect stories and chants. In 1892, he and Tregear co-founded the Polynesian Society, with the aim of promoting "the study of the Anthropology, Ethnology, Philology and Antiquities of the Polynesian races," and launched *The Journal of the Polynesian Society* as a venue for articles, commentary, and transcriptions of traditional lore.

Like Fornander, whom he greatly admired, Smith was committed to the authenticity of Polynesian oral traditions, viewing it as axiomatic that "all tradition is based on fact—whilst the details may be wrong, the main stem is generally right." In a series of influential books and articles published between 1898 and 1921, he laid out his version of Polynesian history, closely following the outline Fornander had established. This included a remote and ancient origin in India; a migration to Indonesia around 65 B.C.; arrival in the Fiji/Tonga/Samoa region by A.D. 450; and a "heroic period" of voyaging, during which the major island groups of Polynesia were settled. Smith then turned his attention to the peregrinations of his own local branch of the Polynesian family, and his most significant contributions revolve around what he liked to call "the whence of the Maori." The "whence" consisted, essentially, of the *where* and the *when*, two things that oral traditions are particularly bad at encoding (by contrast, they are quite good at the *who* and the *why*). Smith agreed with Fornander that without dates and locations there could be no history, and so he set about establishing both a route and a chronology for the settlement of New Zealand.

One of the central problems for European interpreters of Polynesian voyaging traditions was the location of a place known in the lore as Hawaiki. In stories from the central and eastern Pacific, Hawaiki, or one of its cognates—Havaiki, Havaiʻi, Avaiki—is the name of the land from which the great voyagers depart. It is often described as an ancestral homeland, but in many cases it is much more than that. In cosmogonies from the Society Islands, it is the first land to be created: "Havaiʻi, the birthplace of lands, Havaiʻi, the birthplace of gods, Havaiʻi the birthplace of kings, Havaiʻi the birthplace of men." In a myth from Mangareva, it is a sort of world tree, "whose roots are in the Po, whose topmost branches touch the sacred sky of Tane." Good things—pigs, kumara (sweet potato), special kinds of yams—are said to come from Hawaiki, as are treasures like greenstone and red feathers, and special bodies of knowledge like that of *tā moko*, the Māori tattoo. In a story from Manihiki, the hero Maui brings back fire from Havaiki; in tales from the Marquesas, men follow their dead wives to Hawaiki or travel there in search of lost sons. A homeland and a source, it is both a paradisal land of plenty and, like Te Pō, a land of spirits and of generations waiting to be born.

In most stories, Hawaiki is described as lying somewhere in the west—the direction associated in Polynesia with the passage of the dead to their last resting place—though sometimes it is said to be in the east or in the sky, or even underground. But there are also a number of real islands in the Pacific that go by the name of Hawaiki (or one of its cognates), most obviously the Big Island of Hawaiʻi and the Samoan island of Savaiʻi, but also the island of Raʻiatea, in the Society Islands, which was formerly known as Havaiʻi.

The first European to put two and two together regarding this legendary location was Horatio Hale, the insightful philologist with the United States Exploring Expedition of 1838–42, who also had interesting ideas about Tupaia's chart. In the course of his travels around the Pacific, Hale learned from the inhabitants of Aitutaki, in the Cook Islands, that their ancestors had come from

Avaiki. In the Marquesas he was told that Havaiki was the name of the underworld. Being American, he was familiar with the island of Hawai'i, and, being a linguist, he recognized that these were all variants of the same name. It was only when he got to Savai'i, in Samoa, however, that it occurred to him that Hawaiki might be the "key-word" that would unlock "the mystery of the Polynesian migrations." On the principle that people name new lands after the lands they have left behind—Plymouth, Venice, New Amsterdam, New Mexico—one had only to follow the trail of Hawaikis in order to trace the different branches of the Polynesian family "back to their original seat."

Hale believed he had found this "original seat" in Savai'i, the largest and most westerly of the Samoan islands. But, plausible as this was, it did not satisfy Smith and Fornander, whose Aryan thesis required a much older and remoter Polynesian homeland, a Hawaiki much farther to the west, at least in Indonesia if not in India itself. Fornander had alighted on the idea of Java as the original root, tracing the place name through a series of phonetic transformations—Java, Jawa, Hawa, Hawa-iti, Hawaiki—and Smith followed his lead in tracing the ancestral homeland back to the Indonesian islands of Sumatra and Seram. But, when it came to the voyaging stories, Smith also argued that the Hawaiki from which any given hero had departed might not be this *original* Hawaiki but one of the many *other* Hawaikis named by ancient voyagers along the way. Thus, a Māori voyager who claimed to have come from Hawaiki might actually be said to have come from Havai'i (a.k.a. Ra'iatea), in the Society Islands. This conveniently allowed Smith to fudge both dates and locations, an approach he also took with legendary figures when he concluded, in cases of conflicting genealogical evidence, that there must have been more than one person with that name. It was the same problem that Fornander had wrestled with, and the more Smith insisted on the strict historical veracity of the traditions, the more contorted his interpretations became.

· · ·

INTERESTINGLY, WHILE FORNANDER'S work set the stage for these attempts at chronicling the Polynesian past, he himself was somewhat lost to history, and his narratives largely subsumed by time. In New Zealand, on the other hand, Smith's account of the discovery and settlement of New Zealand was widely accepted, even celebrated, as the orthodox version of Māori history. Taught to schoolchildren, repeated in histories, commemorated on plaques, it functioned throughout most of the twentieth century as a national myth of origin.

Smith's story was based on the teachings, recorded in 1865, of two eminent East Coast *tohunga*. It begins in the year A.D. 925 in the ancient homeland of Hawaiki and concerns a man named Kupe, who becomes embroiled in an argument about an octopus. The octopus—a giant with eyes like abalone shells and arms "five fathoms long"—is interfering with Kupe's fishing grounds and Kupe decides that he will have to kill it. So he prepares a great canoe and tells his men to gather plenty of provisions. When everything is ready, he embarks with his wife and his friend Ngahue. Out at sea, Kupe spies the octopus, which he knows by the reddening of the ripples on the water, but as soon as the canoe draws near, the monster swims away—so straight and fast that Kupe knows it is leading them to some strange country. Eventually, when they have been at sea for quite some time, Kupe's wife catches sight of land, "like a cloud on the horizon." Thus the name Aotearoa, which Smith interprets as "the long white cloud." (Other interpretations include "the cloud hanging over a body of land discovered at the end of a long journey" and "the distant land to windward.")

Smith later conceded that some aspects of this story partook "of the marvelous" and sought to ground it more firmly in reality by suggesting that the real reason for Kupe's exploratory voyage southward was that he had observed "the flight of the *kohoperoa*, or long-tailed cuckoo," coming from the southwest. Knowing the habits of this bird, he argued, Kupe would certainly have realized that this meant there must be land somewhere to the southwest. In any case, having reached Aotearoa, Kupe discovers that the country is uninhabited—or, rather, that it is inhabited only by birds. He makes an exploratory circuit of the islands, and when this is done he sails back to Hawaiki and reports what he has found. There he lives out his life, for, according to the story, Kupe never returns to Aotearoa. Thus the rhetorical question *E hoki Kupe?* (Will Kupe return?), which is an ironical proverb signifying that one has no intention of revisiting a place.

According to Smith, Kupe's discovery of New Zealand was followed by two separate waves of immigration from Hawaiki: one in A.D. 1150, when a wayfinder named Toi set sail in search of a grandson who had been swept away in a storm; and another in A.D. 1350, with the arrival of the Great Fleet. The story of Toi almost seems an afterthought in Smith's version, but the Great Fleet is a cherished piece of modern New Zealand mythology. It recounts the arrival of an armada of seven great voyaging canoes carrying men, women, and children—as many as seventy to a vessel—with all their gods, plants, animals, food, water, implements, and tools. The canoes, which arrive more or less together, separate once they reach Aotearoa, each one traveling to a different part of the coast, where the occupants alight and settle, thereby establishing the land rights and lineages of people who would later trace their descent from these founding figures. For most of the twentieth century, the arrival of the Great Fleet was considered to be "the most famous event in Māori history because," as one eminent Māori scholar put it, "all tribes trace their aristocratic lineages back to the chiefs of the voyaging canoes." It was also the capstone of the Polynesian migration story and the end of the great voyaging era. New Zealand was the last of the Polynesian islands to be settled; following the arrival of the Great Fleet, in the words of a Māori proverb, "The *tapu* sea to Hawaiki is cut off."

• • •

FOR DECADES THE stories of Kupe and the Great Fleet were accepted as a true and faithful account of Māori history. But there were reasons to be skeptical. Later scholars, looking at "traditional" accounts compiled in the nineteenth and early twentieth centuries by men like Fornander and Smith, began detailing the many ways in which these stories had been altered. Names, words, paragraphing, punctuation, and grammar had all been tampered with; stories were re-sequenced and whole passages bowdlerized. Some of this, argued the classicist Agathe Thornton, may have been the natural consequence of converting oral narratives to written texts. Oral narratives (one can think here of the *Iliad* or the *Odyssey*) are famously non-chronological, beginning in the middle of an action and unfolding in a zigzag fashion, frequently detouring from the main events to fill in background or explain important information. Traditional Māori narratives were similar, and when they were edited by Europeans (with a European audience in mind), many of these structural kinks were ironed out. The effect was to turn "terse, cryptic and audience-centred originals" into smooth, exegetical narratives, making them more like history and less like myth.

Another problem with these Europeanized histories is that they are often composites. In a close textual study from the 1970s, D. R. Simmons argued that the much-loved stories of Kupe the discoverer and the Great Fleet did not actually represent any particular Māori tradition. Rather, they had been cobbled together from many different sources, often with interpolations by the compilers. Simmons also rejected the dates that Smith had assigned to these events, pointing out that Smith's date of 925 for Kupe was arrived at by working backward from purported settlement events in the twelfth century and was partly driven by the idea that Kupe had found the islands uninhabited and so had to have arrived before anyone else. As for the Great Fleet, Smith had settled on a date of 1350 by taking the mean of a large number of genealogies—some of which had as few as fourteen lines, while others had as many as twenty-seven—a process that, in Simmons's view, rendered it valid "only as an exercise in arithmetic."

Simmons was careful to say that his conclusions did not mean that Māori did not have traditions of settlement or discovery, or that they did not commemorate the voyages of heroes or particular canoes. But he was firm on the point that the orthodox stories of Kupe and the Great Fleet were modern myths that had arisen "out of the desire of European scholars to provide a coherent framework by which to interpret the prehistory of New Zealand" and had gradually become "more and more accepted as 'factual' and 'historical'" as time wore on.

Thus, over the course of the twentieth century, the prestige of histories based on Polynesian oral traditions gradually diminished. The uncritical acceptance of Polynesian traditions that had characterized the work of men like Tregear, Fornander, and Smith came into disrepute, while the messiness of the process—the fragmentary nature of the texts, the layers of translation, uncertainty about the value of genealogical dating—led more scientifically minded scholars of the twentieth century to devalue the discovery and settlement narratives that the traditions had given rise to. Gradually the "heroic" account of bold Polynesian seafarers and their daring journeys—Fornander's Vikings of the South Seas—faded, and a new, more skeptical perspective, one with a preference for "facts" over "rumors," emerged.

# Part IV

# THE RISE OF SCIENCE

# (1920-1959)

*In which anthropologists pick up the trail of the
ancient Polynesians, bringing a new, quantitative
approach to the questions of who, where, and when.*

# SOMATOLOGY

## *The Measure of Man*

*"Polynesian women from the Marquesas (Type I),"*
*photos by E. S. C. Handy and Ralph Linton,*
*in "Marquesan Somatology" by Louis R. Sullivan (Honolulu, 1923).*

**THROUGHOUT THE NINETEENTH** century, the question of who Polynesians were had been addressed by amateurs: missionaries, traders, colonial officials. Isolated from the intellectual mainstream but immersed in Polynesian cultures, they had pursued the question with great passion, clinging fiercely to some fairly idiosyncratic ideas. All this changed in the early decades of the twentieth century with the rise of anthropology as a discipline. The Pacific—one of the great loci of early ethnological research, along with Africa and the Americas—was suddenly awash in professional anthropologists who brought with them a new scientific approach. The problems were all still the same—Who were the Polynesians? Where had they come from? How and when had they colonized the Pacific? What was different was the methods used to address them.

In 1922, Herbert E. Gregory, director of the Bernice Pauahi Bishop Museum, in Honolulu, wrote that the history of Polynesia was "fundamentally a field problem" that could be solved only through "the accumulation of facts." One popular approach was to send teams of researchers from different subdisciplines out into the field to collect information, and in the early twentieth century scores of British and American scientists traveled to remote corners of the world on large anthropological expeditions, many of which were named for wealthy benefactors. Funded by bankers, industrialists, and department store owners, these ventures reflected the confluence of three fin de siècle trends: the vast fortunes accumulated during the Gilded Age, a growing interest in the so-called primitive (many of the great museum collections of art from Africa, Oceania, and the Americas were made around this time), and the professionalization of social sciences like anthropology and sociology, which promised to bring the rigor of the physical sciences to the study of humankind. For the right kind of donor, it was a highly attractive sort of philanthropy, combining fashionable intellectual inquiry with rugged adventure in exotic locales.

Gregory was fortunate in having just such a benefactor: Bayard Dominick Jr., scion of an old New York family, partner with his father and uncle in the brokerage firm Dominick and Dominick, member of the New York Stock Exchange, philanthropist, and big-game hunter. In 1920, Dominick donated forty thousand dollars—the equivalent of half a million dollars in today's money—to Yale University to finance a major anthropological expedition to the South Seas. The money, to be administered by the Bishop Museum, would support the Bayard Dominick Expedition, "the first comprehensive attack on a large scale on the problem of Polynesian origins" and a "systematic investigation" into the physical, cultural, and environmental characteristics of the Polynesian people.

Of course, quite a lot was already known about the peoples of

Polynesia. Anecdotal information about everything from Tahitian dietary habits to the monolithic sculptures of Easter Island could be culled from the journals of countless explorers, missionaries, memoirists, and travel writers. But it was all rather scattered and fragmentary and, above all, unscientific. What was wanted was detailed, systematic studies that assembled large bodies of information in ways that made them easy to classify and compare. The plan of the Bayard Dominick Expedition (actually a series of expeditions) was to describe a number of Polynesian cultures as completely as possible. Four teams of scientists, including ethnologists, archaeologists, and botanists, were sent to four different parts of the Polynesian Triangle: Tonga in the west, the Marquesas in the east, the Australs in the south, and Hawai'i in the north. Most of the participants were in their late twenties or early thirties; some were still graduate students; several were accompanied by their wives, who were listed officially as "volunteers." Each of the groups was to stay put for at least nine months, during which time they were to gather as much information as possible—for if the Bayard Dominick Expedition was anything, it was an exercise in data collection.

In practice, the brief of the expedition was so broad that there was room for members to investigate whatever they wanted. The anthropologist Edward W. Gifford made an extensive study of Tongan social structure and customs relating to law, property, religion, and war. Ralph Linton, an archaeologist with the Marquesan team, examined stone walls, terraces, platforms, sculptures, petroglyphs, and fortifications. Robert Aitken, in the Australs, studied mythology, while the botanist Forest B. H. Brown and his wife undertook a survey of the flora of southeastern Polynesia, with particular attention to local botanical knowledge and nomenclature.

One member of the Bayard Dominick Expedition was the ethnologist Edward S. C. Handy, who, with his wife, Willowdean, spent nine months in the Marquesas. The two of them made a formidable pair, he focusing much of his attention on Marquesan myths and religious practices while she made detailed studies of string figures and tattooing. Although the practice of tattooing had been outlawed by the French government in the late nineteenth century, Willowdean managed to find more than a hundred Marquesans with significant tattoos. She persuaded them to let her document these extraordinary designs, meticulously copying them onto paper when she discovered that the blue-black markings did not show up well in photographs. Years later, she recalled what it had been like to drop down into the middle of a Polynesian society in 1920. Much of her energy, she wrote, had been spent trying to figure out the social behaviors—what was considered polite, what was offensive, what was the true meaning of the things people said and did. But part of the learning curve had to do with her own shifting perspective: she had come to the island, she wrote, thinking of its inhabitants "as repositories of information" and departed nine months later thinking of them as friends.

Still, the purpose of the expedition was to collect information, and the Handys dutifully went about this task, inquiring about dances and dress styles, witchcraft, fish poisons, boxing, bird catching, ideas about time—anything and everything they could think of. They were especially interested in Marquesan legends, which seemed to Willowdean unlike anything she had ever encountered, with a louche, casual violence and a sexuality so explicit that some of the stories were "unpublishable" in English. Marquesan myths had gone underground in the 1920s in much the same way as tattoos, and many of the stories the Handys collected during this period were recounted by a man known locally as "a great liar," meaning, wrote Willowdean, that "he told the stories of the old-time people which the missionaries called 'lies.'"

Each of the Bayard Dominick teams was expected to complete a "physical survey" of the islanders and was provided with a special set of instruments for the purpose: calipers for measuring faces and heads, standing rods for determining height, pigmentation charts for classifying skin color, and special "anthropometrical cards" on which to write it all down. The data, which included numerical codes for attributes like hair form and skin tone as well as a standard set of body measurements, were to be gathered and sent, along with hair samples and photographs, to the expedition's "somatologist," Louis R. Sullivan of the American Museum of Natural History, who was tasked with compiling and publishing the results.

The Handys quickly realized that they would need to measure every full-blooded Marquesan who came their way if they were to meet their quota of three hundred "samples." Edward busied himself with calipers and standing rod while Willowdean wrote down the numbers on a chart, which, as she put it, "covered every feature of the human body from the crown of the head to the soles of the feet." Then she would snip off a bit of hair (she was surprised that the Marquesans allowed her to do this, since hair was known to be used by sorcerers "as bait to entrap the spirit of a man"), paste it onto a card, and try to match the subject's skin color to a scale of pigmentation shades. This last, as it turned out, was one of the most difficult parts of the job.

Several different systems existed for assigning skin tones a numerical value. They included Broca's Couleurs de la Peau et du Système Pileux (Colors of the Skin and Body Hair), published in Paris in 1879; a color panel designed by the German anatomist and physiologist Gustav Fritsch, consisting of forty-eight shades painted in oil on special paper in a handy pocket-size case; and Felix von Luschan's Hautfarbentafel, or skin-color panel, a seven-by-three-inch brass tray containing thirty-six glass mosaic pieces in shades from ivory to nearly black, which also came in a smaller, double-sided version fitted with a sliding brass sleeve. Von Luschan's Hautfarbentafel was considered the gold standard, but it was not available to the Bayard Dominick teams, who used Fritsch's kit instead.

Willowdean was often flummoxed by her assignment. At first, she thought it would be easy with the help of a pigmentation chart, but all too often she could not identify the right number. "Everyone complains about being unable to match Polynesian skin colors with the standard chart," her husband told her. "Put down the number of the nearest match." Sometimes she would put down two numbers with a plus sign between them. "Once," she wrote, "I was tempted to write a fraction." Held up against the cheek of a living person or against the inside of the upper arm—the two preferred locations for measuring "exposed" and "unexposed" skin—the flat, painted colors of the little paper blocks were woefully inadequate. Most of the Marquesans, Willowdean wrote, "had skins that were glowing, golden, light, yellow, brown—how describe them? Copper-colored under sunlight?" She wondered how an artist would handle the situation: "Would a painter mix chrome yellow with sepia, perhaps a bit of rose madder?" The adjectives that came to mind were all poetic, "but we were dealing with scientific data. I had to put down the approximate number."

SOMATOLOGICAL STUDIES—THAT IS, studies of the human body such as those undertaken in Polynesia by the anthropologists of the Bayard Dominick Expedition—were made of many different classes of people in the late nineteenth and early twentieth centuries. Typical subjects included women, children, athletes, "mental defectives," ethnic subgroups like Scandinavians and Eskimos, twins, Neanderthals, and the criminally insane. There were studies of distinctive physical features—palms, soles, teeth, ears—and a great deal of interest in skulls, crania, and the brain weights of various types of people, including artists, scholars, scientists, and "distinguished educated men." The ostensive purpose of all this activity was classification, the establishment of the range of variation, and an exploration of the mechanisms by which variation occurred.

Some somatological studies were purely descriptive—studies of the angle of the elbow, for instance, or the comparative growth rates of girls and boys. But many were driven by sociological questions: attempts, for example, to establish links between physical attributes (like stature or head shape) and mental states (like insanity) or social conditions (like poverty or being firstborn) or cultural customs (like nomadism). The idea that complex questions about the human condition could be answered by measuring people's bodies was not new. Johann Blumenbach's classic eighteenth-century division of humanity into five distinct types (Caucasian, Mongolian, Malayan, Ethiopian, and American) had been based on craniometric data—taken, apparently, from his own extensive collection of skulls. But in the latter half of the nineteenth century, debates about evolution and heredity had ignited interest in the notion that heritable physical characteristics could be definitive when it came to human populations. What was needed to prove this was data, and many large-scale studies were undertaken (including a census of the eye and hair color of six million German schoolchildren, which gave rise to a rumor that the king of Prussia had staked and lost forty thousand fair-haired children in a card game with the sultan of Turkey).

One of the many pernicious aspects of this research was the way it was used to classify human "races." In biology and anthropology, race has long been abandoned as a meaningful category; indeed, although the term has been in use since the seventeenth century, it has never been precisely defined. There has never been any agreement about the number of human races, or what the definitive characteristics of a race might be: skin color, hair type, head shape, etc. Genetic research in the twentieth century has shown that there are no genes that correspond to racial types and that the range of variation within so-called races is greater than the variation across them. But scientists in the early 1920s were working with an essentialist model of race as something immutable, definitive, and grounded in biological reality.

The framework within which the anthropologists of the Bayard Dominick Expedition operated was that there existed a certain number of "pure" human races. The minimum was generally considered to be three: Caucasoid, Mongoloid, and Negroid. But many of the world's peoples did not fit clearly into any of these categories, and scientists frequently invented additional racial types—Malayan, Indonesian, Austronesian, Negrito—or argued that these unclassifiable people represented populations that were "racially mixed." Polynesians (along with Native Americans, Melanesians, and Australian Aborigines) were one of the ambiguous groups, and one goal of the Bayard Dominick Expedition was to ascertain, using anthropometric data, what unique medley of existing races had "combined to make the Polynesian physical types."

It had long been observed—indeed, it is a cliché of early descriptions of Polynesians—that the islanders of the remote Pacific all looked remarkably alike. And yet, beyond the fact that they were tall, strongly built, dark-haired, brown-skinned, and generally handsome, there was little consensus among Europeans about how to describe them, especially when it came to the color of their skin. Nor could Europeans agree about who else in the world they most closely resembled, with some saying they looked like American Indians and others that they were more like Indonesians or Filipinos. Ideas about Polynesians' racial makeup were equally muddy. Many scientists, influenced by the still powerful Aryan theory, considered them Caucasian. Others described them as Mongoloid (i.e., Asian), while a third group identified them as belonging to the same stock as the indigenous peoples of the Americas—though, as no one was quite clear what race *they* belonged to, this was hardly a helpful idea. Most, however, concluded that Polynesians were "a hybrid people," a mixture—or layering, as one theorist imagined it—of Caucasian, Mongoloid, and Negroid elements in some combination.

Sullivan, whose job it was to crunch the data delivered to him by the Bayard Dominick field teams and bring some clarity to the situation, had a difficult task. The data sets ran to thousands of numbers: hundreds of subjects analyzed in terms of dozens of features. To begin with, there were the body measurements: stature, shoulder height, arm length, sitting height, head length, face width, nasal height, ear width, as well as the "bigonial diameter at the angles of the mandible." Then there were all the nonquantitative features: skin tone, hair form, eye color, tooth shape—all of which were assigned numerical values. Sullivan also calculated a whole series of ratios with exotic-sounding names like the "transverse fronto-parietal index" and the "zygomatico-mandibular index" and tried grouping subsets of the data in all different ways, noting the hair form and cephalic index of the men with the longest arms, or the stature and pigmentation of women with the shortest heads, seeking, quite hopelessly, as it turned out, to identify significant clusters or correlations.

The results were presented in a series of studies based on anthropometric data from Samoa, Tonga, and the Marquesas and published by the Bishop Museum between 1921 and 1923. (A fourth study, of Hawaiian data, was in preparation when Sullivan died, prematurely, in 1925.) The conclusions are complex—inscrutable, even—but it is interesting to trace the evolution of Sullivan's thinking as he worked his way through this mass of statistical information.

Beginning with the observation that Polynesians were commonly described as having "European racial affinities" (a gesture toward their supposed Aryan roots), Sullivan first concluded that the evidence from the Bayard Dominick Expedition contradicted this. Based on his analysis of Samoan and Tongan data, he found that, on the contrary, they were "most closely allied to the Mongoloid race of mankind"; in other words, they were essentially Asian. In the case of the Samoans, Sullivan found that, to the extent that they diverged from this type, it was in the direction of the European. When it came to the Tongans, however, the variation tilted in a "Melanesian" direction, meaning that Tongans were a little more black. (It is worth noting that Tongans were considered one of the "purest" Polynesian populations. Tonga, which is the only island nation in the Pacific never to have been ruled by outsiders, had a population in 1920 of more than 23,000 Tongans and only 347 Europeans. Compare this with the 1920 census for Hawai'i, which lists 41,000 Hawaiians, 54,000 Europeans, and more than 150,000 combined Filipino, Japanese, and Chinese.)

Sullivan next turned his attention to the Marquesas, where the situation was complicated by the cataclysmic population collapse of the nineteenth century and the high rates of intermarriage between the Marquesans and both Europeans and Chinese. Here, perhaps under the influence of Edward Handy, Sullivan introduced an entirely new model. The Marquesans, he decided, could be divided into two types: one characterized by taller stature, longer heads, narrower noses, straighter hair, more body hair, and lighter skin color (all classic "Caucasian" markers) and the other by shorter stature, broader heads, wider noses, wavier hair, less body hair, and darker skin color (all stereotypical "non-Caucasian" features). To the first he gave the name "Polynesian"; to the second, "Indonesian." This led Sullivan to rethink his earlier analyses of Samoa and Tonga, and, with the benefit of hindsight, he now realized that these two types—a taller/lighter, and a shorter/darker—had been present all along in all these other populations. The upshot of all this was to shift the primary racial category of the Polynesians back to Caucasian from Mongoloid, making them once again "white" and Indo-European rather than Asian, while still allowing for a "blackish" element or strain.

WHAT IS PAINFULLY clear from Sullivan's attempts to rationalize all this anthropometric data—so many numbers, so laboriously collected, so tirelessly grouped and regrouped—is how entirely futile it seems to be. In fact, no analysis of head shape or nose width or cephalic index was ever going to produce anything but a murky result. No tabulation of pigment would ever correlate with arm span or ear height in the way Sullivan hoped, because, even if the patterns he was looking for were there, the tools available to him in the 1920s were incapable of revealing them. All of Sullivan's calculations had to be done by hand, and neither the statistical methodology nor the computational power that would have enabled him to extract meaningful results from this data had yet been invented. And so instead, what we see is a jumble of results reflecting not some truth about the data but a set of underlying assumptions about the people themselves.

In his Marquesan study, Sullivan directed the reader to a group of photographs at the end of the volume that had been sorted into his "Polynesian" and "Indonesian" types. These photos, consisting of head shots of men and women, face-on and in profile, resemble nothing so much as mug shots or passport photos. The subjects stare at the camera with serious expressions, some look a little worried or annoyed, a few wear the tiniest of smiles. Although many appear to have dressed up for the occasion, you could never mistake these images for portraits. They are clearly specimen studies, designed to be as consistent and uniform as possible in order to facilitate comparison and classification. Sullivan's somatological studies were published in large quarto volumes, allowing for as many as twelve, fifteen, even sixteen head shots per page, and this presentation encourages the reader to judge for himself whether what Sullivan said—that there can be "no doubt that at least two separate and radically different groups . . . are represented"—is borne out by the photos.

And the truth is, when you look at these arrays of Polynesian faces, you really cannot see what Sullivan was talking about. All of these people look sort of alike, and yet, as one would expect, they are also all different. One has a longer nose, another a broader; one's hair is wavy and a bit disheveled, another's is straighter, perhaps more carefully combed. Looking at these pictures, one cannot help seeking a sense of the person behind the shot. Who were these men and women? What were they thinking? Willowdean Handy wrote that among the Marquesas there was great demand to be photographed and that each of the sitters received a print. (The Marquesans, it seems, *did* think of these photos as portraits.) And other anthropologists have also described these measuring and photographing sessions as popular social events, with lots of joking and banter from the assembled crowd. None of this comes through in the photos, however, and it is interesting to speculate about what else has been eliminated in the drive to achieve strict standardization. But even putting aside one's natural human sympathy and viewing these images as they are meant to be viewed—as type specimens—it is impossible to see in them any of the classificatory systems Sullivan described.

The somatological studies of the Bayard Dominick Expedition were a key piece of the plan to put the study of Polynesian origins on a scientific footing. As quantitative studies based on large amounts of data, they promised objective, replicable insights into the history of the Polynesian peoples, potentially confirming (or not) the Aryan theory of Polynesian origins and revealing the precise nature of the relationship between Polynesians and their neighbors in Melanesia and Southeast Asia. Reading this work, one feels the intensity of effort, the commitment to the method, the devotion to the idea of science—as one anthropologist of the period put it, "There is only one way by which we can arrive at an understanding . . . and that is by measurements, measurements, and yet more measurements." And yet it is also obvious that these studies were not a success.

Much of the problem was simply methodological, but at least part of the issue was the way they were formulating the question. The classes or groups into which scientists were trying to sort Polynesians were not the objective categories they appeared to be; they were fluid, socially conditioned, historically constructed, and astonishingly easy to fudge—a point that goes some way toward explaining Sullivan's imprecise and constantly shifting terminology.

From the perspective of the twenty-first century, a lot of this work looks creepy, and for good reason. Physical anthropology in the early twentieth century was closely associated with eugenics and with attempts to legitimize racist claims using scientific methodologies. But this is not to say that the whole project was irredeemably flawed. Later scientists, using better tools and larger data sets, would succeed in deriving statistically meaningful information from biometric information, and with the sequencing of the human genome, the role of biological evidence in the search for answers about human history would leap to the fore. Although these early attempts to use biology to answer questions about origins, ancestry, and heredity were clumsy, the questions they sought to answer were not going away.

# A MĀORI ANTHROPOLOGIST
## Te Rangi Hiroa

*Peter Buck studying Paratene Ngata making a* hinaki
*(wickerwork pot for trapping eels), ca. 1922,*
*by an unidentified photographer.*

**THE QUESTION OF** who Polynesians were—in a biological sense—
was of particular interest to one of the period's leading anthropologists, a man who went by the names of both Peter H. Buck and Te
Rangi Hiroa. Born in New Zealand to an Anglo-Irish father and a
Māori mother, he was the only anthropologist of the early twentieth century who could claim Polynesian descent and, thus, the only
one with a personal stake in the problem of Polynesian origins.

Te Rangi Hiroa had one of those remarkable lives: arising from
nowhere and ascending, on the strength of ability alone, to the very
pinnacle of his profession. His father was an itinerant worker who
had followed the gold rush to Australia and, failing to strike it rich,

crossed over to New Zealand, where he settled down with a Māori woman from the Taranaki region. As a child, Te Rangi Hiroa was deeply attached to his mother and grandmother, who were his first teachers of Māori language and custom. He attended a primary school for European children, and after his mother died in 1892— he would have been about fourteen or fifteen at the time; his actual birth date was never recorded—he left with his father to go work in another part of New Zealand. A few years later, having concluded that the shearing life was not for him, he applied to Te Aute College, a famous secondary school for boys that produced many of the most prominent Māori leaders of the early twentieth century. From there he went on to the University of Otago, where he studied medicine, receiving his bachelor's degree in 1904 and his doctorate in 1910.

He often described himself as being conscious of "an internal struggle." "Sometimes," he wrote, "the Irish in me criticized the Maori, and at other times the Maori differed from the Irish." But this sense of belonging to two different worlds was central to his identity and, later, to his authority as an anthropologist. He believed that his biculturalism gave him an edge—"the inside angle," as he once put it—and that he could see things that European scientists missed. It also occasionally made for odd situations, as on the day he first entered "the taboo precincts" of the Otago Medical School and saw, at the top of the stairs, a notice "offering various prices for Maori skulls, pelves, and complete skeletons." He read it "with horror," he wrote, and almost abandoned his quest for Western medical knowledge there and then.

He did not abandon the quest, however, and went on to become a physician and medical officer with the New Zealand Department of Health. He was always interested in cultural issues: large chunks of his doctoral dissertation addressed the history of traditional Māori medicine, and even while he was still working as a doctor, he was publishing descriptions of tattoo patterns and house panels, basketry, and weaving, and notes on small outrigger canoes. He also, on his own initiative, conducted one of the largest somatological studies of a Polynesian population in this period. He had served as a medical officer in the Maori Pioneer Battalion in World War I, and in 1919, at the end of the war, it occurred to him that he would have a large sample population on board the troop ship returning home to New Zealand. Borrowing a Flower's craniometer and a von Luschan color panel, he undertook the measurement of no fewer than 814 Māori soldiers, amassing by far the largest sample of Polynesian biometric information to date. (His conclusions, once he had collated the results, were no less murky than Sullivan's.)

In 1923, at a Pan-Pacific Science Congress in Melbourne, he came to the attention of Herbert Gregory of the Bishop Museum, and the next year he was invited to join an expedition to the Cook Islands as a follow-up to the Bayard Dominick Expedition. A few years later, Gregory asked him to join the museum's staff in Honolulu. This marked a turning point in his career; he left both New Zealand and the practice of medicine and turned his focus entirely to anthropology. Over the next few years he traveled widely, writing papers on the ethnology of Samoa, Aitutaki, Tongareva, Manihiki, Rakahanga, and Mangaia. By the mid-1930s his reputation as one of Polynesia's leading ethnologists was secure, and in 1936, when Gregory stepped down, he became director of the Bishop Museum, a post he held, along with the prestigious Yale professorship that went with it, until his death, in 1951.

NATURALLY, TE RANGI HIROA was interested in the problem of Polynesian origins; not only was this one of the dominant questions in Pacific anthropology, it was the story of his own kin. He had been raised with a reverence for the traditions of his mother's people, and he had a deep admiration for the work of men like Fornander and Smith, whose historical narratives formed the backdrop for research into Polynesian origins in the 1920s and '30s. But while he never questioned the authenticity of the Great Fleet story, he was uneasy about many of the details. He noted that some of the narratives on which Smith had based his account were uncomfortably close to biblical tradition, while others contained a knowledge of geography that could only have come from European sources. He also questioned some of the extremely long genealogies that had been used to date Polynesian migrations. While he felt sure that genealogies did serve as a kind of chronology of Polynesian history, he doubted whether any people could keep an accurate oral record of events for more than two thousand years. "With all my love for my mother's stock," he wrote, "my father's unbelieving blood gives me pause."

Te Rangi Hiroa himself had come to the problem of origins not through folklore and mythology but through disciplines like anatomy and epidemiology. He believed that theorizing should begin with evidence, and that the best evidence was material. He liked things that were measurable (like bodies) or concrete (like fish traps) and felt that the history of nonliterate peoples could best be deduced from the "objects which people of past generations have made with their hands." And not just the objects, but the living technique: a weaver might use modern materials, "but the fingers and the mind express themselves in the culture technique that her mother handed on as it was handed on to her."

In time, Te Rangi Hiroa became so knowledgeable about these things that he could tell at a glance what part of Polynesia an artifact belonged to, and on trips to see the great Polynesian collections in European and American museums, he routinely discovered items that were mislabeled. In a diorama at the American Museum of Natural History, in New York, he noted that a Tahitian figure making a pandanus thatch was posed with the wrong implement in his hand. In the Berne Historical Museum, in Switzerland, he found a typical Hawaiian adze with the label A HATCHET FROM OTAHEITE. In the same museum he also found a Native American cape from the Pacific Northwest and a Māori cloak with a taniko border, both of which were described as Tongan. "Imagine," he wrote to his friend Apirana Ngata, "the atrocities that could have been committed by an academic student in Berne writing a thesis on the textiles of Tonga!"

He was most famous, however, for the "unwearying patience" with which he studied how these objects were made and for his mastery of a vast array of Polynesian handicrafts. He could weave floor mats, cloaks, and baskets; make seine nets, scoop nets, trap nets, and crayfish pots. One colleague described how he would stand for hours, notebook in hand, observing the construction of some complicated object, recording each stage of the work with sketches, photographs, and descriptions. Then, when it was all finished, he would start from the beginning, repeating the entire process himself on the principle that "the best way to describe an operation is to do it from personal working." So complete was his understanding of how to make house panels, boats, clothing, furniture, weapons, baskets, and tools that it was said he could have lived "like one of his ancestors if he had been cast away on an atoll."

Ngata, the great Māori statesman and his closest friend, urged Te Rangi Hiroa to go beyond the "packed store-houses of facts" to "conclusions that will compel anthropologists to readjust their Western angle to the facts of a wider humanity." And in the 1930s he did make a stab at a general theory of Polynesian origins. This was always going to be interesting because of his deep knowledge of Polynesian cultures, but it ended up being interesting because of his emotional investment in the problem itself.

Like most anthropologists of the period, Te Rangi Hiroa still accepted the basic tenets of the Aryan thesis, though he was never much interested in the very earliest stages of this tale. What did interest him was the pathway that the ancestors of the Polynesians had taken once they began migrating out of Southeast Asia. The most obvious route passes through Indonesia and the Philippines, along the north coast of New Guinea, through the Bismarck Archipelago to the Solomons, Vanuatu, New Caledonia, and Fiji, and thence to Tonga, Samoa, and the rest of the Polynesian Triangle. This path through the heart of Melanesia presents the fewest and smallest gaps between islands and offers the advantage of abundant natural resources: many kinds of plant and animal food, access to fresh water, a variety of useful materials like wood and stone.

But Te Rangi Hiroa did not believe that his ancestors had followed this path. He thought they had taken a more northerly route, island-hopping from the Philippines through Micronesia—from Palau to Yap to the Caroline, Marshall, and Gilbert Islands—on the way to Samoa and the Polynesian Triangle. But this region is not called Micronesia for nothing. Not only are the distances between islands enormous, the islands themselves are minuscule coral atolls with extremely limited natural resources: plentiful in fish, shellfish, and sharks, but poor in soil, plants, animals, water, wood, and stone.

There are countless problems with the idea of a primary Polynesian migration through Micronesia. But the most insurmountable, as Te Rangi Hiroa himself noted, is that virtually all the Polynesian food plants—breadfruit, banana, cassava, sweet potato, most varieties of taro—will grow only in continental or volcanic soils and could not have been transported along an "atoll-studded route." His solution was to argue for two separate waves of migration: a foundational wave of original settlers who "steered their ships . . . from atoll to atoll" and a later wave of people who brought food plants and domestic animals by the more southerly route. But this was not, as one anthropologist puts it, "a parsimonious explanation."

One has to wonder why Te Rangi Hiroa would tie himself in knots in this fashion, and the Occam's razor answer is that he objected to the idea of his Polynesian ancestors migrating through the islands of Melanesia. But to understand why this might be so, we have to take a step back and look at the history of this region.

ALMOST FROM THE very beginning, European travelers had noticed a curious thing about the Pacific: the inhabitants of the central and eastern islands (the Polynesian Triangle) looked different from their neighbors in the islands immediately to the west. To Cook's naturalist, Forster, the Pacific appeared to be inhabited by two great "Varieties" of people: "the one more fair, well limbed, athletic, of a fine size . . . and the other, blacker, the hair just beginning to become woolly and crisp, the body more slender and low." This idea was further reinforced in the early nineteenth century by the French navigator Jules Dumont d'Urville, who proposed a set of divisions and a nomenclature that are still with us today. It was d'Urville who gave us the three "'nesias"—Polynesia, Micronesia, and Melanesia—the first named for the "many islands" of the central and eastern Pacific; the second for the "little islands" to the north and west; and the third for the "black islands" of the western Pacific. D'Urville considered Micronesia to be a sort of extension of Polynesia, and so the primary contrast was between the lighter-skinned people of the open ocean—d'Urville called them "*la race cuivrée*," or "the coppery race"—and the darker-skinned people at the western edge.

This idea of two distinct varieties of people (which quickly hardened into a Polynesian/Melanesian divide) turns what is, in fact, a spectrum of skin tones and peoples across the Pacific into a more or less binary division between black and white. With this binary came a tangle of other ideas about morality, intelligence, temperament, beauty, social and political complexity, even depth of time. Melanesians were routinely described by Europeans as not just dark-skinned, but "primitive" in their political, economic, and social structures. In eighteenth- and nineteenth-century accounts, they are depicted as small, dark, and mistrustful, the women "ill-favoured" and "ugly," the men "despotic" and cruel. Banded together in small, autonomous groups, they appeared to Europeans to lack any form of law, government, or organized religion and compared unfavorably with their larger, fairer-skinned, more hierarchical neighbors the Polynesians, differing from them, in one unforgettable formulation, "as the wolf from the dog."

The term "Melanesian" had thus long served in European discourse as a marker for otherness and inferiority, and in the racially charged climate of the early twentieth century, Te Rangi Hiroa could hardly fail to be aware of this. When the anatomist J. H. Scott (the probable author of the Otago Medical School notice offering to buy Māori skeletons) asserted, "We know the Maoris to be . . . the result of the mingling of a Polynesian and a Melanesian strain," or when Sullivan argued for a "Melanesian element" in his Tongan or Samoan data sets, Te Rangi Hiroa would certainly have recognized the subtext. And in his own early somatological studies, which were written explicitly with the work of these other men in mind, you can see him struggling with the problem.

It would be both simplistic and patronizing, however, to see Te Rangi Hiroa's views on the Melanesian question purely in terms of an internalization of racist European ideas. His own attitudes about race and racism were, not surprisingly, complex. He regarded his own biracial heritage as advantageous—"I am binomial, bilingual, and inherit a mixture of two bloods that I would not change for a total of either," he once wrote, and "any success I may have achieved has been largely due to my good fortune in being a mongrel." But being "half-caste" in the 1930s and '40s definitely had its disadvantages. One of the great irritations of Te Rangi Hiroa's life was the refusal of the U.S. government to grant him citizenship, on the grounds that he was not more than 50 percent Caucasian, as U.S. naturalization laws then required. The irony of this, of course, was that most anthropologists of the period, including Te Rangi Hiroa himself, believed that Polynesians *were* Caucasian, being part of the great Indo-European diaspora. But the U.S. government of the 1940s classified them as "Asiatics" and barred them from becoming citizens on these grounds.

Even his ever-increasing eminence—half a dozen major academic prizes, a bestselling book, four honorary doctorates, and a knighthood—could not entirely protect him from insult. And, while he was famously genial and good-natured in public, he occasionally unleashed a torrent of resentment in his private correspondence. As he put it to Ngata, "the Pakeha [European] attitude towards the native races is on the whole saturated with the deepest hypocrisy. . . . Even in ethnology, I doubt whether a native people is really regarded as other than a project to give the white writer a job and a chance for fame." But Polynesians, too, had their own systems of ranking and classification. Te Rangi Hiroa described "Melanesian" physical characteristics as conflicting with "the Polynesian idea of beauty" and wrote that among Māori, "a fair skin was admired," while those at the darker end of the spectrum had "to put up with the humorously disparaging remarks of their lighter tinted friends."

In the end, it is quite impossible to tease apart the strands of his thinking, or to know with any degree of certainty how much of what he thought was derived from customary Māori attitudes and how much from European prejudices. Nor, frankly, does it really matter, since both seem to have led him to the same point.

TE RANGI HIROA'S Micronesian theory was ultimately another of those red herrings, like drowned continents or the Beringian route: provocative but almost certainly wrong. It did, however, highlight an important issue: What *was* the nature of the relationship between Polynesians and their neighbors to the west? Might the Polynesians have originated in Melanesia? Did they pass through it on their way from someplace else? And what, in either case, did that actually mean, both culturally and biologically?

It was impossible to address any of these questions without also knowing who the inhabitants of Melanesia were, and this, too, was something of a mystery. Curiously enough, Forster, way back in the 1770s, had proposed what would prove to be a strangely prescient idea. He hypothesized that the darker-skinned peoples of the western Pacific, many of whom lived in the mountainous interiors of the larger islands, were "the more antient inhabitants," while the lighter-skinned coastal peoples, who were related, he thought, "to the various tribes of Malays," had arrived in the region more recently. No one would be able to prove it for nearly two centuries, but there was actually something to this idea.

We now know that the islands of western Melanesia (New Guinea and the Bismarck and Solomon Islands) have been occupied for tens of thousands of years—ages and ages longer than the islands of Polynesia. Modern archaeological evidence reveals that New Guinea and Australia, which were joined by a land bridge when sea levels were much lower, were settled at least forty thousand years ago, by people who then managed to spread themselves right out to the end of the Solomons. So there is an ancient substrate to this population. But forty thousand years is a long time, and it is quite inaccurate to suggest that the modern inhabitants of Melanesia can simply be equated with this very ancient population. There are not now, as Forster suggested, two great varieties of people in the Pacific: there is one quite homogeneous group in the central and eastern Pacific (Polynesians), and, thanks to the incredibly long time they have had to diversify, a hugely complex and heterogeneous mix of peoples and cultures in the Melanesian islands to the west.

One index of this complexity was actually recognized by both Forster and d'Urville, though neither of them understood it at the time. This was the extraordinary proliferation of languages in Melanesia. It had been the similarity of languages across the islands of Polynesia that had first led to the idea of a single Polynesian "nation," but no such unity exists in the islands to the west. Even today on New Caledonia—an island roughly the size of New Jersey—between thirty and forty languages are spoken. One hundred and ten languages have been recorded in the islands of Vanuatu. And in New Guinea, which is famous for being the most linguistically diverse place on earth, there are more than 950 languages belonging to a still unknown number of language families. To a linguist, what such extreme diversity indicates is depth of time. Languages are always changing—splitting and morphing and turning into new languages—and the more time they have in which to do this, the more languages there are. Consider the changes that have occurred in English just since Chaucer's day, and then imagine what might happen if this process were to continue for, say, forty thousand years.

All of this would prove important to the story of the Polynesian migrations, but in the 1930s the methods that would bring these facts to light had not yet been discovered. Although the impulse to use science to answer some of these questions was strong in the first half of the twentieth century, the early results were generally disappointing: some mystifying claims based on the measurement of bodies; a number of confusing attempts to deduce migration patterns from comparisons of ethnological traits; much speculative theorizing based largely on prejudice. But there was one branch of anthropology that had not yet really been brought into play, and over the next few decades, all the most exciting discoveries would be made by people wielding shovels and sieves.

# THE MOA HUNTERS

## Stone and Bones

*Rock painting of moa, in "The Material Culture of
the Moa-Hunters in Murihuku" by David Tevitodale,*
Journal of the Polynesian Society *(1932).*

**FOR A LONG** time, no one thought that archaeology was worth doing in the Pacific. Well into the twentieth century, it was assumed that there would be little to find (no ceramics or metal); that the history of occupation was not long enough to be interesting; and that the cultures of the Pacific were so static and unchanging that any archaeological discoveries would only duplicate what had already been revealed by other means. There was one exception to this, however, and that was New Zealand, where archaeology got a dramatic early start in the nineteenth century, when human artifacts were discovered mixed in with the bones of giant prehistoric birds.

The moa was quite a mystery in early colonial New Zealand. None of the early explorers appears to have known anything about it, but once settlers began arriving in the early nineteenth century, reports of mysteriously large bones quickly began to surface. An English settler by the name of Joel Polack described the "large fossil ossifications" that were shown to him by Māori, who told him that there had been very large birds in New Zealand "in times long past." Polack also recorded a tale, then still current among the very old, of "Atuas [gods], covered with hair, in the form of birds, having waylaid former native travellers among the forest wilds, vanquishing them with an overpowering strength, killing and devouring [them]." A missionary traveling in the same region at about the same time was similarly treated to the story of "a certain monstrous animal."

> While some said it was a bird, and others "a person" all agreed that it was called a Moa;—that in general appearance it somewhat resembled an immense domestic cock, with the difference, however, of its having a "face like a man";—that it dwelt in a cavern in the precipitous side of a mountain;—that it lived on air;—and that it was attended, or guarded, by two immense *Tuataras* [lizards], who, Argus-like, kept incessant watch while the moa slept.

The people who reported this also said that they made fishhooks from the creature's bones, which were sometimes discovered among the sandbars and shallows of the river.

Polack shrewdly observed that these bones appeared to belong to an extinct "species of the Emu." But no one seems to have paid any attention to this remark, and it was Sir Richard Owen, the famed British comparative anatomist and paleontologist (it was Owen who gave us the classification Dinosauria), who got the credit for identifying the bird. In 1839, Owen received a fragment of moa bone from a New Zealand traveler. It was a section of femur about six inches long and five and a half inches in circumference. At first he dismissed it as a piece of common beef bone, "such as is brought to table in a napkin." On closer inspection, however, he concluded that it did not, in fact, resemble the long bones of a mammal, that it was even less like the bone of a reptile, and that if it did belong to a bird, it was not a species that had ever known flight. Owen eventually concluded that the bone belonged to a large struthious (that is, ostrich-like) bird, which he christened *Dinornis novaezea-landiae*, by which he is said to have meant not so much "Large and Terrible" as "Surprising" Bird.

This was all quite wonderful in its own right, but then, in the 1840s and '50s, evidence began to emerge that man and the moa had actually coexisted. In both the North and South Islands of New Zealand, moa bones were discovered in middens, that is, heaps of shell and bone left over from centuries of prehistoric meals. They were found in or near ancient cooking pits and ovens, mixed in with shells and the bones of ducks, dogs, rats, porpoises, and seals. Flaked stone knives lay scattered nearby, and enough pieces of egg-shell were discovered to reconstruct at least twenty moa eggs, some of which showed signs of having been drilled. The eggs looked, wrote one observer, "as if a hole had been artificially formed for the purpose of extracting the contents," or "perhaps to allow of the shell being used as a water vessel." But the coup de grâce was the discovery, a decade or so later, of a human skeleton buried with a moa egg in its hands.

Although some in the mid-nineteenth century held out hope that a species or two of moa might have survived into modern times—a few irrepressible hoaxers actually claimed to have chased one—most scientists accepted that the moa had been extinct for a period of time. The question was how long? And, even more in-triguingly, who were these people, these moa hunters, who had killed and eaten them?

ONE SUGGESTION, REMARKABLE because it shows just how unclear the timelines for human settlement of the Pacific were, was made by a Prussian geologist and immigrant to New Zealand named Ju-lius von Haast. Haast was strongly influenced by theories then being advanced in Europe about the ages of prehistoric man. Finds of prehistoric animal bones and human artifacts in France had led researchers to conclude that the Stone Age should properly be divided into two eras: an Old Stone Age, or Paleolithic, when primitive humans had hunted prehistoric beasts like mammoths and cave bears using only rudimentary flaked knives, and a New Stone Age, or Neolithic, when they had advanced to making tools of polished stone and bone.

The Māori, Haast reasoned, clearly belonged to the later Neolithic era, as evidenced by their beautiful greenstone pendants and finely polished stone adzes and clubs. But the moa, as a species of megafauna—New Zealand's equivalent of "the huge *pachydermata* and other gigantic forms . . . in the northern hemisphere"—was obviously Paleolithic. And if the moa was Paleolithic, that meant that whoever killed and ate the moa was also Paleolithic. This, in turn, led Haast to the conclusion that there must have been an earlier, more primitive people in New Zealand who had lived—on the strength of the European analogy—perhaps as long as ten thousand years ago.

Haast believed that these Paleolithic people had hunted the moa to extinction and that they had died out long before the Māori arrived. He argued that many Māori seemed to know little about the moa and often did not recognize moa bones when they found them, believing them to be the bones of horses or cows and even misidentifying fragments of moa eggshell as pieces of human skull. But the real key to his argument was the ubiquitous presence of flint knives—the classic Paleolithic technology—at moa-hunter sites all across New Zealand. Haast considered this artifact diagnostic, proof of an essential primitivism in the tool makers. When it was discovered that some of the stone flakes found in South Island sites were made from a type of obsidian that could be obtained only on the North Island, he even suggested that this proved the antiquity of the moa hunters. Too primitive to have crossed a large water gap like Cook Strait, they must have occupied

New Zealand in some geologic era before the North and South Islands had been divided.

This, of course, was absurd, and Haast's timeline was controversial even in his own day. Few critics accepted that New Zealand had been occupied for anything like ten thousand years, or that the moa had been extinct for anywhere near that long. Some noted the "remarkably perfect" moa remains that had been discovered in caves, including some with ligaments, skin, and feathers all still attached, which appeared far too well preserved to have been around for millennia. Others felt that Māori tradition, though thin on the subject of the moa, should not be entirely dismissed. Sir George Grey, an important collector of oral traditions, was firmly of the opinion that the Māori people knew perfectly well what the moa was and that it was extinct, and that this knowledge had been handed down to them from their ancestors, who had encountered the creature when they first arrived. He noted that *moa* was a Polynesian word meaning "chicken" or "fowl," and that it was "the very word which new comers to the islands of New Zealand would have been likely to apply to the *Dinornis*, if they had found it in existence there."

But if the moa hunters were not primitive Paleolithic hunters, who were they? Independent of the timeline, Haast's theory had raised an important question: Were the Māori the original settlers of New Zealand, or had they been preceded in the islands by somebody else? The issue was very much muddied by the claim, made by S. Percy Smith in his history of New Zealand, that the islands were already inhabited when the first settlers from Hawaiki arrived. According to Smith's account, these first settlers were tall and thin, with black skin, flat noses, and lank hair. They lived in lean-tos, wore little or no clothing, and did not know their own genealogies or grow any of their own food. No one knew where they had come from, but they were believed to have been blown to New Zealand from some larger, warmer country to the west. According to this tradition, when the later, more sophisticated immigrants from Hawaiki (i.e., the ancestors of the Māori) arrived, they easily overpowered and enslaved these earlier arrivals, taking their women as wives and their boys as servants and killing whoever was left.

This obviously post-contact narrative, with its racist invocation of the Melanesia/Polynesia divide, had worked its way into New Zealand's settlement story. Although it had nothing to do with moas or archaeological sites, it effectively cemented the idea of the moa hunters as a distinct, ethnically different (i.e., possibly Melanesian) people from the Polynesian Māori. This, then, was how things stood when the problem was taken up by the professionals.

THE FIRST SYSTEMATIC attempt to sort out some of these issues was made by a University of Otago anthropologist by the name of H. D. Skinner. Skinner, who held the first—and, for a long time, only—anthropology lectureship in New Zealand, was more of an ethnologist than an archaeologist, but his passion was for the classification of objects that survived in archaeological contexts: fishhooks, files, needles, awls, and especially adzes. Adzes—smooth, dark, heavy blocks of fine-grained stone, polished, in some cases, to a satin gloss—were one of the more important artifacts uncovered in moa-hunter sites. Haast had considered their presence there confusing, considering them too "sophisticated" to be associated with New Zealand's first settlers, and one of the tasks Skinner set himself was to determine whether these objects could legitimately be associated with the moa hunters.

The obvious way to do this is through stratigraphy: the principle that, in undisturbed ground, older things lie beneath things that are more recent. If adzes and other sophisticated tools belonged to later occupants, they should be found only at higher levels in these sites. But the situation was confusing. Stratigraphy was not much on the minds of nineteenth-century curio hunters, and there had been a great deal of indiscriminate digging and mucking about, with the consequence that, as one of New Zealand's modern archaeologists puts it, "many of the rich collections from this time are now of limited use."

As a partial solution, Skinner and his colleague David Teviot-dale came up with an ingenious idea. They realized that the mere presence of moa bones could not be taken as an indication of moa hunters, since anyone could scavenge old bones. But some parts of a moa were more useful than others: leg bones, for example, were good for making tools, but vertebrae were not. They therefore applied the following rule: an object could safely be associated with moa hunters only if it appeared in a site with "refuse" bones—ribs, vertebrae, pelvic bones, and so on—the presence of which strongly suggested that living moas had been butchered on the site.

Slowly, Skinner and Teviotdale began to piece together a sketch of the people widely presumed to be the first settlers of New Zealand. They noted their use of earth ovens, their fondness for dogs, the evidence in their middens of other extinct creatures, including *Harpagornis moorei*, the giant eagle, and *Cygnus sumnerensis*, the giant swan. Although there was no way to be absolutely certain, they believed that the moa hunters had left a record of themselves in drawings on the walls of rock-shelters and caves, depicting hunters and short-legged moas with plump, ovoid bodies and long, sinuous necks.

Based on an exhaustive study of artifacts—more than ten thousand in the Otago Museum alone—along with some more conscientious excavations, Skinner and Teviotdale ultimately concluded that the moa hunters were indeed New Zealand's first colonists and settlers; that they had hunted the moa to extinction, along with a number of other large birds; and, most importantly, that they were culturally Polynesian. The similarities between their artifacts and those of both Māori and other Polynesians (including, surprisingly, far-off Easter Islanders) were too obvious to be ignored, and there was nothing whatsoever to link them to Melanesia or anyplace else, or to suggest that anyone had ever reached New Zealand before them.

Then, one day in 1939, a thirteen-year-old schoolboy named Jim Eyles stuck his shovel into the ground on his family's farm and hit something that at first he believed to be the shell of a dried gourd. It turned out to be not a gourd at all, but a large and almost perfect moa egg. Continuing to dig, he uncovered the bones of a human skeleton, then a necklace made of seven large beads in whale-tooth ivory, with a central pendant made from a sperm whale tooth. He had discovered what is still considered the most important archaeological site in New Zealand, the "type-site of the earliest phase of New Zealand's prehistory."

The Eyles farm sat on a strip of land—a sand-and-boulder bank about four and a half miles long—known as Wairau Bar. Formed at the mouth of the Wairau River and built up "during the ages of ceaseless struggle between the river and the sea," the bar separates the waters of Cloudy Bay, on the south side of Cook Strait, from a series of estuarine channels and lagoons. It is a barren, windswept place, but rich in marine resources, including kahawai and whitebait, eels, herring, flounder, and shellfish. Swans and ducks flock to the lagoons, and it appears to have been a good place for hunting (or perhaps preserving) the innumerable moas whose bones were strewn across the bank. Many of these were first uncovered when the area was plowed in the 1920s, but no one seems to have known, until Eyles made his startling discovery, that just below the surface lay the remnants of an entire settlement: middens, ovens, house posts, and more than forty graves.

Eyles's find generated considerable local interest; moa eggs were a rarity, and the whale-tooth necklace was virtually unique. In order to keep the artifacts safe, the family packed them into a biscuit tin and deposited them at the National Bank. For a while they were exhibited in the window of a fish shop; Eyles recalled watching one woman stroke the egg as if it were a holy relic. Several museums expressed interest in the find, and when a deal was eventually struck with the director of the Dominion Museum, in Wellington, the egg and the ivory necklace were carried across Cook Strait in the family fishing boat.

Early in 1942, Eyles again took up his shovel, this time in an

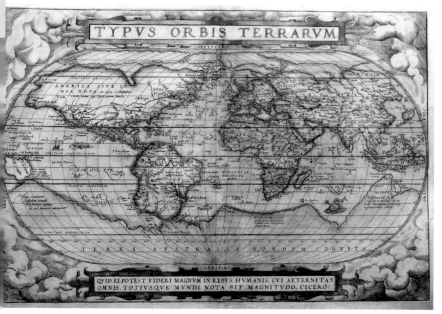

Map of the world showing Terra Australis Incognita, 1570.

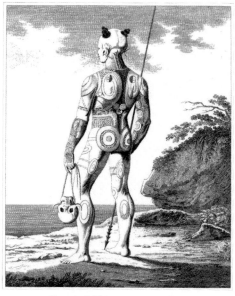

Tattooed Marquesan, ca. 1804.

Easter Island *moai*, ca. 1776.

Nukutavake canoe, ca. 1767.

Nukutavake canoe detail.

Capt.ⁿ James Cook
of the Endeavour.

Portrait of Captain Cook by William Hodges, 1775–76.

Tupaia's drawing of a Māori trading with Joseph Banks, 1769.

Peter H. Buck
(Te Rangi Hiroa),
ca. 1904.

Von Luschan
skin color panel.

Richard Owen
and moa, ca. 1879.

Moa egg found by Jim Eyles at
Wairau Bar in 1939.

Necklace of moa bone and stone "whale tooth"
pendant from Wairau Bar.

"The Arrival of the Maoris" by L. J. Steele and C. F. Goldie, 1898.

Reconstructed Lapita pot from Vanuatu.

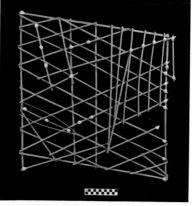

Micronesian stick chart.

*Hōkūleʻa* passing the Statue of Liberty in 2016.

attempt to dig an air-raid shelter, and once again, like a diviner, he came upon a trove. About twelve inches below the surface, in an area not far from the site of the 1939 discovery, he found the crushed remnants of another egg and then a second skeleton—a young man, it would later prove to be, in the prime of life. The body had been interred with a spectacular array of grave goods: two "whale tooth" necklaces, one in moa bone and one in whale ivory; two necklaces made from hundreds of drilled porpoise teeth; one necklace of eleven large moa-bone beads, with a central whale-tooth pendant; and fourteen argillite adzes, including five that were between twelve and eighteen inches long and weighed between five and ten pounds.

This time the news was so exciting that Roger Duff, ethnologist at the Canterbury Museum, traveled up from Christchurch to see the objects. Duff, who had been one of Skinner's students at the University of Otago, was aware of the earlier discovery but had considered it "a chance, isolate find." Realizing now that he'd been wrong, he impressed upon the young man the very great significance of his discovery, saying that it "surpassed anything else in New Zealand." Eyles, who had been out fishing when Duff arrived, later wrote that he wished he'd been there "to see Duff's expression when he first saw the hoard of material confronting him on the kitchen table."

Over the next two decades, Eyles and Duff together excavated a series of sites at Wairau Bar, uncovering more than two thousand objects, including drilled moa eggs, adzes, fishhooks, and a stunning array of bracelets, necklaces, pendants, and amulets in whale ivory, moa bone, and stone. Among the most intriguing were a number of massive ridged tubular beads, known as "reels," made from sections of moa femur (the same bit of bone that Professor Owen had used to diagnose the bird). These "enigmatical" objects had been seen before only in stone, and their purpose had never been fully comprehended. Some Māori claimed that they were used as part of a cord drill, others that they were "connected with genealogical matters," but no one within the historical period had ever seen them worn or strung on necklaces—as they were in the graves—with sperm whale teeth or large, tusklike pendants of highly polished stone.

There was something quite fantastical about these discoveries. Duff referred to a "tradition of gigantism" in both ornaments and tools; the adzes in particular were so large and heavy, it was hard to imagine using them. This, along with the fact that so many of the objects had never been seen in New Zealand before, seemed to lend credence to the still popular (though officially discredited) idea that the moa hunters represented some distinct, perhaps foreign population. Duff, however, suggested that there might be a different principle at work. "No culture," he wrote, "at any one time manages to stand completely still." Rather, it evolves spontaneously and continually in response to the environment and to outside stimuli, and because change is the nature of life. This perspective enabled Duff to think—pretty much for the first time—less in terms of a distinct moa-hunter *culture* and more in terms of a moa-hunting *phase*. Moa hunters and Māori were not two different peoples; they were two different stages in a sequence.

Looking back on it, this shift toward a more evolutionary way of thinking about human culture seems obvious, but at the time it was not. Nor was it immediately obvious what the implications of such a paradigm shift might be. One underappreciated aspect of early anthropological models of Polynesian history, which envisioned the settlement of the islands in terms of a series of migratory "waves," is that they implicitly supported the idea of Polynesian voyaging. They were consistent with traditional accounts of navigators who set out to explore and colonize new islands, who packed up their families and emigrated and traveled back and forth with comparative ease. But the idea that Polynesian cultures might have *evolved locally* opened the door to quite a different story.

All of a sudden, it became possible to envision a much smaller number of settlement events and, therefore, a great deal less voyaging. As one archaeologist calculated it, even "a single canoe-load" of young men and women might have had "a reasonable chance of establishing a viable population" in New Zealand. Assuming an initial settlement date of A.D. 1000 and a "modest" growth rate of between 1 and 2 percent per year, a founding group of just twenty young people might have reached a population of 100,000 by the beginning of the historical period. It was not at all clear that this was what *had* happened, but it was now viewed as something that *could have* happened. A more evolutionary model made the chronology—indeed, the whole history—of Polynesian settlement much simpler. Instead of a confusing sequence of hypothetical migrations back and forth from Hawaiki and other places, there was now, conceivably, just an initial arrival, followed by a long, slow evolution in place. It was different from any of the stories that had been told so far, and it was especially different from the story that had been drawn from the oral traditions. Of course, none of this said anything about *when* any of this had happened, but the key to that particular puzzle was right on the horizon.

# RADIOCARBON DATING

## *The Question of* When

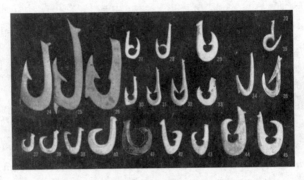

*Fish hooks from South Point, Hawai'i, in* Fishhooks
*by Kenneth P. Emory, William J. Bonk, and*
*Yosihiko H. Sinoto (Honolulu, 1959).*
BERNICE P. BISHOP MUSEUM, HONOLULU, HAWAI'I.

**THE FIRST EDITION** of Duff's book about the discoveries at Wairau Bar, *The Moa-Hunter Period of Maori Culture*, was published in 1950. In 1951, the first radiocarbon date from the Pacific was reported by Willard F. Libby's lab at the University of Chicago. Based on a sample of charcoal from the lowest layer of an excavation of the Kuli'ou'ou rock-shelter, on the island of O'ahu, it fixed the earliest occupation of this Hawaiian site at A.D. 1004, plus or minus 180 years.

The development of radiocarbon dating, for which Libby won the Nobel Prize in Chemistry in 1960, was "a godsend" to archaeology, particularly in those parts of the world without a written history. For the first time, it was possible to know, given a few ounces of organic matter—some wood from a coffin, a handful of barley, a deer antler, an oyster shell, a sample of peat—when, in calendrical terms, something in the undocumented past had actually happened. One could know when a fire had been lit or an animal slaughtered, when a house or canoe had been built, when a settlement had been founded or abandoned. Of course, the numbers were only approximate, and there were tricks and difficulties to the method that would take years to sort out, but the fact that it was possible at all was a game changer.

The method of radiocarbon dating arose out of work in the rarefied field of atomic physics and was challenging to prove experimentally, but the principles behind it are fairly straightforward. Early in the twentieth century, it became apparent that the earth was being bombarded by cosmic rays, which set off atomic reactions when they came into contact with the earth's atmosphere. One of these reactions produced small quantities of carbon-14, a radioactive isotope of carbon, also known as radiocarbon. Radiocarbon is rare—for every atom of carbon-14 in the earth's atmosphere, there are a million million atoms of carbon-12, the ordinary form of carbon—but the chemical behavior of the two isotopes is identical. Both combine with oxygen to produce carbon dioxide, which (through the process of photosynthesis) is taken up by plants, which are eaten by animals, which are eaten by other animals, and so on. Thus, the different isotopes of carbon all enter the food chain in the same way, and the ratio of carbon-14 to carbon-12 in plants and animals is the same as it is in the atmosphere that surrounds them.

There is one key difference between these isotopes, however. Radiocarbon (carbon-14) is not stable like ordinary carbon (carbon-12); it is radioactive, meaning that it slowly and steadily decays. The rate at which this happens is known, although it was one of the many early unknowns for Willard Libby, whose first guess was that the half-life of carbon-14 was three months. In fact, the half-life of carbon-14—the amount of time it would take for half of a given quantity to disappear—is around 5,700 years.

When a plant or animal dies, it no longer takes up carbon-14 and thus becomes a "closed system." The existing carbon-14 in its structure continues to decay, and, since it is no longer being replaced, the ratio of carbon-14 to carbon-12 begins to change. This happens at a steady and predictable rate, and the "beautifully simple principle" of radiocarbon dating is that by measuring the proportion of the remaining carbon-14, one can tell how much time has elapsed. As the archaeologist Colin Renfrew explains,

> We know the initial proportion when it was living, since this is a constant figure through time. When we know the proportion left in the sample now, we can calculate how long the radioactive decay process has been going on. This is the same thing as the age since death of the sample; when we know this, we have dated it.

The first radiocarbon date to be reported, known officially as C-1, was from a piece of cypress wood from the tomb of the Third Dynasty Egyptian king Djoser. It had been sent to Libby in early 1947 by a curator in the Department of Egyptian Art at the Metropolitan Museum, in New York. Djoser's tomb, at the time considered one of the earliest monumental stone structures, was thought to be datable to about 2700 B.C. "I shall be very much interested to see what your finds turn out to be when compared with our own records," the curator wrote. "If we could get scientific evidence for even an approximate date in the period before 2000 BC, it would be of considerable use to us." The radiocarbon age of this sample, determined on a hot Chicago afternoon in July 1948, put the date of the tomb (or at least the wood fragment) at 2029 B.C., plus or minus 350 years.

Over the next eighteen months, a wide variety of materials were tested: charcoal from the famous Lascaux cave in France (more than fifteen thousand years old); a pair of rope sandals from a cave in Oregon (more than nine thousand years old); the dung of a giant sloth from a cave in Chile (more than ten thousand years old); charcoal from Stonehenge (roughly 3,700 years old); wood from the heart of a giant sequoia felled in 1874 (roughly 2,700 years old according to the radiocarbon dates and known from its rings to be more than 2,800 years old); and a piece of linen wrapping from the Dead Sea Scrolls (dated to within two hundred years on either side of A.D. 33).

**THE HAWAIIAN SAMPLE** submitted for radiocarbon dating (known in the literature as C-540) had been sent to Libby's lab in Chicago by a Bishop Museum anthropologist named Kenneth P. Emory, who played a key role in Polynesian research in the mid-twentieth century. Emory had grown up in Hawai'i and had joined the staff of the Bishop Museum in 1920, just as the Bayard Dominick Expedition was setting out. He spent the next three decades doing fieldwork in some of the remotest corners of Polynesia, and in 1925 he met and married a half-French, half-Tahitian woman named Marguerite Thuret. (Like Te Rangi Hiroa, Thuret was initially denied U.S. citizenship on the grounds that, as a Polynesian, she was "Asiatic." This decision was later overturned, thanks to arguments made by an expert in physical anthropology who asserted that "the color of Marguerite's skin, the shape of her nose, and the configuration of her head" showed her to be "more Caucasian than anything else.")

In 1941, when the Japanese bombed Pearl Harbor, Emory was living with his family in Honolulu. At forty-four, he was too old to enlist, so he took it upon himself to protect the museum's collections, including thousands of pages of typed chants and legends, field notebooks, journals, reports, and unpublished manuscripts, which he painstakingly microfilmed and sent for safekeeping to his alma mater, Dartmouth College, on the grounds that, whatever happened, Hanover, New Hampshire, would probably "be safe from bombs."

Not long after America's entry into the war, Emory was having dinner with a naval officer when the conversation turned to the question of what would happen to U.S. airmen if they were shot down over the Pacific. The officer argued that even if they managed to find "a desert island," they would certainly perish from starvation or thirst. Emory pointed out that Polynesians had been managing just fine for hundreds, if not thousands, of years and that there was food and water to be had on even the smallest islands if you knew where to look. Coconuts alone provided food, water, containers, and fuel for a fire; the problem was that most American servicemen had no idea how to husk one. Asked if he could teach them, Emory replied, *Of course*—all that was needed was a pointed stick. And so began his stint as survival instructor to the U.S. military in the Pacific theater.

Emory compiled a little manual of the basics, entitled *South Sea Lore* (known in its first incarnation as the *Castaway's Baedeker to the South Seas*). It was based on a combination of firsthand experience and ethnological research and contained information on which plants to eat (pigweed and pandanus kernels); which fish to avoid (stonefish and puffer fish); how to dig and line a well; how to make sandals from coconut husks and weave a coconut-leaf shelter; how to treat a coral cut (never use iodine); and what to drink for an emetic (salt water). He pointed out that a magnifying glass was more useful than a box of matches and suggested that the only piece of equipment anyone actually needed was a machete (though if you also had a pocketknife, you would be "well equipped").

Enthusiasm for Emory's little book was overwhelming. *The Honolulu Advertiser* ran a story under the headline "Invaluable Advice for Unfortunate Airmen, Coconuts Sufficient to Sustain Life," and the Honolulu Academy of Arts mounted an exhibition featuring Emory as a modern-day Robinson Crusoe, making sandals and weaving coconut fronds. Soon he was giving four, then five, then as many as eight lectures a day, to "fliers, chaplains, nurses, infantrymen, gunners, sailors," while articles about Emory's "school for castaways" began appearing in the national press.

Anthropology had proven unexpectedly useful in war, but the war was also changing the Pacific in ways that were disheartening to anthropologists. Runways were being built on islands to supply and move American troops, and distances that had once taken weeks to cross by sampan or schooner could now be traversed by air in a matter of days. The swarms of GIs who flooded into the region—not unlike the whalers of old—brought quantities of money and manufactured goods, precipitating a second great wave of cultural change. For men like Emory and Te Rangi Hiroa (who, as director of the Bishop Museum from 1936 until his death, in 1951, was Emory's boss), the feeling was of an era come to an end.

**ONTO THIS RATHER** gloomy prospect, the development of radiocarbon dating cast an unexpected ray of light. Te Rangi Hiroa, who lived just long enough to learn the news, read Libby's letter containing the first dates for the Kuliʻouʻou rock-shelter aloud to Emory, who immediately understood that "a whole new vista of possibilities" had suddenly opened up. Emory quickly embarked on an ambitious program of excavations throughout the Hawaiian Islands, using students from the University of Hawaiʻi as laborers and assistants.

One of his most promising helpers was a Japanese graduate student named Yosihiko Sinoto, who had worked on archaeological digs in Japan and whose first question for Emory was "Where is the pottery?" In early Japanese archaeological contexts, as in classical archaeology, pottery was a key indicator of relative age. It was the artifact of choice for a technique called seriation, which involved sorting objects by shape or style or some other formal feature and then ranging them in series, on the principle that things that are alike probably belong to the same period and that changes in style are often incremental. Like stratigraphy, seriation is a means of establishing relative chronologies; combined with the new technique of radiocarbon dating, it could be used to nail down whole stretches of cultural time. There was, however, no pottery in Hawaiʻi, and Sinoto wondered what else could be used as a "diagnostic" artifact. The answer was fishhooks.

Like Skinner with his adzes, Emory and Sinoto sorted thousands of fishhooks to establish typologies—one-piece, two-piece, barbed, unbarbed, notched, knobbed. Sinoto even devised something he later described as a "poor man's IBM": a card file containing 3,500 entries, with either holes or slots cut into the top of each card. A metal rod inserted into the file would lift out only those cards with holes, leaving behind those with slots, thereby selecting a particular subset of the entries.

The Hawaiian site that produced the most spectacular array of fishhooks was a parched corner of the Big Island known as South Point. The southernmost point in the Hawaiian Islands, South Point is famous for its clash of ocean currents and the fish this attracts, and excavations in the area produced thousands of fishhooks in a wide variety of styles. But when charcoal from the South Point sites was sent for radiocarbon dating, it returned a confusing set of results. One sample suggested that South Point had first been occupied in the tenth century A.D., while another put the date as early as the second century. A single sample from a nearby site that was sent to two different laboratories for analysis returned dates that differed by more than four hundred years. All of this confirmed what was rapidly becoming apparent: that radiocarbon dating was subtler and more complicated than it had first appeared.

It had been understood from the beginning that there could be counting errors and issues of sampling and contamination, but what soon became evident was that there were also built-in errors in the method itself. One of Libby's key assumptions had been that the quantity of carbon-14 in the atmosphere was constant, but this, as it turned out, was not true. Changes in the earth's magnetic field, sunspot activity, even human activities like burning fossil fuels, exploding atom bombs, and testing nuclear weapons, altered the atmospheric concentration of radiocarbon. Unless radiocarbon dates were corrected using a known formula (i.e., calibrated), they could be off by significant amounts (as much as seven hundred years in the case of dates around 3000 B.C.). Gradually, other complexities revealed themselves, including the marine reservoir effect, which lowers the proportion of radiocarbon (and therefore increases the age) of marine organisms, and the "old wood problem"—the fact that wood from a long-lived species of tree could actually be hundreds of years older than a house that was built from it or than charcoal from a fire in which it was burnt.

**OF COURSE, EMORY** was not the only one requesting radiocarbon dates for Polynesian materials. In New Zealand, Roger Duff sent samples of charcoal from an earth oven at Wairau Bar to two separate laboratories, one in Wellington and the other at Yale, obtaining two date ranges: A.D. 1015 ± 110 from the Yale laboratory, and A.D. 1225 ± 50 from the lab in Wellington. These correlated well with Emory's date of A.D. 1004 ± 180 for the Kuliʻouʻou rock-shelter. But the most tantalizing early radiocarbon dates came from the Marquesas.

The archaeologist attached to the Bayard Dominick's Marquesan team had reported in 1925 that the Marquesas offered "few opportunities for archaeological research." But in 1956, a new expedition set out to reexamine the possibilities in these islands at the eastern edge of the Polynesian Triangle. An energetic Columbia University graduate student named Robert Suggs was sent ahead to reconnoiter, and he quickly discovered that the previous generation had gotten it all wrong. Everywhere he looked, he saw archaeological potential. "We were seldom out of sight of some relic of the ancient Marquesan culture," he writes. "Through all the valleys were scattered clusters of ruined house platforms. . . . Overgrown with weeds, half tumbled down beneath the weight of toppled trees and the pressure of the inexorable palm roots, these ancient village sites were sources of stone axes, carved stone pestles, skulls, and other sundry curios." There were ceremonial plazas "hundreds of feet long" and, high on the cliffs above the deep valleys, "burial caves containing the remains of the population of centuries past."

The coup de grâce came when Suggs and his guide followed up on a report of a large number of "pig bones" in the dunes at a place called Haʻatuatua. This windswept expanse of scrub and sand lies on the exposed eastern corner of Nuku Hiva. A decade earlier, in 1946, a tidal wave had cut away part of the beach, and since then bones and other artifacts had been washing out of the dunes. Not knowing quite what to expect, Suggs and his guide rode over on horseback. When they came out of the "hibiscus tangle" at the back of the beach and "caught sight of the debris washing down the slope," he writes, "I nearly fell out of the saddle."

> The bones that were scattered all along the slope and on the beach below were not pig bones but human bones! Ribs, vertebrae, thigh bones, bits of skull vault, and innumerable hand and foot bones were everywhere. At the edge of the bank a bleached female skull rested upside down, almost entirely exposed.

Where the bank had been cut away, a dark horizontal band about two feet thick could be seen between layers of clean white sand. Embedded in this band were bits of charcoal and saucers of ash, fragments of pearl shell, stone and coral tools, and large fitted stones that appeared to be part of a buried pavement. They had discovered the remains of an entire village, complete with postholes, cooking pits, courtyards, and burials. The time was too short to explore the site fully, but the very next year, Suggs and his wife returned to examine it.

There were several interesting things about the objects that emerged during the excavation of Ha'atuatua. Many were classically Polynesian: beautifully curved, nearly circular one-piece fishhooks; pearl-shell points and shanks of two-piece lures; saw-toothed coconut graters of nacreous shell. But some were surprising: a unique form of snail-shell vegetable peeler; "some very peculiar stone adzes" with "Melanesian" shapes; large ornamental pearl-shell disks with notched edges, from a kind of headdress that was common in the islands of Vanuatu but unknown in Polynesia. Like the reel-and-whale-tooth necklaces in the burials at Wairau Bar, in New Zealand, these artifacts seemed to hark back to an early period of Polynesian history and also to suggest a direct link with islands far to the west.

But what was really astonishing was the dates obtained for the samples of ash, charred bone, and charcoal from Ha'atuatua that were sent for radiocarbon dating. They suggested that these Marquesan artifacts were far and away the most ancient cultural materials to have been discovered in eastern Polynesia, pushing the occupation of the islands back to the second century B.C. Even Marquesan traditions did not suggest such early settlement. "According to the most trustworthy genealogies," writes Suggs, "the settlement of the archipelago by Nuku, the traditional first settler, occurred about A.D. 950," whereas the carbon-14 dates suggested that at that point the islands had already been occupied for a thousand years.

But an even more startling discovery awaited Suggs in his second season of work at Ha'atuatua. Returning in 1957, he began a systematic examination of the site, methodically trenching, digging, sifting, and recording what he found. At first this was comparatively little: "a few fragmentary pearl-shell fishhooks, and a coral file or two," plus some postholes indicating buildings and a pit that might have contained a burial but didn't. Then one day, as he was watching one of his workers sift a shovelful of earth, something among the rocks and sand caught his eye, "a flat fragment of some brick-red substance," which appeared briefly and then disappeared. It looked, thought Suggs, exactly like a piece of pottery. But that couldn't be—pottery was found throughout Island Southeast Asia and much of Melanesia, but it had never been seen east of Samoa. And yet, there it was: an unmistakable potsherd from the lowest level of the dark band of sand that indicated human habitation. Almost immediately, a second, larger fragment emerged, then a third: a piece of an ancient pot rim with a grooved and rounded lip and marks on the inner and outer surfaces, "from the hand of the potter who had smoothed this vessel in the dim past."

In all, five fragments of pottery were discovered, belonging to just three vessels: a poorly fired, crumbly brown pot with a coarse temper; a well-fired reddish-brown bowl with a flared rim; and a fine-tempered fragment, also reddish brown, with marks that showed it had been polished using some kind of tool. Modest though they were, these ceramic tidbits changed "the complexion of Polynesian prehistory"—though, as was so often the case, it was not immediately clear in precisely what way. Had the ancient Marquesans made these pots, and if so, why were there not more? Or had they been in trading contact with islands thousands of miles away to the west where pottery was known to have been made? Or might these be fragments of pots that were brought by the very first settlers to the Marquesas? And if so, did that mean that the original settlers had come direct from the western edge of the Polynesian Triangle, bypassing the intermediate, apparently aceramic islands of the mid-Pacific—Tahiti, the Cooks, the Australs, and the Tuamotus?

It was impossible to say. But combined with the dramatic early dates from Ha'atuatua, the discovery of pottery at the far eastern edge of the Polynesian Triangle was a sensation. Among the immediate implications was the possibility that the Marquesas, rather than pottery-less Tahiti, might be the Hawaiki of legend, the original dispersal point for all the islands of eastern Polynesia. And yet there was something counterintuitive about this idea. All one has to do is look at a map to see that sailing from Samoa or Tonga direct to the Marquesas—straight into the wind for more than two thousand miles—and then doubling back to reach Tahiti and the other islands at the triangle's center feels like an unlikely path.

But there it was. There was no getting around the fact that, based on the radiocarbon dates, Ha'atuatua was the oldest known cultural site east of Samoa and the only one at which even the smallest sherd of pottery had ever been found. "The big question now," writes Suggs, "was: Just how did this find alter our ideas and theories concerning the origins of the Marquesan people and the Polynesians in general?" Pottery, it turns out, was to be the key.

# THE LAPITA PEOPLE
## A Key Piece of the Puzzle

*Lapita patterns from Site 13, in "Archaeological report"*
*by Christophe Sand,* Journal of the Polynesian Society *(1998).*
COURTESY OF THE AUTHOR.

**IN ORDER TO** understand the significance of pottery for Polynesian history, we have to leave the Polynesian Triangle and travel west to the tiny Melanesian island of Watom. This speck of land, barely three miles wide, lies off the north coast of New Britain, which is itself an island off the north coast of Papua New Guinea, in what is known as the Bismarck Archipelago. One day in 1908, a German priest by the name of Father Otto Meyer was digging a foundation for his church when he uncovered a number of finely decorated potsherds. Father Meyer was not at all sure what exactly he had discovered: "I, poor hermit, what do I know of these scientific questions which are still so perplexing?" But it occurred to him that the sherds might be evidence of contact between the people of Watom and the inhabitants of South America, so he sent a few of the fragments to the Musée de l'Homme, in Paris.

A few years later, in 1920, the Bayard Dominick Expedition's Tongan team reported the discovery of decorated pottery on the island of Tongatapu. Pottery was not considered to be part of the Polynesian "cultural complex," but early European explorers had reported seeing small earthenware pots in the Tongan archipelago. Cook's naturalists, who saw them there on the second voyage, thought they might be "memorials" of Tasman's passage through the archipelago in 1642, while nineteenth-century Europeans who saw pottery in Tonga generally believed it to have come from nearby Fiji, where there was a robust and ongoing ceramic tradition. None of this prepared the Bayard Dominick team for the quantity of pottery they discovered once they started to dig. They collected no fewer than 1,577 pieces of a "highly porous, lightly fired, fragile ware," ranging in color from red through brown to dark brown to black. Most of the sherds lacked decoration and were, in the words of one of the team members, "rude, indifferently made, and serviceable rather than ornamental." But a few displayed a highly refined and distinctive type of ornamentation made up of small dots arranged geometrically in lines and curves, which appeared to have been stamped into the clay.

The senior member of the Tongan team was a man named Edward W. Gifford, a methodical, data-driven anthropologist with a curious claim to fame. An amateur ornithologist and conchologist whose first academic paper—on the mollusk *Epiphragmorphora fidelis*—had been published when he was only fourteen, Gifford took a job right out of high school at the California Academy of Sciences. He was then steadily promoted through the ranks until, at the age of fifty-eight, he reached the rank of full professor at the University of California, Berkeley without ever having attended college himself.

In 1947, Gifford returned to the Pacific on the first of a series of three archaeological expeditions to Fiji, New Caledonia, and Yap.

He was hoping to establish a "succession of cultures," following a path backward in time (and westward in space) from the western edge of Polynesia. On his first expedition, he discovered that what had been true for Tonga was even more true for Fiji: the "chief characteristic of Fijian archaeology" was "pottery, above all." Potsherds were everywhere, in the dunes and rock-shelters and riverbanks, "conspicuous on the surface" and "abundant beneath." Discovered in digs at depths of up to twelve feet, they were vastly more common than any other kind of artifact. Although Gifford also found tools and ornaments made of stone and shell, the ratio of these to potsherds was on the order of one to ten thousand. Present in all places and at all points in time, Fijian pottery came in a great variety of styles, including some with a distinctive geometric patterning made up of straight and wavy lines, arcs, dashes, and dots that appeared to have been stamped or pressed into the clay using some kind of tool.

Following his star westward, Gifford next embarked in 1952 for New Caledonia. New Caledonia, with its neighbor Vanuatu, occupies an intermediate position between the Polynesian Triangle and the Bismarck Archipelago. Like New Zealand, it is a piece of old Gondwana, and, also like New Zealand, it has a strange and unique natural history. It is home to an unusual number of curious animals and plants, including a "mistletoe-like" parasitic pine and a famous tool-using crow. Before the arrival of human beings, New Caledonia had one of the most diverse collections of reptiles anywhere on the planet, including a giant horned turtle with a spiked tail, a twenty-pound monitor lizard, and a rare pygmy land crocodile, all of which—along with a giant megapode, a flightless swamp hen, two falcons, a scrub fowl, and several other species of bird—are now extinct.

As soon as Gifford and his colleague Richard Shutler Jr. arrived in New Caledonia, they began touring the island in search of suitable archaeological sites, traveling around in a 1951 Chevy half-ton truck that had been shipped over from California. Setting out from the capital, Nouméa, they traveled up the wetter, more heavily forested east coast, crossed over the central mountain range, and made their way back down the drier, savanna-like western side, stopping at various points along the way. At the edge of an eroding beach on the Foué Peninsula, they picked up their first piece of decorated pottery. The spot, to which they would later return, was known as Site 13.

OVER THE COURSE of the next seven months, the two anthropologists, with their teams of local helpers, as well as their wives, who had come out from California to join them, surveyed fifty-three sites and excavated eleven. They put more than fourteen thousand miles on the truck—on an island just 250 miles long—and collected more than seventeen thousand artifacts, including sinkers, knives, peelers, bracelets, scrapers, choppers, grinders, and adzes. But, once again, the most common artifact was pottery. The majority of sites were what Gifford described as "coastal kitchen middens," which could be recognized by surface scatterings of potsherds and shells. Almost all of these sites, he observed, shared three characteristics: they were close to the sea, they were near a source of fresh water, and there was good gardening land nearby.

It was during this expedition that Gifford received news of the first radiocarbon dates from his earlier excavations in Fiji. Anticipating the possibility as early as 1947—before the method of radiocarbon dating had even been experimentally proved—he had been careful to collect charcoal samples for testing but had been thwarted in his attempts to get them dated when he returned from the field. Libby's lab at the University of Chicago was swamped, and requests made to both the California Institute of Technology and the Radiation Laboratory at Berkeley were turned down. "I am afraid," wrote an assistant at the Rad Lab unhelpfully, "that our answer . . . will have to be in the negative. If, however, you are able to assign a student or technician to the problem of developing the apparatus and method for performing these determinations, we will be happy to consult and advise."

Eventually, Gifford secured the assistance of the University of Michigan's Memorial Phoenix Project, a research institution launched in 1948 to support "peaceful uses" of atomic energy. When tests of the first Fijian sample found it to be approximately 950 years old, he immediately dashed off a note to *The Journal of the Polynesian Society*. The date, Gifford wrote, was "of considerable significance, since it implies a much greater age for the deeper parts of the deposit." And, indeed, subsequent analyses of charcoal from the same location later demonstrated that the site had first been occupied nearly a thousand years earlier, around the first century A.D.

At the end of six months, even as preparations for their departure were getting under way, Gifford and Shutler returned to Site 13 for the second-to-last dig of the expedition. They had plenty of workers and the site was easy to excavate; elsewhere there had been cave-ins and pits that continually filled with water. They marked out a number of rectangles along the sloping edge of the beach and across the isthmus in a low, overgrown area between the mudflats and the sea that showed signs of having recently been used as a yam field. Almost immediately it became clear that Site 13 was different from all the other sites they had examined. As in Tonga and Fiji, more than 90 percent of the pottery found in New Caledonia had been of a plain, undecorated kind, with only small amounts showing any form of decoration. But what emerged from the ground at Site 13 was not only a vastly greater percentage of decorated pottery—roughly a third of the total—but an entirely new class of ceramics that were "vastly superior" to anything the researchers had yet seen.

Richly and completely decorated—sometimes on both the inside and the outside of the pot—with delicate patterns of circles, semicircles, diamonds, squares, triangles, zigzags, palmettes, and "eye" designs (almonds with a circle inside), the pottery from Site 13 was reminiscent, some thought, of Corinthian vases from the seventh century B.C., or the black Etruscan pottery known as *bucchero nero*. Others described it as similar in style, and perhaps technique, to Polynesian tattooing. The patterns, which were both intricate and regular, seemed to have been imprinted on the clay using a tool with teeth and then filled with a white paste of coral lime—a technique strikingly similar to the traditional Polynesian method of tattooing using a sharp, toothed instrument to puncture the skin and rubbing dye or charcoal (or, in nineteenth-century New Zealand, gunpowder) into the wound.

On the last day of the dig, Gifford noted in his field book that "Lapita was name of village at this site," thereby christening (unintentionally) not only the distinctive type of pottery that had been found at Site 13 but the as yet unknown people who had left it there. In his final report, he made several important connections, noting the stylistic continuity between the pottery from this site and sherds he had seen in Tonga and Fiji, and connecting the dots between his work and French discoveries on the nearby Isle of Pines, which, in turn, had been linked to Father Meyer's Watom sherds in the Musée de l'Homme. Gifford and Shutler's feeling that this was all quite significant was more than confirmed when the results of the radiocarbon tests came back, showing that by far the oldest New Caledonian samples were those from Site 13. But what was really surprising was how early the dates were: at 2,800 years before the present, they pushed the occupation of New Caledonia back to the end of the first millennium B.C.

IN THE YEARS that followed, Lapita sites would be discovered on the Mussau Islands off Papua New Guinea, the Reef and Santa Cruz Islands, Tikopia Vanuatu, Fiji, Tonga, Futuna, and Samoa—in other words, virtually everywhere between the Bismarck Archipelago and the western edge of Polynesia. Dates from these sites confirmed the age of the culture represented by these ceramics, but they also revealed an unexpected pattern: Lapita settlements across a 2,500-mile swath of the western Pacific—from roughly the Solomon Islands to Samoa—seem to have appeared *almost simul-*

*taneously* around 1000 B.C. Furthermore, east of the Solomons, they appeared to represent a cultural horizon: no one predated them in these islands, archaeologically speaking; no cultural artifacts underlay theirs. Whoever they were, the so-called Lapita people appeared to be the first people on the scene in these places, and this, in turn, meant that not only were they the true pioneers of the remote Pacific—the first people to sail over the horizon to islands that were too far away to see—but they were also the first people to reach the Polynesian Triangle. And this meant that they were the immediate precursors and ancestors of the Polynesians.

All of a sudden it was possible to track the Polynesian migrations backward some two thousand years with near perfect certainty. The Lapita people were, you might say, Polynesians in an earlier incarnation. So what can we say of them, beyond the fact of their taste for fine decoration? We know they were colonists, movers, migrants, settlers, explorers, pioneers. We know they had a technology that enabled them to travel and a culture neat and transportable enough to take with them wherever they went. We know they were denizens of the coast, occupants of a narrow band of shoreline between the forest and the sea. Almost all the Lapita settlements that have been discovered are located on beaches or beach terraces, or in places that were beaches two thousand years ago. We know they liked spots at the edge of a lagoon, in proximity to fresh water and arable land, often opposite an opening in the reef that gave access to the open ocean. We know they trolled the deep sea, cast nets in the lagoon, and fished at night by torchlight on the reef. We know they had a few domesticated animals—pigs, chickens, and dogs—that would have fossicked and foraged along the shoreline, while their owners divided their time between gathering seafood and tending their yam beds and taro plantations.

Although it is pottery that has come to define them, the crowning technological achievement of the Lapita people must have been their canoes. Almost all the islands in the one-thousand-mile chain that begins in the Bismarcks and ends in the Solomons are intervisible, with water gaps generally smaller than forty miles. But from there to the next group of islands, the distance is 250 miles, and it's 500 miles from there to the group after that. No one has ever uncovered even a scrap of a Lapita canoe—it has been too long, the materials are too perishable, the atmosphere too damp— but words for sail, outrigger, boom, washstrake, rib, caulking, paddle, bailing, and cargo can all be reconstructed in Proto-Oceanic, a hypothetical language (like Proto-Indo-European) that is associated with the Lapita expansion.

Proto-Oceanic is the theoretical mother tongue of the Oceanic peoples and the language from which all the Oceanic languages are thought to descend. It is a huge family, encompassing more than 450 languages, including those spoken on all the islands of Polynesia, most of the smaller islands of Melanesia, and all the islands of Micronesia except two. It is itself a branch of the larger Austronesian language family, a truly stupendous grouping of more than a thousand languages, which includes, in addition to all the Oceanic languages, those of the Philippines, Borneo, Indonesia, Timor, the Moluccas, and Madagascar. The very oldest Austronesian languages—and thus, in a sense, their geographic root—are a group of languages known as Formosan, a few of which are still spoken by the indigenous inhabitants of Ilha Formosa (Beautiful Island), an old Portuguese name for the island of Taiwan. Thus, at least from a linguistic point of view, the path back from Polynesia to the ultimate homeland proceeds through the Melanesian and Southeast Asian archipelagoes to an island off the coast of China, where the trail goes cold around 5000 or 6000 B.C.

The splitting off of the Oceanic branch of this language family is thought to have taken place in the neighborhood of the Bismarcks around the time of the first Lapita settlement, and it is strongly linked with the rapid colonization of the islands between there and Samoa between 1500 and 1000 B.C. Thus, the reconstruction of Proto-Oceanic opens a window onto the otherwise fairly mysterious Lapita world. Little survives in archaeological contexts in the tropics—none of the baskets or cordage or wooden housewares, no foodstuffs or clothing, no buildings apart from stone foundations and the dark impressions left by long-decayed posts. But something of the texture of these people's lives can be extracted from their reconstructed vocabulary, working back through the ages via whatever was essential enough to pass on.

It seems, for example, that they had terms for two particular times of day: the period from dawn to midmorning and that from midafternoon to dusk—both good times for getting things done in the tropics. They had a word for a water container made from a calabash or coconut shell and a word for the bung or stopper used to seal it. They had words for wooden bowls and coconut cups and for tongs that could be used to lift food out of an earth oven. They had a word for a conch- or triton-shell trumpet and another for a coconut-leaf torch. They had words for clearing and hoeing and weeding and for the fences they built around gardens, perhaps to keep out the pigs. They had a large number of words for types of wind, including strong wind, storm wind, light wind, dry wind, winds from various directions, and wind bringing rain. They had a constellation known as Big Bird, which overlaps our constellations Orion and Canis Major, and they gave the same name to the planet Venus that we give it: Morning Star.

Not all these concepts are attested in every Oceanic language, but enough traces exist to enable linguists to follow the trail. Some concepts that one might have expected to find have proven surprisingly difficult to reconstruct: there is no obvious Proto-Oceanic term for tidal wave or volcano, although words can be reconstructed for both earthquake and flood. It has also been difficult for linguists to identify specialized navigational terminology. Two possible reasons for this might be that, like politics, all navigation is local, and that what is true in one geographical region is not necessarily true in another. The night sky in New Zealand is not the same as the night sky in Papua New Guinea, which is not the same as the night sky in Hawai'i. The winds and currents in the Solomons are not the same as those around Rapa Nui or in the Marquesas. A second consideration might be that in many Oceanic societies, navigational knowledge is believed to have been privileged and known to only a few, which may mean that it was especially easy to lose once it was no longer central to a society's survival.

There are some very important notions, however, that can be traced back almost to the dawn of Oceanic time: the word for land, as in "not sea" but also "inhabited territory"; the word for canoe, meaning a large sailing vessel for going on the open sea; the word for star, along with terms for rising and descending; and a word for sky or heavens that, once you get out into the remote islands of Polynesia, doubles as the name of a primordial god.

THE KEY TO the migrations of the Lapita people (or, more properly, peoples) was their ability to replicate their lives—their houses, gardens, customs, modes of travel, their whole way of interacting with the world—on island after island, beach after beach. Although they actively sought out a particular kind of setting—coastal plains, tidal rivers, lagoons—they were always adapting to new environments, responding to both the opportunities and the disadvantages presented by new lands. One salient feature of the Pacific region is the steady diminishment in the number of species as you move eastward away from the continental edge. The point is often illustrated with reference to bird species, which, on the large, ecologically opulent island of New Guinea, number some 520. Just a few hundred miles east in the Solomon Islands, the number of bird species drops to 127; then 54 in Fiji, 33 in Samoa, 20 in Tonga, 17 in the Society Islands, 11 in the Marquesas, and at the extreme southeast end of the Polynesian Triangle, on remote Henderson Island, just 4. What is true for birds is also true for corals, plants, reptiles, insects, echinoderms, and vertebrates, with the consequence—at least for human colonists—that the farther they went, the less there was to work with and the more resourceful they had to be.

The Lapita colonists and their descendants solved this problem by transporting everything they needed to reestablish the life they had left behind: breeding pairs of animals, root stocks, seedlings. They also carried a whole host of other life forms: weeds, mollusks, insects, microbes—the entire "portmanteau biota," to use Alfred Crosby's charming formulation, that colonists take with them wherever they go, intentionally or not. Crosby coined the phrase in an account of the impact of European expansion on, among other places, the Pacific, but it applies equally well to these earlier colonists. The portmanteau biota of the Lapita peoples included not just their valued dogs, pigs, chickens, taro, breadfruit, sugarcane, and banana, but a little brown stowaway known as *Rattus exulans* (the Pacific rat) and an assortment of geckos, skinks, and snails.

The Lapita peoples did not just arrive and adapt; they also changed each of the new places they discovered. Humans are notorious for altering the environments into which they move, and the Lapita peoples were no exception. Pollen cores on islands in Lapita territory show a dramatic increase in charcoal particles around the time they arrived, which has been interpreted as evidence of widespread burning to clear land for gardens. Layers of mud, clay, and other "erosional debris" also point to forest clearing, but the most dramatic impact was on the wildlife, particularly the birds. One account of the extirpation of land birds in Polynesia describes it as perhaps "the most extreme example of late Quaternary vertebrate extinction." The evidence shows overwhelmingly that the Lapita peoples and their descendants, the Polynesians (with help, no doubt, from the omnivorous Pacific rat), wiped out innumerable varieties of birds, including rails, pigeons, parrots, fruit doves, and megapodes, either by hunting them to extinction or by destroying their habitat. Humans will eat whatever they find and will do whatever it takes to make their environment more habitable; the biologist Tim Flannery famously describes the species—our species—as "Future Eaters." It should therefore come as no surprise to learn that the Lapita peoples ate not only the birds but the turtles, lizards, mollusks, fish, and even the large land crocodile of New Caledonia, thereby irrevocably altering every one of the environments they encountered.

One can look at these facts from one of two points of view. Like all other humans, the Lapita peoples and their descendants were a powerfully transformative force in Oceania, responsible for much alteration of the landscape and the destruction of many life forms. But one can also think about what it took to be so successful, to *be able to* wreak this kind of havoc in so many places, so far apart. Nothing about this stupendous migration—over thousands of miles of water to islands that no one could have known existed—was either obvious or, seemingly, necessary. And so one of the most tantalizing questions of all must be *Why?* Why leave the safety of the intervisible lands, where, even if there is water between you and the next shore, you can still see the dark peaks of your destination?

One reason may have been that when the speakers of these Austronesian languages—the precursors of the Lapita peoples—first arrived in the islands of the western Pacific, many of these were already occupied and had been for tens of thousands of years. Perhaps the newly arriving immigrants showed such a strong preference for coastal niches because that was what was available. Rather than try to colonize already inhabited interiors or compete with established populations, they kept to the edge of the islands and moved on. But this rationale fails once these oceangoing settlers moved beyond the inhabited islands—out past the intervisible islands of the Solomon chain to the uninhabited Reef and Santa Cruz Islands, to Vanuatu and New Caledonia, to Fiji, and on to the islands of Polynesia.

Some of these islands were large and promising, and one wonders what it was like to discover them. It must have been great—lots of food, plenty of land, good water supplies—so why did they keep going? Given the size of some of these islands, it could not have been population pressure; it would have taken hundreds of years before a scarcity of resources forced them to leave. A more interesting notion is that they were "pulled" into the unknown by a "founder-focused ideology," meaning that the impetus for movement was embedded in the way they constructed their world. Many Austronesian cultures show a deep reverence for founder figures; this is certainly true in Polynesia, where lineages are named for founders whose names and deeds are the very backbone of the mythology. Founders hold positions of rank and command material advantages, and over time these benefits accrue. As one anthropologist put it, the original settlers of New Zealand, whose journey constitutes the final chapter in this great migration, "would have been heirs to perhaps 3,000 years of successful Austronesian expansion"—three thousand years of founder tales "stacked one upon the other." Under such circumstances, what "ambitious young man of a junior line" would *not* seek to become a founder himself by setting off in search of his own island, no matter how far away?

# Part V

# SETTING SAIL

# (1947–1980)

*In which we set off on an entirely new tack, taking to the sea with a crew of experimental voyagers as they attempt to reenact the voyages of the ancient Polynesians.*

# KON-TIKI

## *Thor Heyerdahl's Raft*

*The* Kon-Tiki, *1947.*
THE KON-TIKI MUSEUM, OSLO, NORWAY.

**THE DISCOVERY OF** the Lapita peoples yoked Polynesian prehistory firmly to the western Pacific and thus, ultimately, to Asia. But it could not entirely put to rest a competing notion that there was a link between Polynesia and the continent on the other side, namely South America. It had been popular in the nineteenth century to argue that the strength and prevalence of the easterly winds "most preposterously" conflicted with the idea of anyone sailing eastward across the Pacific and that the inhabitants of Polynesia must therefore be "descended from the aborigines of Chili and Peru." This notion continued to percolate in the early twentieth century, and in the 1930s and '40s it attracted the attention of the Norwegian adventurer and anthropologist Thor Heyerdahl.

Heyerdahl had made his first foray into the Pacific in 1936, when, at the age of twenty-two, he went to live on the island of Fatu

Hiva, in the Marquesas, with his twenty-year-old bride. The two had decided to abandon civilization and return to nature; leaving behind "the chains" that bound them to the modern world, they would "enter the wilderness empty-handed and barefoot." It was, Heyerdahl wrote many years later, "a hippy's dream, a trip deep into an utterly different existence." And it did not go very well. Ants ate up the bamboo house they tried to live in; the Marquesans mistrusted them; cuts and scrapes they got from going barefoot became infected; and they finally ended up in a cave, ill, afraid, and desperate for a boat to come and rescue them. It was during this period, however, that Heyerdahl first concocted the theory that would bring him immense celebrity and, at the same time, estrange him from the majority of his academic peers.

About a year into their sojourn on Fatu Hiva, Heyerdahl and his wife, Liv, were sitting on a beach in the moonlight, watching the waves. "It's queer," said Liv, "but there are never breakers like this on the other side of the island." "No," Heyerdahl replied, "but this is the windward side, there's always a sea running on this side." This prompted him to begin thinking about the geography: how the sea was always "rolling in from eastward, eastward, eastward" and how the "eternal east wind" was always pushing it up over the horizon to the islands.

> The first men who reached these islands knew well enough that this was so. . . . And we knew ourselves that far, far below the horizon to eastward, where the clouds came up, lay the open coast of South America. It was 4,300 sea miles away, and there was nothing but sea between.

An old Marquesan who was sitting with them then offered this tidbit of information: "Tiki," he said, "was both god and chief. It was Tiki who brought my ancestors to these islands where we live now. Before that we lived in a big country beyond the sea."

That night when Heyerdahl went to bed, the stories of Tiki and his ancient homeland swirled in his mind, "accompanied by the muffled roar of the surf in the distance," sounding, he thought, "like a voice from far-off times which . . . had something it wanted to tell." Suddenly it struck him that the sculptures he had seen up in the forest, "the huge stone figures of Tiki," as he called them, were "remarkably like the gigantic monoliths which are relics of extinct civilizations in South America." And so, he wrote, "the whole thing began."

When the pair got back to Europe, Heyerdahl decided that he wanted to study the peoples of Polynesia. "The unsolved mysteries of the South Seas had fascinated me . . . and I had made my objective the identification of the legendary hero Tiki." According to the ethnologist Edward Handy, Tiki was one of many gods in the Marquesan pantheon. He was a trickster figure who was also known as the first ancestor of men, whom he created through his union with a heap of sand. The word *tiki* was also used generically in the Marquesas, as it is in other parts of Polynesia, to mean figures carved in human or animal form that depict deified ancestors or family gods. In the past, Handy believed, the word had likely meant "a figure or design representing a procreating human progenitor, referring back always to the ultimate origin of man." Heyerdahl, however, became convinced that Tiki was a historical figure. With the fresh gusts of the trade winds and the breakers uppermost in his mind, he concluded that Tiki was a founder figure who had come to the Marquesas from the east and that his roots should be sought in South America.

Over the next few years, Heyerdahl assembled a theory about the settlement of Oceania based on a mix of his Marquesan insights, observations about the weather, some not very good linguistics, nineteenth-century theories about the diffusion of knowledge, and some dubious Spanish conquistador lore. It had all begun, he argued, high up in the Andes on the shores of Lake Titicaca, on what is now the border of Bolivia and Peru. There, in the days before the rise of the Inca Empire, a remarkable collection of megalithic monuments had been erected by a mysterious people. Almost nothing was known about them save for a garbled conquistador claim that they were led by the high priest and sun king Viracocha—described by Heyerdahl as a tall white man with red hair and a beard—who also went by the name of Kon-Tiki. Around the sixth century A.D., Heyerdahl argued, Kon-Tiki and his followers had been routed by an invading force. Fleeing their high, dry plateau, they descended to the sea and set sail across the Pacific on balsa-wood rafts, becoming the first settlers of Polynesia.

Heyerdahl was, of course, aware of the great mass of evidence that by now linked Polynesia to Southeast Asia—including the Asian origin of virtually all Polynesian food plants and domesticated animals and the well-established linguistic arguments— and in order to account for these inconvenient facts, he posited a second wave of settlement from the Asian side. These secondary immigrants, Heyerdahl argued, had followed something very like the Beringian route proposed by the nineteenth-century missionary William Ellis, traveling north along the Asian mainland and across the Bering Strait to North America, then over the ocean to Hawai'i, from which they dispersed to the rest of Polynesia. There, he believed, these Asiatic arrivals had mixed and mingled with the red-headed, white-skinned followers of Kon-Tiki, so that when Europeans arrived in the Pacific, the people they discovered in the islands were a combination of these two groups.

Heyerdahl marshaled various bits and pieces of evidence in support of his thesis—the occasional appearance of red-haired Polynesians; the presence of megalithic sculptures on Easter Island; certain cultural similarities between Polynesians and the Kwakiutl and Haida tribes of the Pacific Northwest—but the primary driver of his theory was the direction of the Pacific's currents and winds. Heyerdahl believed that the human settlement of the Pacific had to have followed the path of these meteorological forces. As he put it, "The decisive factor is not distance but wind and current," the pattern of which was determined by the rotation of the earth itself.

. . .

IN 1947, HEYERDAHL famously put the South American portion of his theory to the test. Together with five other athletic and daring Scandinavians, he built a large balsa-wood raft, which he christened *Kon-Tiki*, after the mysterious pre-Incan sun king. Measuring thirty by fifteen feet, it was made from nine huge balsa trees, which Heyerdahl and his companions found and felled (with the help of some local labor) in the Ecuadoran jungle and floated down a river to the sea. These were planked over with smaller balsa logs, followed by a layer of split bamboo, which was then covered with reed matting for a deck. Two tall mangrove-wood masts tied together at the top held a bamboo yard from which hung a large square sail printed with an image of the bearded Kon-Tiki. A large wooden steering oar projected from the stern, and, to protect the men from sun and rain, a small bamboo hut was erected on the deck.

The expedition was supported by a remarkable collection of official and semi-official figures from several nations. Heyerdahl had help from members of the Explorers Club, in New York; the research laboratory of the U.S. military's Air Materiel Command; the Norwegian military attaché in Washington; the U.S. Navy Hydrographic Office; the British Military Mission; a Chilean assistant secretary at the United Nations; "the balsa king of Ecuador," Don Gustavo von Buchwald; and even His Excellency Don José Luis Bustamante y Rivero, president of Peru. Some donated money, others provided advice or material support, including U.S. military gear and rations, which the members of the expedition agreed to test.

On the afternoon of April 28, before a crowd of enthusiastic onlookers, the *Kon-Tiki* was towed out of the harbor at Callao, Peru. Although no metal had been used in the construction of the vessel, which was held together entirely with rope, the crew did have a compass, a sextant, watches, and charts to work out their position, as well as a radio to keep in touch with the outside world. Fifty miles off the coast, their escort left them; they had been towed out into the middle of the Humboldt Current, which would sweep them along until they hit the westward-setting South Equatorial Current, which would, in turn, pull them to Polynesia.

For the next three months, they lived in a small, self-contained world consisting of six men and a parrot, their raft, and the creatures that surrounded them in the sea. Heyerdahl wrote of the isolation and the way it affected his sense of time: "Whether it was 1947 B.C. or A.D. suddenly became of no significance." The trade winds blew steadily and they were never becalmed, though about halfway through the voyage they were hit by two ferocious storms, during one of which the parrot was lost overboard. The raft averaged about fifty miles a day, and they never saw another ship or a plane or any other sign of human activity. The sea around them, however, was teeming with life. Every night, flying fish leapt onto the raft, and every morning it was someone's job to collect them for breakfast. Most of the time, they were accompanied by schools of iridescent mahi-mahi; sharks were also frequent companions. Large squid sometimes floated up from the depths at night, "their devilish green eyes shining in the dark like phosphorus"; whales occasionally sported about the raft; and, once, they were visited by an enormous whale shark, which passed slowly beneath them before one of the crew members gratuitously jabbed it with a harpoon.

The "waves and fish and sun and stars came and went," and as he floated across the Pacific, Heyerdahl returned to one of his favorite themes. "The closer we came into contact with the sea," he wrote, "the more at home we ourselves felt." They were learning "to respect the old primitive peoples who lived in close converse with the Pacific and therefore knew it from a standpoint quite different from our own." And the conclusion Heyerdahl reached was that "the picture primitive peoples had of the sea was a truer one than ours." It was much the same view of paradise lost that had inspired him to go to the Marquesas and seek out an untrammeled world, the same mistrust of modernity, the same hunger for a "truer," more elemental way of life. No doubt the horror of two world wars had something to do with this, inspiring a deep, atavistic longing for some earlier, more innocent time. "Life," wrote Heyerdahl rather sadly, "had been fuller and richer for men before the technological age."

When they were still hundreds of miles from Polynesia, the crew of the *Kon-Tiki* had their first harbingers of land: frigate birds, followed by two boobies. With every passing day, larger and larger flocks of seabirds appeared, hightailing it away to the west as the sun set. The next thing was a "curious stationary cloud" that hung in the sky while "small feathery wisps of wool" blown by the trade winds passed by. They had reached the Tuamotu Archipelago, the screen of atolls between Tahiti and the Marquesas that so many of the early Europeans explorers had found in their path. Beneath the cloud lay Puka Puka—one of Magellan's Desventurados and the Dog Island of Schouten and Le Maire. Smoke rose above the treetops, and "a faint breath of burnt borao wood" drifted over the water. A little while later, they caught the scent of leaves, greenery, and freshly cut wood. But with no way to steer, they drifted on, and soon the island lay astern.

They drifted past the atoll of Fangatau, from which a number of islanders came out to meet them in canoes. But still they were unable to maneuver the raft against the wind and current. Soon they began to realize what they were facing. Although they could see the quiet waters of the lagoons and the sand beaches and the bright green forests of coconut palms, they could not reach them, kept off as they were by "the viciousness of the red reef." Canoes could come and go, but it would never be possible to steer the raft through one of the openings into a lagoon.

Then, on the 101st day of the voyage, the inevitable happened. Stretching across their path like an impenetrable wall was a forty-five-mile section of coral reef. There was no way of getting around it; it was now, Heyerdahl wrote, "a question of saving our lives." The *Kon-Tiki* began to pitch up and down as the swell became complicated by waves bouncing back off the coral. Dead ahead they could see "the blue Pacific being ruthlessly torn up and hurled into the air all along the horizon." Closer and closer until, with a violent blow, the *Kon-Tiki* crashed onto the outer reef of Raroia and was instantly submerged under a mountain of water as wave after giant wave broke over the raft. Heyerdahl and his companions clung on for dear life and, miraculously, no one was washed overboard and smashed onto the wall of coral. Though the raft was pounded nearly to pieces, it was just buoyant enough to ride up over the reef, allowing the men to scramble off into the lagoon and make their way through shallow water to a little islet. "I shall never forget that wade across the reef toward that heavenly palm island," wrote Heyerdahl.

> When I reached the sunny sand beach, I slipped off my shoes and thrust my bare toes down into the warm, bone-dry sand. . . . Soon the palm-tops closed over my head, and I went on, right in towards the centre of the tiny island. Green coconuts hung under the palm-tufts, and some luxuriant bushes were thickly covered with snow-white blossoms, which smelt so sweet and seductive that I felt quite faint. . . . I was completely overwhelmed. I sank down on my knees and thrust my fingers deep down into the dry warm sand.

FROM A PROMOTIONAL point of view, the voyage of the *Kon-Tiki* was a roaring success. The story of the expedition, published first in Norwegian in 1948 and translated into English in 1950, sold millions of copies and was eventually reprinted in more than sixty languages, including Mongolian and Esperanto. It was described by the *New York Tribune* as "great as few books in our time are great," and by the London *Sunday Times* as "certain to be one of the classics of the sea." Praised by Somerset Maugham as both incredible and true, it was also admired by Harry S. Truman, who observed that it was "a wonderful thing to have people in the world who can still take hardship." A year later, the film *Kon-Tiki*, based on footage shot aboard the raft, won the Academy Award for Best Documentary Feature. Soon "Kon-Tiki fever" broke out around the world: there were Kon-Tiki hotels and Kon-Tiki cocktails, Kon-Tiki bathing suits and Kon-Tiki floats. Heyerdahl became a worldwide celebrity, but this did not necessarily translate into academic respectability.

One of the first to pooh-pooh the significance of the voyage was Te Rangi Hiroa. "A nice adventure," he was quoted as saying. "But you don't expect anyone to call that a scientific expedition. Now do you?" Much of the initial attention had been focused on technical issues—specifically, whether a balsa-wood raft would make it across four thousand miles of open ocean without either breaking up or becoming waterlogged and sinking. Then there was the question of whether the crew would starve to death or die of thirst; one naval attaché at the dockyard in Callao bet them all the whiskey they could drink for the rest of their lives that they would never reach Polynesia alive. But, while there was some grumbling about the use of modern navigational instruments and cans of preserved food, as well as the fact that they'd been towed out to catch the current, most of the technical questions had been answered by the voyage itself. A balsa-wood raft set adrift on the South American coast *could* end up in Polynesia, and humans *could* carry or forage all they needed to stay alive for the three months it would take to get there.

This was really all the general public cared about, but among anthropologists, the larger question was whether the theory behind the voyage made sense. And the answer, at least for the majority, was no. As one critic put it: Heyerdahl's arguments could not be supported "chronologically, archaeologically, botanically, racially, linguistically, or culturally." Heyerdahl always insisted that the academy was arrayed against him, but many of his key points were indefensible, and those that were not were often unacceptably stretched. In 1952, he published an eight-hundred-page defense of his ideas, entitled *American Indians in the Pacific: The*

*Theory Behind the Kon-Tiki Expedition.* Reviews of the volume were harsh. As a writer in the *American Anthropologist* put it, "The author's unquenchable enthusiasm for his theories is evident on every page. Again and again the 'possibility' cited in one paragraph becomes a 'probability' in the next and an established fact half a page later." Another, writing in *American Antiquity,* complained that "every straw is seized, bent, and twisted to suit the author's purposes. Tenuous evidence is pushed beyond reasonable limits; conflicting data are given scant attention or omitted, and the manuscript abounds with incautious statements."

Many of the things Heyerdahl claimed were simply not true. Polynesians were not sun worshippers; the Tahitian word *pahi* did not translate as "raft"; the *moai* of Easter Island were not identical, or even very similar, to the megalithic sculptures of Tiwanaku; the languages of the Pacific Northwest were not related to those of Polynesia. And then there was the cringe-making problem of the "white god" Kon-Tiki. Much of Heyerdahl's argument rested on the need, as he saw it, to explain the presence of sophisticated megalithic masonry and sculpture on the islands of eastern Polynesia. His solution——the arrival of a mysterious white civilization that then inexplicably vanishes, leaving behind evidence of its superior know-how and taste——is a familiar European fantasy trope of the 1920s and '30s. Among professional anthropologists of the 1950s, it was impossible to take seriously, and a few were prepared to concede what is now obvious: that it was difficult "to avoid reading racism from this work."

There was, however, one piece of evidence that no one could argue with, and that was the presence in central and eastern Polynesia of a key American food crop: the sweet potato. This sweet, starchy, nutritious member of the morning glory family, officially known as *Ipomoea batatas,* was first cultivated by indigenous peoples in the Americas and was already widely established there by the time Europeans arrived. The first European reference to the plant is, in fact, from Christopher Columbus, who brought back a sample for Queen Isabella as an example of the products of the New World.

A century or two later, when they began reaching the islands of Polynesia, European observers found that the sweet potato was an important staple in many of the islands of the central and eastern Pacific. At Easter Island in 1722, Jacob Roggeveen was offered sweet potatoes in trade; in Hawai'i, one of Cook's officers reported that they were so plentiful "the poorest natives would throw them into our Ships for Nothing"; and in New Zealand, where many traditional Polynesian food crops would not grow because of the climate, visitors found extensive sweet potato plantations. Indeed, the first "absolute botanical proof" of the plant's presence in Polynesia— proof that these early observers were not conflating it with the visually similar but botanically distinct yam—is an herbarium specimen collected in New Zealand in 1769 by Joseph Banks.

None of this would be in any way remarkable were it not for the fact that every other Polynesian food crop comes from the opposite side of the Pacific. Assuming that Polynesians carried all their most important plants—bananas, breadfruit, taro, sugarcane, yam, and so on—into the Pacific from Asia, how did they come to be growing the American sweet potato? How, in other words, did the sweet potato get to Polynesia?

Botanists have long argued that the sweet potato could not have dispersed throughout the Pacific without human assistance. It does not float and could not have drifted, nor, as is sometimes the case with plants, does it appear to have been carried in seed form in the guts of birds. Assuming that humans are the vector, there are just three possibilities: the Spanish; indigenous South Americans; or Polynesians. For a while, it was argued that Spanish explorers, who are known to have transported the plant to the Philippines, might have planted the first sweet potatoes in the Marquesas when they discovered the islands in 1595. But this does not seem a very likely origin story, for it is hard to imagine how the plant could have become so widespread in Polynesia just a century or so later. Much more ink has been spilt debating the other two possibilities: that the sweet potato was conveyed to the islands by some unknown indigenous inhabitants of South America, or that it was picked up by Polynesians who reached South America and returned to eastern Polynesia with their prize. Logic favors the seafaring Polynesians with their large canoes and penchant for travel, rather than the coast-hugging South Americans who only had rafts. But there is still no absolutely watertight evidence placing Polynesians on South American shores. Very recently arguments have even been made for the natural long-range dispersal of sweet potato seeds, meaning that there would be no need to invoke a human carrier at all. But nothing about this is settled, and the sweet potato remains just as tantalizing a mystery as it was when Heyerdahl deployed it in support of his views.

INSIDE THE SCHOLARLY community, Heyerdahl's theories were met with everything from polite skepticism to outright disdain. One of his harshest critics, the anthropologist Robert Suggs, describes the Kon-Tiki theory, with its mishmash of Marquesan, Easter Island, Tiwanakan, and Incan components, and its mysterious vanished race of "white and bearded men," as about as plausible as the idea "that America was discovered in the last day of the Roman Empire by King Henry the Eighth, who brought the Ford Falcon to the benighted aborigines." But in the court of popular opinion, Heyerdahl's ideas lived on—and on. As one historian put it as recently as 2003, "If an opinion poll today asked citizens on the streets, 'Where did the Polynesians come from?', it is my bet that . . . the most likely response would be 'South America.'"

But there was another aspect of Heyerdahl's theories that did not attract quite so much attention but was, in its way, even more important. This was his insistence that the first settlers of the Pacific were at the mercy of the elements and that no matter where they had originally come from—Asia, Peru, British Columbia—they could only ever run before the wind. Although Heyerdahl sometimes asserted that "the old Polynesians were great navigators," he did not actually credit them with much ability. As one writer put it, Heyerdahl "systematically underrated" both the Polynesians' skill as sailors and "the excellence of their sea-going craft." But he was not alone. Following nearly two centuries in which Polynesian navigational ability had been largely taken for granted, the mid-twentieth century saw a lurch in the direction of doubt about their capacities as the question of whether Polynesians were really navigators at all—whether they had ever been sailing, as opposed to drifting—suddenly took center stage.

# DRIFTING NOT SAILING

## *Andrew Sharp*

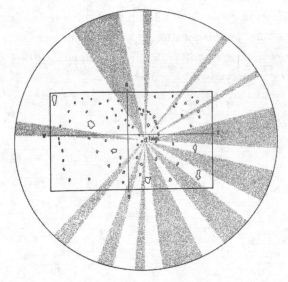

*Tupaia's map with island screens, in* The Settlement of Polynesia:
A Computer Simulation *by Michael Levison, R. Gerard Ward,
and John W. Webb (Minneapolis, 1973).*
THE UNIVERSITY OF MINNESOTA PRESS.

**IN 1956, AN** iconoclastic New Zealand historian by the name of Andrew Sharp published what would come to be seen as "one of the most provocative studies ever in Pacific history." His book, inoffensively titled *Ancient Voyagers in the Pacific*, argued that the longest intentional journey ever made by any Polynesian voyager was no more than three hundred miles; that no sea gap larger than this had ever been crossed on purpose; and that there had thus been "no deliberate colonization" of Fiji, Tonga, Samoa, Tahiti, the Tuamotus, the Marquesas, New Zealand, Hawai'i, or Easter Island.

Inside certain island clusters, like the Fiji–Tonga–Samoa region and the Tahiti–Tuamotu archipelagoes, Sharp conceded that Polynesians had been able to travel backward and forward, to set out for islands, find them, and safely return. But beyond the three-hundred-mile limit, he argued, any kind of intentional navigation was impossible. The problem, in Sharp's view, was the absence of instruments; without sextants, compasses, and something to keep time, it was simply not possible to keep track of where one was on the open ocean. There were invisible currents, fluctuating winds, and no fixed reference points apart from the celestial bodies, which were useful only up to a point. "Stars do not shine during the day, daytime is much longer than the night, and the sun is a poor navigation guide." Fogs, cloud cover, and storms were a perpetual hazard, and a clear, continuous view of the heavens was a "miraculous event." Even European navigators with instruments were often metaphorically *at sea*. While Polynesian sailors deserved their reputation as "outstanding voyagers" within the defined three-hundred-mile limit, "the myth of deliberate long off-shore voyages in the days before navigation instruments" was not, Sharp insisted, "supported by any evidence."

The issue *was* evidence—specifically, which kinds of evidence Sharp considered admissible. He begins—as does almost everyone who tells this story—with the testimony of the ur-eyewitness, Captain Cook. But the passage that interests Sharp comes not from Cook's first voyage and his encounter with Tupaia, but from his third and final voyage, and it involves a different Tahitian, known as Mai. Mai had been brought to England in 1774 by the captain of one of Cook's companion vessels and, against all odds, had survived the experience. (Banks had arranged for him to be inoculated against smallpox, which certainly helped.) A year later, when Cook set out on his last voyage to the Pacific, one of his tasks was to return Mai to Tahiti.

On the way, Cook passed through what are now known as the Cook Islands, a scattered archipelago of islands lying to the south and west of Tahiti. On the island of Atiu, Mai discovered four of his countrymen—four Tahitians—who told him that about ten years earlier they had set out on a journey from Tahiti to Ra'iatea, a comparatively short passage of 130 miles. They had somehow missed their target, and after a long period at sea, they sighted Atiu. By this time they were nearly five hundred miles southwest of where they wanted to be; just five of the original twenty were still alive, and these were clinging to the hull of their overturned vessel. The people of Atiu rescued them and absorbed them so completely into their own society that the castaways no longer had any desire to return home. "This circumstance," wrote Cook in his journal, "very well accounts for the manner the inhabited islands in this Sea have been at first peopled; especially those which lay remote from any Continent and from each other." Here, in other words, was a method by which the remote islands of Polynesia might have been settled—by voyagers who'd become lost at sea.

This was quite a different conclusion from the one Cook had reached on his first voyage to the Pacific, when, in conversation with Tupaia, he first turned these ideas over in his mind. Then he had written: "From all the accounts we can learn, these people sail in those seas from Island to Island for several hundred Leagues [about a thousand miles], the Sun serving them for a compass by day and the Moon and Stars by night. When this comes to be prov'd we Shall be no longer at a loss to know how the Islands lying in those Seas came to be people'd."

Cook is certainly the most knowledgeable and trustworthy eyewitness of the period, but even his testimony can be tricky. In between these two voyages there had been another, a long, arduous expedition with two island sweeps and a frigid circumnavigation of the South Pole. Thus, by 1777 he had been at sea almost continuously for a decade, thousands of miles from home in unknown waters, often in dangerous circumstances, responsible for the lives and health of hundreds of men. The man who emerges from the journal of the third voyage is not the same as the one who first took such a keen interest in Tupaia's lists and charts. He is, as his biographer puts it, "a man tired, not physically in any observable way, but with that almost imperceptible blunting of the brain . . . His apprehensions as a discoverer . . . not so constantly fine as they had been; his understanding of other minds . . . not so ready or sympathetic." The Cook of the third voyage is harder, crankier, less given to wonder, and less inclined to give Polynesians—or anyone else, for that matter—the benefit of the doubt.

Sharp, however, saw the matter differently. In the passage from Cook's third journal he read a necessary and corrective shift away from conjecture and speculation and toward concrete and objective evidence. Sharp argued that in what he called the "authentic record"—meaning the written record of the Pacific in the post-European period—there was not a single instance of deliberate long-distance voyaging. There were, however, innumerable examples of drift or accidental voyages. Drawing from the accounts of missionaries, whalers, naval captains, and other early European observers, Sharp recounted a number of stories about Polynesian castaways: a group of Tahitians blown more than thirteen hundred miles to an island just east of Samoa; a family from the Tokelaus swept more than twelve hundred miles southeast to Mangaia; a canoe from Aitutaki that finished up a thousand miles west in the Tongan archipelago after nearly five months at sea.

He related in detail a story about three canoes from an island in the Tuamotus that set out for Tahiti (240 miles west) with 150 people on board. They had almost reached Mehetia (the first signpost, at 170 miles) when a westerly gale sprang up. The canoes were battered by ferocious winds and swamped by enormous seas; the three lost sight of one another, and two were never seen again. The third, with its complement of forty-eight men, women, and children, survived the storm and bravely set sail again, only to be becalmed. Then the food and water ran out and half the people died. A second storm came, bringing "life-giving" rain but also driving them still farther back in the direction from which they'd come. By the time they finally cast up on an uninhabited atoll, they had traveled more than 400 miles in the wrong direction and were now 650 miles from where they wanted to be.

This, then, was Sharp's model for how the islands of Polynesia had been settled: *accidentally*, through voyages arising from exiles and storms. Many of Sharp's critics later referred to these journeys as "drift voyages," though Sharp himself was adamant that there was an important distinction between "drifting" and "accidental voyaging." Polynesians, he insisted, were able seamen who knew very well how to control their canoes. It was just that, over long distances or in bad weather, they could not keep track of where they were. They could not "re-set their courses when blown away . . . or when committed to unfamiliar waters." They could "exercise a choice" about the direction in which they sailed, but since they soon became lost "in the trackless wastes of the vast Pacific Ocean," they could not know where to go.

This distinction between sailors who had lost their way and hapless drifters was not so clear to some, however, and there were implications of Sharp's argument that he seemed unwilling to acknowledge. "No Polynesian," he wrote complacently, "need be in the slightest degree disturbed about the impact" of this accidental voyaging theory "on his genealogy or his tribal history. Obviously the Polynesians had ancestors, and obviously they came in canoes. The only thing that needs to be revised is the manner of their arrival." They could not take credit for deliberately exploring the Pacific or discovering their islands, but they should take pride in the fact that their ancestors had survived "such a long succession" of unintentional voyages. New Zealand Māori, as the inhabitants of the last islands to be settled, were the inheritors of a particularly impressive record of survival and adaptation. They might not have been deliberate navigators, Sharp argued, but they were "healthy, hardy and optimistic, taking life as it came, as their forebears who were borne to distant islands had done many times before."

There is something quite tone-deaf about this, even for 1956.

The argument, wrote one of Sharp's critics, owed more "to ancient prejudices which seem now to be deep-rooted in the European psyche" than "to any genuine understanding of Oceanic life and culture." The Māori scholar Pei Te Hurinui Jones was more direct: "My first reaction to the theme of the book," he wrote, "was decidedly hostile. I felt that Andrew Sharp had set out with the purpose of discrediting the achievements of our Polynesian ancestors." Like many, Jones considered the term "accidental," when applied to Polynesian voyaging, to be "unfortunate" and suggested that the voyages that had led to the discovery of islands "were as deliberate as the first voyage of Christopher Columbus." A better term for such journeys, he suggested, might be "voyages of exploration."

THERE CAN BE little doubt that Sharp enjoyed setting the cat among the pigeons. The historian K. R. Howe tells a funny story from his own undergraduate days at the University of Auckland in the mid-1960s. Sharp, who had been invited to give a history lecture, introduced himself to the students with a wave of his hand, declaring, "I stand before you as a heretic!" "None of us had heard of him before," writes Howe, "and because we had done Luther in the previous lecture, we thought we were about to get a talk on the Reformation." But while undergraduate history majors might not have realized it, Sharp's book had generated so much heat among professional anthropologists and historians that a special volume of responses was even then being prepared, one that would run to three editions. In response to this, Sharp rewrote and reissued his own book, noting in the preface to the new volume that the first edition had received "upwards of a hundred published notices" and that he had engaged in "a dozen protracted and interesting exchanges of letters" and "2,191 oral discussions" of his ideas. None of these had caused him to change his view on any of the essential points. "I have yet to hear of a fact or read an argument," he wrote, "which impugns the basic contentions of the former book."

But Sharp, in his queer, intransigent way, had crystallized some important problems. One of his most "heretical" assertions was that Polynesian oral traditions were essentially of no use in determining what had happened in the past. It was a fundamental mistake, he argued, to seek answers to historical questions in this quarter. "Polynesians," he argued, "were making stories and poetry, not writing history." Their voyaging tales were filled with "mystical and figurative" elements—ancestors who traveled by rainbow or on the backs of birds, or who floated across the sea on a piece of pumice or traveled from island to island by bending a tree. It was neither "scientific" nor "objective" to cherry-pick these accounts, selecting only those bits that seemed to support the theory of long-range voyaging and discarding the rest as so much embellishment, as, he claimed, "traditionalists" like Smith and Fornander had done.

Sharp had staked out an extreme and in many ways unpopular position. And yet, he also seemed to have tapped into a broad concern. For some time, the feeling had been growing among anthropologists and historians that the so-called traditionalists of the late nineteenth century had given too much credence to Polynesian accounts and that the time had come for a reevaluation of the conclusions that had been drawn from this material. Sharp, for all his irritating tendentiousness, wrote one anthropologist, "echoed the doubts of many other scholars who have not had the courage to place their views in print."

Sharp's intervention had the effect of opening a floodgate, and a torrent of books and articles followed, questioning the "authenticity" of canonical sources of Polynesian mythology. This was an easy one for European scholars because, of course, it was quite true that Smith, Fornander, and the others had been unsophisticated in their methods and had brought their own ideas and longings to the project. But for Polynesians, the implications of this new angle were complex. On the one hand, it led to a more thoughtful approach to Polynesia's oral history and a deeper appreciation of the complex process by which Polynesian traditional knowledge had been converted to historical documents—including the role that Polynesians themselves had played. At the same time, some of the stories being "debunked" had come to be understood as cherished history, and the idea that profound and seemingly ancient Polynesian traditions had been "invented" by nineteenth-century Europeans was, quite naturally, felt as a blow.

The nuanced view, as represented by Te Rangi Hiroa, for example, was that the traditions were essentially poetic but that this did not disqualify them as sources for history. It was essentially a matter of interpretation: being too literal put one at risk of losing "the inner thought through the outer garb." Citing a widespread myth in which the demigod Maui fishes up the islands of Polynesia with a magic hook, he suggested that the idea of an island being pulled from the sea is so obviously untrue that we overlook its real meaning as "the echo of a traditional Polynesian explorer who by discovering a new island literally fished it up out of the depths of the unknown." But this kind of argument was gradually losing its appeal in a world increasingly preoccupied with "precision and definiteness." What anthropologists and historians in the mid-twentieth century seemed to want was something almost *mathematical*, and in 1964 that was exactly what emerged.

**SHARP'S ARGUMENT HINGED** on the idea that the original settlers of Polynesia had been carried to the islands by currents and blown there by winds. But while vast numbers of claims and counterclaims had been made regarding the influence of meteorology, no one had ever attempted to assess the statistical probability of a canoe being driven from one part of Polynesia to another.

Then, one morning in 1964, two geographers at University College London met over coffee to discuss the value of computer simulations in solving certain kinds of problems. The ideal type of problem would be one involving a system with known dynamics but many variable elements. Its complexity would be such that only by running a huge number of scenarios could the likelihood of any given outcome be determined—a problem, in other words, with too many permutations for the human mind to manage. One of the geographers, John Webb, was visiting from the United States, but the other, Gerard Ward, was a New Zealander, and later, during a relaxing soak in the tub, it occurred to him that the drift hypothesis of Polynesian settlement was a problem of precisely this type. A well-designed simulation, even if it could not provide "an unqualified yes or no," might give a persuasive answer to the question of whether the islands of Polynesia could have been discovered by drift voyaging alone.

Of course, such a project could not be undertaken without the help of a computer scientist with access to a large computer, and so Michael Levison, of Birkbeck College, came on board. Levison, who worked for many years on computing applications in the humanities—one of his projects concerned the authorship of the Epistles of St. Paul—remembers the period as one in which researchers were just beginning to realize what computers could do. "All sorts of people would show up" with projects, he recalls, some of which were quite interesting, while others were "decidedly odd." The Polynesian problem fell into the former category, and Levison agreed to begin writing and testing a program while the geographers set about amassing the data required to make such a simulation work.

The data for this model consisted primarily of information about winds and currents over the test area, which is to say, most of the Pacific. It was gathered from more than five thousand tables of meteorological information collected by British naval and merchant vessels since the mid-nineteenth century and tabulated by the Marine Division of the United Kingdom Meteorological Office. For the purpose of the study, a vast rectangle from Australia to South America and from Hawai'i to New Zealand was divided up into five-degree "Marsden squares," boxes defined by lines of latitude and longitude. Wind and current probability matrices were devised for every month of the year for every one of the 392 squares. For winds, these included both speed (measured from 0 to 9 on the

Beaufort scale) and direction (any one of sixteen compass points, plus "calms and variable winds," a no-direction category). Currents came in eight different speeds (0–7) and from any one of sixteen compass points.

On top of this, the model also required geographical information on the location of 994 islands and coasts and a variety of factors affecting survival at sea. These last were combined into a "risk probability table," compiled with the help of the Naval Life Saving Committee of Bath, which took into account "the fact that some vessels will carry provisions, water, or fishing equipment, and that some will have luck and others none." The table suggested that the probability of dying increased substantially after about seven weeks at sea, and that by week 25 the chances of survival were effectively nil. Risks to the vessel itself—of swamping or breaking up—were envisioned as a function of wind; the model assumed that a wind of Force 9 or greater gave the vessel "a 50 percent chance of surviving to the next day."

The process of transcribing nearly 800,000 separate entries on winds and currents, keypunching, assembling onto magnetic tape, and checking was a "mammoth task," and it was not until 1967 (three years from conception) that the researchers were finally ready to run their first computations. The volume of data was also too great for the computer they were using—a Ferranti Atlas that occupied two floors of a house owned by the University of London—to store in its main memory. Considered the fastest computer in the United Kingdom at the time, the Atlas was so much in demand that Levison had to run his program in the middle of the night. "Once a week for several weeks," he writes, "I had to leave my London suburban home at 3.00 a.m., drive 45 minutes into Central London, run the program, and arrive home around 5.30." But the results, when they finally came in, were worth the trouble.

Out of more than 120,000 simulated voyages, begun at points all over the Pacific and conducted at all times of the year, some highly likely drift routes did emerge. These included Tonga to Fiji, Pitcairn to the Tuamotus, the Marquesas to the Tokelaus, and several others, all of which entailed travel from east to west. Almost no drifts going the other way, from west to east, emerged from the experiment. The results gave "no support" to the possibility of drifting along what was then envisioned as a likely Polynesian pathway from Samoa to the Marquesas, while the chance of drifting from Samoa to the Society Islands was less than one in seven hundred.

Then there were the islands to which it was impossible to drift no matter where you started. One of these was Hawai'i. Out of sixteen thousand drift experiments begun at points all along the northern boundary of central and eastern Polynesia, with extra experiments starting in the Line Islands and the Marquesas, not one ever reached the Hawaiian Islands. In fact, almost no voyages begun in central and eastern Polynesia ever managed to get north of the equator; even those begun on Christmas Island (around 2 degrees north latitude) never got farther than about 10 degrees north.

Nor would a drifting canoe ever be likely to reach New Zealand. None of the many thousands of drift voyages begun on the southern margin of tropical Polynesia—the presumed starting point of New Zealand's first settlers—ever reached Aotearoa. This was a surprise to the New Zealander Ward, who had seen the trunks of coconut palms washed up on a beach at Opotiki, in the Bay of Plenty. But the only drift path from the tropics that led to New Zealand in the simulation came from the Kermadecs, a string of tiny, uninhabited islands halfway between New Zealand and Tonga.

As for Easter Island, the third point of the Polynesian Triangle and one of the most isolated islands in the world, the chance of drifting there from anywhere in Polynesia was next to zero. It was also "virtually nil" from the coast of South America: with a single exception, every one of the more than four thousand drift voyages begun on the coast of Peru landed farther north on the South America coast or in the Galápagos or were lost at sea. This would seem to contradict Heyerdahl's experience in the *Kon-Tiki*, but it's important to recall that Heyerdahl's raft had been towed well out to sea before the start of his epic journey. The computer simulations confirmed just how necessary this had been; in the experiment, the only voyages from South America that succeeded in making landfall in Polynesia were begun 450 miles off the Chilean coast.

The authors of this study acknowledged that the whole problem of Polynesian voyaging might well be one that, by its very nature, "defies proof." But their results were still compelling. Based on the computer simulation, the chance of settling Polynesia by drift voyaging alone looked infinitesimally small. Even Sharp, however, had allowed that it was not *purely* a matter of drift: some human decision-making had to be taken into account. To address this, Ward, Webb, and Levison devised a variation of the main experiment, which they referred to as "voyaging with intent." In these experiments, they added the capacity to steer as close as possible to a specified direction, allowing the vessels to hold a course of 90 degrees or greater to the wind.

Under these conditions, it proved quite probable that a canoe starting in Samoa and traveling east would reach the islands of eastern Polynesia—Tahiti, the Marquesas, the Tuamotus, the southern Line Islands, and the Northern Cooks—and a handful even went on to the coasts of Panama and Colombia. It was also possible (an 8.5 percent chance) for a canoe traveling north-northwest from the Marquesas to reach Hawai'i, while a canoe traveling southwest from Rarotonga would reach New Zealand more than half the time. Thus, the researchers concluded, while the settlement of Polynesian by drift alone was a nonstarter, there were "good chances of successfully crossing all the major ocean stretches within and around the Polynesian Triangle, with a very limited degree of navigational skill, within a reasonable survival period, and in craft which have poor capability of sailing to windward." As a standard for Polynesian voyaging, it was a pretty low bar, but it did appear to settle the question of whether some degree of seamanship and navigation had been necessary to reach the islands of Polynesia, and, as an example of cool, quantitative reasoning, it was difficult to refute.

# THE NON-ARMCHAIR APPROACH

## David Lewis Experiments

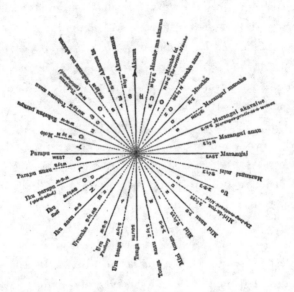

*Polynesian wind compass, in* Myths and Songs from
the South Pacific *by the Rev. William Wyatt Gill (London, 1876).*
HARVARD UNIVERSITY LIBRARY.

IT WAS ONE thing to assert that "some navigational ability" had been
required to settle the islands of Polynesia, and quite another to artic-
ulate how it had worked. What actual navigational methods might
the original settlers of Polynesia have used? What conceptual tools
did they have in their tool kit? How seaworthy, really, were their
canoes? The inspired intervention of Ward, Webb, and Levison had
brought a breath of fresh air to a debate that had become "stultified by shortage of facts." But the computer simulation had never
been designed to answer the question of *how* such voyages might

have been accomplished. For this, something quite different was needed—perhaps even a return to voyaging itself.

"Most scholars are landlubbers," wrote one of the people involved in this new phase of the inquiry. And it was quite true that, since the early nineteenth century, almost everyone writing about Polynesian voyaging had been an armchair theorist (with the obvious exception of Thor Heyerdahl). That all changed in the 1960s and '70s, thanks, in large part, to Sharp's provocations and to the man who emerged as his archnemesis in the drift debate, a physician and blue-water sailor named David Lewis. Lewis had been born in the United Kingdom but had grown up in New Zealand and lived for a time as a child in the Cook Islands. He described himself as having been interested from a young age in Polynesian seafaring—a subject he associated with memories of "trailing my toes luxuriously through the warm red dust, clad only in a pareu [sarong], and on moonlit nights, surreptitiously watching, with my friends, parties of silent men illegally poisoning lagoon fish with crushed *utu* fruit, or equally secretly, from the under the palms, watching the hula dancing."

Following the Second World War, Lewis set up as a doctor in London, but in 1964 he left his practice to sail around the world with his family—including two daughters, aged three and four—in a catamaran called the *Rehu Moana* (Ocean Spray). A keen yachtsman, he had already made three solo crossings of the Atlantic, but for this particular voyage he had a special plan in mind. During their passage across the Pacific, he would test some of the navigational methods attributed to the ancient Polynesians. Lewis believed that attempts to understand indigenous navigation in the Pacific had been "hampered by too theoretical an approach," and he saw the voyage as an opportunity "to bring academic theories about oceanic navigation down to sea level."

The plan was to retrace the route believed to have been taken by the first settlers of New Zealand—from the Society Islands via the Cook Islands—without using any instruments, thereby testing the accuracy of "star and sun steering by eye alone." Lewis was surprised to find that, in spite of his "inexpert performance and second-hand knowledge of the techniques," the method was surprisingly accurate. At the end of the longest leg of the test segment—a run of seventeen hundred miles from Rarotonga to New Zealand—his landfall was off by less than half a degree of latitude, a mere twenty-six miles. For the next three years, Lewis and his family wandered around in the *Rehu Moana*, visiting many of the remoter corners of the Pacific, where he was further surprised to discover navigators who still used traditional techniques, eschewing modern tools like maps and compasses.

In 1968, he secured a research fellowship from the Australian National University—"a most unusual fellowship," as one of his American colleagues enviously described it, "that allowed him to sail about the Pacific in search of islanders who might still know the old ways." Lewis set out again, this time with his twenty-year-old son in a ketch called the *Isbjorn*, to track down and sail with some of these navigators. Among those who instructed him was a man named Tevake, from a Polynesian outlier in the Santa Cruz Reef Islands. The "outliers" are a scattering of small islands that lie outside the Polynesian Triangle, in what is officially Melanesia, but are occupied by people who speak Polynesian languages and have Polynesian cultural traits. Once thought to represent a breadcrumb trail left by the original Polynesian migrations, they are now understood to be communities of later settlers who traveled—or possibly were swept—back westward from Polynesian homelands like Samoa. The outliers, incidentally, are one of the few categories of Polynesian islands to which, according to Ward, Webb, and Levison's computer simulation, it is actually quite easy to drift.

Tevake, wrote Lewis, was "an old and wrinkled man by the time I knew him . . . the first Polynesian navigator I ever sailed with, and one of the greatest." In his prime, he had made journeys of up to 320 miles, as far as Tikopia and Vanuatu. His thirty-foot outrigger canoe had long since been wrecked, but, "old as he was, . . . he still ranged ceaselessly among the islands." Lewis and his son also traveled to Micronesia, where they sailed with a navigator named Hipour from the atoll of Puluwat, in the Caroline Islands, and took instruction from Iotiebata and others in the Gilberts. Over time, Lewis sought out information (it was "hardly appropriate," he wrote, to describe the men he spoke with as "informants," when they were explicitly master teachers and he explicitly their pupil) in the islands of western Polynesia, Micronesia, Melanesia, Indonesia, even Alaska and the Russian Far East.

The upshot of it all was the realization that the ancient sea lore of Oceania had not been lost, as so many believed, but could still be found scattered among the islands as "a mosaic of fragments . . . only waiting to be put together." The second important realization was that traditional navigational techniques and concepts were remarkably consistent across a huge swath of the Pacific. All the evidence pointed to a single navigational methodology, a "former Pacific-wide system," albeit with local variations. This came as a surprise to Lewis, who had been cautious about assuming that techniques still in use on remote atolls in Micronesia might be the same as those employed in other parts of the Pacific. They all, however, appeared to incorporate a set of key elements that included detailed lists of stars and star paths; sophisticated orientation concepts; and a wide array of landfinding techniques, some of which could be readily translated into Western conceptual terms, but others of which reflected ways of seeing and thinking with no obvious corollary in the European tradition.

Lewis, whose training and cultural background had ingrained in him an attitude of intellectual caution, was persuaded. Based on his own experience and the testimony of those he met, he became convinced that the islanders of the Pacific had had the vessels, the knowledge, and the techniques to traverse the great expanses of the Pacific, to make landfall on islands that were known to them, and to find their way home from those that were not.

. . .

**LEWIS'S CONCLUSIONS WERE** not so terribly different from those that had been reached by others along the way, but the pathway to them was entirely new. He had tested the navigators' methods by putting his own sailboat into their hands and watching them navigate, using nothing but what they could feel and see and the information they held in their minds. He describes how these wayfinders, as they are often called, kept course using the rising or setting points of a succession of stars, which constituted the "star path" from one island to another. About ten stars a night were required to maintain a constant heading, though sometimes as few as five could be used. Even when the heavens were obscured by cloud, he noted, the most experienced wayfinders knew the sky so well that the appearance of just one or two stars was enough to orient them.

On his first night of sailing with Hipour, Lewis observed how he steered first toward the setting Pleiades, then, as they became masked by clouds, how he kept the rising Great Bear to one side, in line with part of the rigging, then held the Pole Star in line with the edge of the wheelhouse, while keeping "the sinking Pollux fine on the starboard bow." At one point, Lewis wrote, "a strange star appeared at which I stared in surprise; but Hipour merely grinned and remarked, unexpectedly in English, 'Satellite.'"

Star lore is the foundation of non-instrumental navigation, but stars, as Sharp had pointed out, are visible only at night, and so another method was required for navigation by day. Navigators could steer by the sun for a few hours at the beginning and end of the day (otherwise it was too high in the sky) and at noon (when the shadow of the mast will give north and south). But they also used another very important—and, to Westerners, much less familiar—technique: that of reading the ocean swells. Swells are not the same as waves. Waves are a local phenomenon thrown up by winds in the immediate vicinity; swells, by contrast, are waves that originate far away and travel beyond the winds that generate them. The important swells, those created by enduring weather patterns like the trade winds or the westerlies in the South Pacific Ocean, tend to have long wavelengths and to move past the boat "with a slow, swelling undulation." This does not necessarily mean they are easy to recognize, for in practice the actual pattern of waves and swells at any particular point will be a complicated mix of "systems that differ in height, length, shape, and speed moving across each other from different directions."

Despite having sailed for years on the world's great oceans, Lewis reported that he could not consistently differentiate the various patterns of waves and swells and would frequently have to have them pointed out. On a passages with Tevake, the navigator showed him how the "Long Swell," from the southeast, and the "Sea Swell," from the east-northeast, passed "through each other like the interlocked fingers of two hands." It was not so much a matter of seeing them as of feeling the changes in the movement of the vessel: which part of it meets the wave first, how it rocks or rolls or corkscrews as it's lifted up and then falls. Sometimes, Tevake told him, he would lie down on the outrigger platform, the more clearly to feel the pitch and roll of his canoe and thus disentangle the different forces. Lewis also reported a bit of wisdom related to him by a "veteran island skipper," who had been told that "the most sensitive balance was a man's testicles."

In addition to sun, stars, and swells, wayfinders used winds to steer, though this was the least accurate, given the frequency of wind shifts on the open ocean. (Lewis reported that on his passage from Rarotonga to New Zealand, there were no fewer than sixty-four changes in the direction of the wind.) Wind compasses are one of the very few bits of navigational lore to have survived in eastern Polynesia, where they were recorded on several islands in the early nineteenth century. These were not physical objects or drawings— though pictures were made of them by European missionaries— but conceptual systems that were visualized, in at least one group of islands, as a series of holes at the edge of the horizon, "some large and some small, through which *Raka*, the god of winds, and his children love to blow."

SO FAR, NONE of this is terribly hard for a Westerner to comprehend, even if he cannot replicate the skills represented. But there is one component of the navigational system described by Lewis that is quite alien to European thinking. It is attested in only one place—the Caroline Islands, where it was first described by the anthropologists William Alkire and Thomas Gladwin in the early 1970s—and may never have existed in precisely this form anywhere else. Nevertheless, it is a salutary reminder of how much more there is in heaven and earth than is dreamt of in our philosophy.

In order to keep track of their progress on a long voyage out of sight of land, Carolinian navigators use a system known as *etak*, in which they visualize a "reference island"—which is usually a real island but may also be imaginary—off to one side of the path they are following, about midway between their starting point and their destination. As the journey progresses, this island "moves" under each of the stars in the star path, while the canoe in which the voyagers are traveling stays still. Of course, the navigators know that it is the canoe and not the islands that are moving, but this is the way they conceptualize the voyage. They organize all the information they need—the distance to be covered, the speed at which they are traveling, the bearing of each star relative to the canoe at each stage of the journey and to the islands at either end—into a mental map made up of *etaks*, or segments, each of which is completed as the reference island passes under each star in the star path in turn.

Gladwin, the anthropologist, wrote a wonderful description of the way voyaging by this method feels. "Picture yourself," he suggested, "on a Puluwat canoe at night."

The weather is clear, the stars are out, but no land is in sight. The canoe is a familiar little world. Men sit about, talk, perhaps move around a little within their microcosm. On either side of the canoe water streams past, a line of turbulence and bubbles merging into a wake and disappearing in the darkness. Overhead there are stars, immovable, immutable. They swing in their paths across and out of the sky but invariably come up again in the same places. You may travel for days on the canoe but the stars will not go away or change their position aside from their nightly trajectories from horizon to horizon. Hours go by, miles of water have flowed past. Yet the canoe is still underneath and the stars still above. Back along the wake, however, the island you left falls farther and farther behind, while the one toward which you are heading is hopefully drawing closer. You can see neither of them, but you know this is happening. You know too that there are islands on either side of you, some near, some far, some ahead, some behind. Everything passes by the little canoe—everything except the stars by night and the sun in the day.

This image of a canoe stationary on the great circle of the sea, while the ocean and all its islands slide past, is reminiscent of Polynesian tales in which islands float away or wander, or appear and disappear in certain places or at certain times of day, or have to be caught and tethered to the bottom of the sea. Islands in these stories are less fixed or stable than one might have expected; they are more like clouds or vapor, which from a distance they resemble. In some stories they are said to hover on the horizon and to be driven through the night sky by wind.

The last piece of the Oceanic navigational puzzle is the set of landfinding techniques, sometimes referred to as "expanding the target." Birds, as one of Lewis's instructors explained, "are the navigator's very best friends." If a low island can be seen at about ten miles, the range of terns and noddies—land birds that return to their islands at night—is twice that, while boobies, which fly "low and arrow-straight for the horizon" at dusk, are known to travel as many as fifty miles from land. The navigator Hipour, Gladwin reported, described the behavior of these birds in "downright affectionate" terms. He explained how, as the day comes to an end and the birds begin heading for home, "a booby which comes upon a sailing canoe will turn and start circling over it. He acts as though he wants to land on it, but does not. At last when the sky is almost dark he finally, perhaps reluctantly, leaves the canoe and heads straight for home." The bird, said Hipour, shows the navigator the way, attracting even the most inattentive sailor by his antics and leading him on a course that is "unerringly true."

In addition to bird lore, there is cloud lore: the way clouds will move slowly over an island "as if stuck" and then speed up once they are past it; or the "brightness" of clouds over an island as compared with those over the sea; or the way a land cloud will lie, at first, like other clouds on the horizon but, if you watch long enough, will appear to hover or keep re-forming while other clouds dissipate or move on. One navigator told Lewis that in calm weather you can sometimes see two clouds "like a pair of eyebrows" low on the horizon, or a tall V-shaped cloud, both of which will point to land. One of the best-known bits of cloud lore has to do with color: clouds over land or reef are said to have a pinkish tinge, while those over a lagoon are green. On a voyage with the Gilbertese navigator Iotiebata, Lewis recalled, the green on the underbelly of the clouds was so striking as they approached the atoll of Tarawa that he was surprised the navigator did not mention it. When asked about this, Iotiebata replied with some hesitation, "I did not wish to embarrass or insult you by mentioning this green. For after all, you are a navigator, of a kind, yourself—and even Europeans notice this obvious sign!"

Other signs include the "loom" of land, which Lewis describes as "a pale, shimmering column" of air, and a mysterious phenomenon known as "underwater lightning," which is different from ordinary bioluminescence and which physicists even now are at a loss to explain. Islanders also speak of "sea marks": places where porpoises or other creatures are known to feed, areas of mist or low visibility, whirlpools, cross seas, shining streaks on the surface of the water, congregations of sharks or jellyfish, and lines of flotsam that collect at the confluence of different ocean streams.

Finally, there is the technique known as "wave piloting." This is a version of navigating by swells, but with the added complication that in the vicinity of islands, waves are both reflected and refracted by the land. This creates complicated patterns of interference, which in the Marshall Islands have historically been depicted by stick charts made from the ribs of palm fronds, with shells to indicate the positions of islands. These stick charts have often been described as maps, but they are not maps or charts in the way we might think of them. They are teaching tools and mnemonic devices, part of an instructional tool kit used by experienced navigators to communicate concepts, and not something that would ever be relied upon at sea. As one anthropologist in the Marshall Islands put it, navigators there would consider it "scandalous to continue to consult a chart when underway."

Micronesian stick charts are one of the very few physical manifestations of Oceanic navigational lore, which is essentially a body of oral knowledge. (Lewis stressed the incredible amount of information committed to memory by traditional navigators and noted that some of them, when reciting certain pieces of lore, would become irritated if they were interrupted and would have to go back to the beginning and start again.) It is not clear whether these stick charts are a local innovation or part of a system that has elsewhere been lost. But they have no connection with European cartography. As Lewis pointed out, "Europeans had no corresponding graphic representation of these phenomena [swells, waves, and their relationships to islands], and could not have had any, since the underlying principles were not generally known."

Taken all together, these landfinding techniques—and perhaps others involving water temperature, color, drift objects, and other signs—can double or triple the distance at which an island can be detected. In some archipelagoes, these expanded targets overlap, creating a kind of "screen," which a trained navigator would find difficult to miss. Ward, Webb, and Levison, who had given some thought to this issue in the design of their computer simulation, make the interesting suggestion that this vision of island screens might be one of the concepts behind the distribution of islands on Tupaia's chart. They note that on the chart more than half the circumference of the sea around Tupaia's home territory of Tahiti is masked by islands—a much greater density of land than actually exists. But perhaps what was being depicted was not the islands themselves so much as the expanded targets they represented. Perhaps it was less a matter of accuracy and more a reflection of the navigator's belief that the sea was full of islands and "that if one landfall were missed another would be made."

WHAT IS NOT easily conveyed in accounts of traditional navigational techniques is a sense of how navigation is *experienced* by its practitioners: not as an array of discrete techniques but as "a unity," "the sum of input from such disparate sources as stars, swells, and birds being processed through training and practice into a confident awareness of precisely where they were at any one time"—a description that, in itself, seems to capture some of the difficulty. Even more elusive is the larger conceptual framework, the deep, inherited cultural understanding of *island* and *ocean* that was shared by those who for thousands of years lived in and with and by the sea.

"When a Puluwatan speaks of the ocean," wrote Gladwin, "the words he uses refer not to an amorphous expanse of water but rather to the assemblage of seaways which lie between the various islands. Together these seaways constitute the ocean he knows and understands." The island of Puluwat, seen in this way, "ceases to be a solitary spot of dry land" and "takes its place in a familiar constellation of islands linked together by pathways on the ocean." The inhabitants of an atoll know, even if they have not been there, that beyond the horizon lies a "world of little islands . . . each in its own assigned place upon the vast surface of the sea."

This view of the ocean as a thoroughfare rather than a barrier, together with the confidence that another island would always rise up over the horizon, makes sense when you think of the settlers of Remote Oceania as having started out in a realm in which islands were everywhere and not far apart. It was a perspective they might easily have developed—along with the necessary fishhooks and outriggers and navigational techniques—in what is sometimes described as the "island nursery" of Island Southeast Asia. But even this is not the whole story, for no matter how accustomed the earliest migrants were to the idea that islands were "inevitable," some of the sea roads they would eventually travel were terrifically empty and long.

Once again, this raises the question not just of *how* but of *why*. Polynesian and Micronesian traditions give a whole raft of reasons for setting sail: procurement of valuable objects, trade, social visits, revenge, desperation, lust, a desire for conquest and war. To this nineteenth-century Romantics added *the love of adventure*, and those who have studied traditional navigation from an anthropological point of view tend to agree. "All over Oceania," wrote Lewis, "a wandering spirit persists to this day." In Puluwat, added Gladwin, voyaging to far islands, while ostensibly undertaken for some purpose like fetching a supply of tobacco or green turtles, was, "in large measure, an end in itself." Far travel is—and surely was—a form of excitement, a measure of status, sometimes a matter of necessity. But it was also woven into the cosmogonic understanding of these sea people as both a beginning and an end. All over Polynesia, spirits of the dead embark on journeys; on the Polynesian outlier of Tikopia, a "sweet burial" was said to be the fate of a man lost at sea. Lewis was saddened but not surprised when, in 1970, the news reached him that his old friend and teacher Tevake had disappeared. Those who knew him said that he had "simply paddled out to sea in the manner of the Tikopians and did not intend to arrive."

# HŌKŪLE'A

## *Sailing to Tahiti*

Hōkūle'a *under sail, Polynesian Voyaging Society Archives.*
KAMEHAMEHA SCHOOLS, HAWAI'I.

**LEWIS WAS NOT** the only person with an interest in testing these ideas empirically; across the Pacific in California, a similar voyaging experiment was also under way. In 1965, an anthropologist named Ben Finney set about re-creating a traditional double-hulled Polynesian voyaging canoe. Finney, a lanky, fair-haired Californian with sailing experience racing catamarans—a "modern descendant" of the Polynesian craft—had been a student of Kenneth Emory's at the University of Hawai'i. Like Lewis, he had been piqued by Sharp's claims about ancient Polynesian navigational capacities and, in particular, the poor seakeeping qualities of traditional Polynesian canoes: their supposed structural fragility, high risk of being swamped, and presumed inability to sail into the wind. "All this seemed absurd to me," he wrote. But he also recognized that no one really knew what the capacities of such a vessel might be, there not having been one in Polynesian waters for hundreds of years. So, with help from some of his students at University of California, Santa Barbara, he built one.

The canoe, christened *Nalehia* (The Skilled Ones) "for the graceful way her twin hulls glided over the swells," was forty feet long and weighed nearly one and a half tons. It was made from modern materials, including fiberglass and laminated oak, but was based on drawings of Polynesian canoes made by eighteenth-century explorers. The idea, wrote Finney, was to focus on sailing performance, "to try out the canoe in a series of trials . . . then sail it, or a larger canoe built from the lessons learned, from Hawaii to Tahiti and return." (The choice of Tahiti was determined by the many Hawaiian legends and chants that refer to voyages back and forth between Hawaiʻi and Kahiki—the Hawaiian name for Tahiti but also the name of a mythical faraway land, home to various ancestors, sorcerers, and gods.)

*Nalehia* never made it to Tahiti, in part because of flaws in the canoe's design. The hulls, which had been made from casts of an old Hawaiian canoe, were U-shaped and too shallow to prevent the canoe from "skidding sideways at an alarming rate" when it was pointed into the wind. But Finney remained committed to the project, and in the early 1970s he returned to Honolulu, where he joined forces with two other people who had also been thinking about canoes: Tommy Holmes, a surfer and paddler from a prominent haole (European) family in Honolulu, and the Hawaiian artist Herb Kāne, whose romantic paintings of Polynesian voyagers were hugely popular in Hawaiʻi. Together they founded the Polynesian Voyaging Society, a nonprofit corporation whose goal was to build and launch a "performance replica" and sail it to Tahiti and back.

The canoe would be named *Hōkūleʻa* (Star of Joy), the Hawaiian name for Arcturus, which is the zenith star of the Hawaiian Islands. At sixty feet long, it would be bigger than *Nalehia* and would cost a good deal more to build; the first estimate came in at $1,000 a foot, for a total that was the equivalent of almost $350,000 in today's money. Finney wrote research grants, describing the project as "an exercise in 'experimental archaeology,'" while Holmes tapped the Honolulu establishment and Kāne printed thousands of posters to sell. Additional funding came in the form of payment for the story rights from *National Geographic*, an advance from Dodd, Mead & Company for the rights to Finney's proposed book, and a grant from the Hawaii Bicentennial Commission, which designated the venture—with the voyage planned for 1976—an official Bicentennial project.

From the very beginning, the voyage of the *Hōkūle'a* was seen as having a dual purpose: it would be the vehicle for experimental research into the seakeeping abilities of a vessel built along traditional lines, and, at the same time, it would encourage a revival of interest in the ancient history of the Hawaiian people. Finney, who was invested in the academic debate, was focused primarily on the experimental dimension, though he understood what the canoe could mean to Hawaiians. He noted that there was much more interest in such a project in the 1970s than when he had first begun to think about it in the late 1950s. In those early days, he wrote, interest in Hawaiian culture had been "minimal" even among Hawaiians, but there was a new feeling in the islands in the early seventies. Decolonization and indigenous rights movements were gaining strength around the world, including in Polynesia. Hawaiians who had only ever spoken English were starting to learn Hawaiian; the study of hula was on the rise; the University of Hawai'i formally recognized the discipline of Hawaiian studies; and activists were engaging in battles over particular pieces of land, most notably the Hawaiian island of Kaho'olawe, which had been used as a bombing range by the U.S. military in the aftermath of World War II.

Kāne, whose own return to Hawai'i from the Midwest was a reflection of this renaissance, was focused on *Hōkūle'a*'s symbolic potential. "The canoe was the center of the old culture—the heart of a culture that was still beating," he is quoted as saying, "and I thought that if we could rebuild that central artifact, bring it back to life and put it to hard use, this would send out ripples of energy." But even he was not prepared for the impact the canoe had on Hawaiians. In preparation for the voyage to Tahiti, *Hōkūleʻa* made a tour of the other Hawaiian islands. When they dropped anchor in Hōnaunau Bay, on the Big Island, so many people came out that Kāne said he thought "the island was going to tilt. You could not see a rock. It was all solid people. They weren't doing anything. They weren't waving. They were just sitting there looking at the canoe." It went on like that for days. "The faces would change but the crowd was still there. Wherever we went it was that way."

There was, however, a dark side to this magnetism, for it was impossible to celebrate the revitalization of Hawaiian culture without recognizing the forces that had brought it to its knees. One of the emotions stirred up by the Hawaiian Renaissance was anger aimed at those who seemed to represent the interests that had reduced Hawaiians to second- or third-class citizens in their own islands. A small but vocal faction of the Hawaiian community began to argue that the entire project should be reserved for Hawaiians only and that haoles should not be allowed to sail on *Hōkūleʻa* or have anything to do with it. "No one could foresee," recalls one of the early crew members, "how pride in the canoe, reviving pride, would turn into possessiveness." Gradually a rift began to form between the leaders of the project and some of the crew, who felt that, as *kanaka maoli* (true Hawaiians), they ought to be in charge. Finney was a prime target of resentment, not only as an outsider and a haole but, as one commentator later put it, as "a professor who seemed to embody a western scientific view of things—who saw the voyage as an 'experiment' of some kind, not the culminating dream of revival that some of the crew considered her to be."

The appointment of a Hawaiian captain, Kawika Kapahulehua, an experienced sailor from Niʻihau who spoke fluent Hawaiian, helped bridge the gap. But there was another crucial position that could not be filled by either a haole scientist or a Hawaiian, and that was the all-important role of navigator. The experimental goal was to reenact a traditional voyage as accurately as possible, and that meant not only replicating a traditional vessel but navigating by traditional means. Nowhere in Polynesia was there anyone who knew how to do this, and so Finney turned to David Lewis for advice. Lewis suggested that they look for a navigator in the Caroline Islands, and the man who ultimately agreed to assist them was a calm, self-possessed man in his forties from the island of Satawal, known as Pius Piailug.

Piailug, who went by the nickname Mau, was an expert canoe builder and the grandson of a famous navigator. He had grown up on a Micronesian atoll and learned everything he knew in the traditional way—listening to the "talk of the sea," watching his teachers, observing the ocean and the sky. To many of the Hawaiians, Mau seemed to embody the very essence of the old ways. "There was something about Mau. . . . He was not like a normal man—he knew things that no one else knew." As for Mau, he, too, recognized his role in the venture: "I made that trip," he said, "to show those people what their ancestors used to know."

ON MAY 1, 1976, *Hōkūle'a* set sail from the island of Maui. Just before their departure, Mau addressed the crew, telling them how to behave while they were at sea. "Before we leave," he told them, "throw away all the things that are worrying you. Leave all your problems on land." On the ocean, he said, "everything we do is different." At all times, the crew would be under the captain's command: "When he says eat, we eat. When he says drink, we drink." For three, maybe four weeks, they would be out of sight of land. "All we have to survive on are the things we bring with us. . . . Remember, all of you, these things," he concluded, "and we will see that place we are going to."

On board, in addition to Captain Kapahulehua and Mau, were Finney, whose job it was to document the voyage, and Lewis, who would make a record of Mau's navigation. Tommy Holmes sailed as a member of the crew, with the particular charge of looking after the animals—a pig, a dog, and "the proper moa" (a chicken)—along with a variety of roots, cuttings, and seedlings, wrapped in damp moss, matting, and tapa cloth to protect them from the sea. Accompanying the canoe in case of trouble, and to keep the detailed record of their position that would later be compared with Mau's daily estimates, was the sixty-four-foot ketch *Meotai*.

The primary navigational challenge was to keep the canoe far enough to the east as it made the long journey south. Hawaiʻi is more than 2,600 miles north of Tahiti, but it is also about 500 miles west. The winds along the route are predominantly from the east—northeast above the equator and southeast below it. Add to this a westward-setting current and the problem was clear. "Our strategy," wrote Finney, "was to sail as hard into the wind as the canoe would point without losing too much speed . . . and then to hold on to as much of that easting as possible." The main worry was that when they reached the latitude of Tahiti, they would find themselves too far west and would then have to beat back into the wind to reach their destination.

One of the biggest unknowns was whether Mau's navigational knowledge would be sufficient, given that the route was entirely unfamiliar to him. "A medieval Tahitian or Hawaiian navigator," wrote Lewis, "would have possessed information about the Hawaii–Tahiti seaway exactly comparable to Piailug's about his own and neighboring archipelagos." He would have known the star path, the winds and currents likely to be encountered, and the distance typically covered in a day's sail; he would be sailing, you might say, in his own neck of the woods. But Mau came from a completely different part of the Pacific, far to the west, where the sky and sea and weather patterns were all different, and his experience covered only some of the latitudes that would be traversed in the course of this journey. This last had significant implications for the navigation—the North Star, for instance, figures prominently in Carolinian navigation, but below the equator it can no longer be seen. Thus, once they crossed over to the Southern Hemisphere, Mau would lose an important celestial reference point. Part of Lewis's job had been to help Mau fill in the inevitable gaps in his geographic knowledge, and one of the ways they did this was by visiting the planetarium at the Bishop Museum. There, using the star projector, they simulated the way the night sky would change as the canoe traveled from the Northern to the Southern Hemisphere. "Once this background was filled in," wrote Lewis, Mau "laid down his strategy for the voyage—the *etak* (the Marquesas) and the star courses to be followed."

Leaving the Hawaiian Islands, Mau steered east-southeast toward the rising point of Antares, "a red giant of a star" in the constellation Scorpius, known to Polynesians as "the Fishhook of Maui." Finney watched Mau watching the sky and the sea, describing it as "a rare privilege" to see a master navigator at work. Gladwin, the anthropologist, had observed that Carolinian navigators remained continually alert during a voyage. "They say," he wrote, that "you can tell the experienced navigators by their bloodshot eyes." Mau, thought Finney, "looks the part," almost never sleeping, just catnapping from time to time. "Most of the time he stands leaning on the deck railing, or sits perched atop it, checking the sea, the sails and at night the stars."

Although some of those on board were experienced sailors— Mau, Kawika, Lewis, Finney—many of the crew were what are known in Hawai'i as "watermen," meaning surfers, paddlers, and lifeguards. They were good swimmers, strong and at home in the sea, but they had never crewed professionally or sailed long distances. Just six days out, one of them startled the relief captain by asking, "Hey, we almost there?" In fact, it would be more than three weeks before they saw land again. As the journey lengthened, this lack of experience began to show. Various minor crises— the discovery of water in a section of the hulls; problems with the food; issues over contraband like radios and marijuana; an argument over the setting of the sails—exposed defects in the chain of command and widened the rift that had opened before the voyage started. A long spell in the Doldrums with fitful, shifting winds and periods of glassy calm—the sea, as one recorder of the story put it, "smoothed to a vast skin of heaving mercury under a copper sun"—only aggravated the situation. One of the crew members became nearly catatonic, while others retreated into a sullen funk, refusing to stand watches and openly defying those in charge. Finney was aggravated by what he saw as a lack of discipline; Mau, though he said little, was worried about the rising tension on the canoe.

As they drew closer to their target, Lewis began to fear that they had been pushed too far west. But Mau seemed "calmly confident," and on the thirtieth day of the voyage he predicted that they would reach the Tuamotus the next day. Not long after this, a crew member spotted some white fairy terns. Then the regular trade-wind swell faltered. "An island lies out there," wrote Finney. "But which island? And how far away?" The next day, the *Hōkūle'a* made landfall on Mataiva, at the extreme northwestern edge of the Tuamotu Archipelago, less than two hundred miles north of Tahiti.

*Hōkūle'a* arrived in the Tahitian capital, Papeete, on the morning of June 4. Unbeknownst to the crew, who had been out of radio communication with the rest of the world, the Tahitians had been avidly following *Hōkūle'a's* progress, posting the canoe's daily position on charts tacked up around the city and broadcasting updates in newspapers and on radio and TV. The governor of French Polynesia had declared the day of their arrival a public holiday; schools and businesses were closed, and the harbor was filled with hundreds of paddling canoes, launches, and yachts. People had begun gathering at the harbor the previous night, and by the time the canoe arrived, wrote Finney, "they were everywhere, standing knee deep in the surf, surging over the reef, jammed along the shore, perched atop waterfront buildings and weighing down the limbs of shade trees lining the water's edge." More than seventeen thousand people—roughly a fifth of the island's population—had come to witness *Hōkūle'a's* arrival. On shore, there was cheering and the beating of drums, then, as the canoe approached, a silence fell over the crowd and a church choir lifted up its voice in a Tahitian hymn of welcome composed specially for the day. The effect, as thousands of singers joined in, was "spine-tingling," according to one eyewitness.

THE SUCCESS OF the voyage was a cultural triumph, the first time in hundreds and hundreds of years that a Polynesian voyaging canoe had made the journey between Hawai'i and the Society Islands. It was also an experimental success: Mau had navigated the canoe 2,600 miles along an unknown sea road; the vessel had performed admirably; even the plants and animals had done well. And yet, all was not as it should be. Shortly before their arrival in Tahiti, Mau had taken Finney aside and told him that he would not be navigating the canoe back to Hawai'i, as planned. He was unhappy with the behavior of the crew, and, not wanting to confront them directly, he recorded a message for them to listen to after he was gone. "When we leave from Maui," he told them, "I say, don't take your problems with you on the trip. Okay, when we leave from Maui, you don't leave the problem in the land. Everybody take the problem to the trip." The crew, Mau said, had been "very, very bad"; even though it would be a different crew for the return voyage, he was not confident that they would be any better. All he wanted at this point was to go home. "Now is last, last I'm see you, you see me," he said on the tape. "Don't ask me to come to Hawai'i ever again."

Mau's departure was an enormous blow; without him, there was no one to navigate the canoe. When *Hōkūle'a* set out for home a month later, it would have to be conventionally guided, using compass, sextant, and maps. There were other changes, too: although Captain Kapahulehua would remain in command, neither Finney nor Lewis would sail on the return trip. On the plus side, the return crew would include a couple of women. (This, too, had been a bone of contention, with some traditionalists arguing that women should not be allowed to sail in the canoe—though, as many pointed out, it was quite unclear how any of the islands would ever have been populated if a prohibition against carrying women had been the rule.)

Out of this breach emerged the person who would, in years to come, lead the Polynesian voyaging movement. His name was Nainoa Thompson, and, like many of those involved with *Hōkūleʻa*, he was a paddler and surfer with little experience on the open sea. He had, however, been present at the first launching of *Hōkūleʻa* and had watched the ritual celebrations, with their prayers and their blowing of conch shells and offerings of food. Nainoa later recalled that he had never heard anything like this before. "I could see what we were doing but I did not understand why we were doing it. . . . It was a brand new experience for me as a Hawaiian. These were ancient traditions that were not valued in modern Hawaiʻi. This was the rebirth of all that."

Nainoa, whose father was Hawaiian and whose mother was part haole, part Hawaiian, was a handsome, self-contained young man with "tremendous intensity." He was good at math and science and had a gift for spatial relations, but he was burdened by feelings of frustration that had to do, in part, with the social conditions of the 1960s and '70s. He was trying, as he later put it, "to understand my place in the larger society where Hawaiians were considered second-rate." The challenge of non-instrumental navigation strongly appealed to him, and on the voyage back from Tahiti, he began to pay attention to the swells and the stars.

Back in Honolulu, Nainoa continued to think about these problems, making himself a star compass big enough to sleep in and testing his navigational knowledge on short trips to sea. He followed Mau and Lewis's example and visited the Bishop Museum planetarium, where he made friends with a lecturer named Will Kyselka. Two or three times a week, he would go to the planetarium and study the night sky, making notes on the positions of the stars while Kyselka ran the projector. Nainoa's notebooks quickly began to fill up, but the true scope of the endeavor was only beginning to reveal itself. "The more I learn, the more I understand," he

had written on the way back from Tahiti, and "the more I understand, the more I know how complicated the heavens are."

IN 1978, THE Polynesian Voyaging Society decided to make a second
voyage to Tahiti. Finney had resigned after the 1976 trip, and this
time *Hōkūleʻa* would be captained, crewed, and guided entirely by
Native Hawaiians. Nainoa would serve as navigator (or wayfinder),
using only traditional techniques, but the canoe would also carry an
instrumental navigator, who would not reveal their position unless
it became necessary for the safety of the crew. In another departure
from the plan of the first voyage, the canoe would not be accompanied by an escort vessel. "We thought we could do without one," recalls Ben Young, then president of the Polynesian Voyaging Society,
"because *Hōkūleʻa* had made the voyage down and back without
any problems."

The departure was set for mid-March, but when the day came,
there was a gale of wind, with rain and whitecaps as far as the
eye could see. "It was blowing like shit," one witness remembered.
"Small craft warnings. The whole nine yards." Several people
thought that *Hōkūleʻa*, which was scheduled to depart after dark,
was overloaded. Finney, who had come down to watch the canoe
being readied for sea, was alarmed. "No escort boat, no Mau, overloaded, in heavy seas and at night," he later recalled. "And the rest
is history."

Around midnight, in winds of up to thirty knots, with ten-foot
swells, *Hōkūleʻa* capsized in the Molokaʻi Channel, about seventeen
miles from the island of Lanaʻi. Water had gotten into one of the
hulls, swamping it, which then cantilevered the other out of the sea.
"It just happened in seconds," remembered a crewman. "The whole
thing just kind of flipped over like a Hobie Cat." The crew managed
to scramble onto the overturned hulls, but, while there was no immediate danger of the canoe sinking, there was also no way to right
it. "We were sitting on the keel of the canoe," Nainoa remembers.
"Windy. Rough. . . . There wasn't much to do, just keep calm."

All through the night, the crew clung to the canoe, occasionally letting off flares, while they drifted farther and farther out of both shipping lanes and commercial flight paths. Around ten the next morning, a crewman named Eddie Aikau, a champion surfer and lifeguard, volunteered to go for help. Nainoa remembers feeling conflicted. "We're tired, we're somewhat in shock, we're in denial." But Eddie "was like a miracle man—he could do anything. . . . I remember grabbing his hand and holding his hand real tight . . . and he said, 'It'll be okay. Everything will be okay.'" Eddie set off on his surfboard, and all that day, the rest of the crew sat on the overturned hulls. None of the planes had seen them, nor had any of the ships that passed within sight. Back in Honolulu, it was assumed that they were observing radio silence, in keeping with the aim of doing things the old way. By nightfall, the crew knew they were in trouble.

Then, around 8:00 P.M., the pilot of a Hawaiian Airlines flight out of Kona just happened to look out his window and see a flash of light down on the water. Circling back to get a better look, he caught the flare of a vessel in distress. The crew knew they had been spotted when the plane turned toward them and blinked its lights. A few hours later, a Coast Guard helicopter arrived to scoop the cold and exhausted sailors out of the sea. But the question on everyone's mind was: *Where is Eddie?*

The loss of Eddie Aikau, whose body was never recovered, changed everyone associated with the Polynesian Voyaging Society. In the wake of the accident, the community was split: one camp felt that the whole project had become too dangerous, while the other believed that if they didn't continue, Eddie's sacrifice would be for naught. Eddie had told Nainoa, in the lead-up to the voyage, that he just wanted "to see Tahiti come out of the ocean," a reference to the mythic vision of pulling an island from the sea. After his death, this idea became a touchstone for Nainoa. "For me," he recalls, "there was no question as to whether we should continue voyaging or not—the question was *how* are we going to do it."

# REINVENTING NAVIGATION

## *Nainoa Thompson*

*Nainoa Thompson, 1989, photo by Ken Ige.*
HONOLULU STAR-BULLETIN ARCHIVES.

IN THE WAKE of Eddie Aikau's death, the man who took charge of the Polynesian Voyaging Society was Nainoa Thompson's father. A social worker and community leader, Myron "Pinky" Thompson knew that Hawaiians needed something to restore their cultural pride, and *Hōkūleʻa* had already demonstrated its capacity to inspire. If the canoe did not sail again, he argued, "if the canoe's legacy is tragedy, that will only confirm the expectation that Hawaiians always fail." Nainoa, meanwhile, redoubled his efforts, returning to the planetarium. There, he and Kyselka studied how the heavens would change as the canoe journeyed south, how the dome of the sky would rotate backward behind them—or, as Nainoa preferred to think of it, how the horizon in front of them would dip—while the stars' rising and setting times would shift a few minutes earlier each day as the earth rotated around the sun. They ran the projector back a thousand years to see what the sky had looked like when Hawai'i was first discovered by voyagers from the south. Then back another two thousand years to the sky as it had looked to the first settlers of Tonga and Samoa.

Three thousand years ago, when the Lapita people were making their way across the western Pacific, the night sky had been quite different from what it is now. Thanks to the slow wobble of the earth's axis, Polaris, now essentially stationary, had been rising and setting, while the Southern Cross, which today lies below the horizon for anyone north of Miami, was so high in the sky that someone in Alaska would have been able to see it. This means that star paths from these earlier periods would have been quite different from the paths that a navigator would use today, and that the corresponding navigational chants—even supposing they could have survived into the modern era—would have been of little use to modern navigators. This may help explain why star and constellation names cannot be traced back very far linguistically, nowhere near as far as, say, canoe parts or food names or fishing terminology. Not only is the sky local—that is, different in different places—but the stars themselves have moved.

Eventually, Nainoa realized that he could learn only so much in the planetarium. "Knowledge alone," wrote Kyselka, "is not wayfinding. How can you know the wind other than by sailing?" He needed an experienced wayfinder to teach him, and the only one he knew was Mau. Taking a gamble, Nainoa flew to Micronesia to ask Mau if he would come back to Honolulu and instruct him. At first Mau put him off, saying he would think it over, but a few months later he turned up in Hawai'i. "I will train you to find Tahiti," he told Nainoa, "because I don't want you to die."

This time the experience was different: Nainoa was the perfect apprentice, but, even more important, the feeling of the endeavor had changed. This was due largely to the leadership of the elder Thompson, who, while encouraging the crew and their supporters to think of the canoe as Hawaiian, was broadly inclusive. "You need to define your community," he told them, "and community is never about what separates you from each other—your race or your culture—it's about what binds you together." Mau could see that they were operating with a new set of values and that, as Nainoa put it, "there were no longer any racial issues among the crew."

In 1980, *Hōkūleʻa* set off again for Tahiti. Mau sailed on the canoe, but the navigation was entirely in Nainoa's hands. Only once during the voyage did Mau step in: at the very end of the voyage—thirty-one days out—when they were barely an hour's sail from their landfall in the Tuamotus. At the time, Nainoa knew they were close, but he was not sure precisely where the island was. The evening before, he had seen birds flying south, heading home for the night, which meant that the canoe was still north of where they wanted to be. The next morning, before dawn, it was all hands on deck, eyes peeled for the first sign of birds. But although they waited and waited, no birds appeared. "I was in near trauma," Nainoa writes, "my first voyage, in my early twenties." Mau, however, was perfectly calm.

At last, a solitary bird was spotted, once again flying south. Since it was now morning and time for birds to go out and fish, Nainoa interpreted this to mean that they had somehow drifted past the island in the night and that it was now behind them. In his panic, he told the crew to turn the canoe around, "to look for the island the bird was coming from. They turned the canoe around—and now we are sailing north, back toward Hawaiʻi." It was at this point that Mau stepped in. "Turn the canoe around and follow the bird," he said. Nainoa was completely puzzled. "I didn't know why. He didn't tell me why, but we turned the canoe around and now we saw other birds flying south. Mau said, 'You wait one hour and you will find an island.'" One hour later he stood up and said, "The island is right there."

"Vision," writes Nainoa, "is not so much about just looking, but knowing what to look for. It's experience. Mau had seen in the beak of the bird a little fish, and he knew that the birds were nesting, so they had flown out earlier that morning and were taking food back to their young before they fed themselves. He just did not tell me that in our training program."

IT WAS A stunning achievement. Without maps or charts or instruments or recording devices, without even paper and pen, an apprentice navigator—the first from Hawai'i in at least half a century—had piloted a canoe more than 2,500 miles, spanning more than thirty-five degrees of latitude, and made landfall on an atoll in the Tuamotus. Mau, who had been the first to accomplish this, had done it on the strength of more than thirty years' experience as a navigator. Nainoa—to an extent that is remarkable in hindsight—was not quite making it up, but not quite navigating in the traditional manner, either. He was weaving together the strands of two very different traditions, combining everything he had learned from school and books and the planetarium with everything he had learned from Mau about looking at the horizon, feeling the wind and waves, and observing the physical world.

Finney had written in some frustration in the 1970s that it had been "naïve" to think that the goals of "scientific research and cultural revival could be easily combined," and there was always tension around the notion that the Polynesian Voyaging Society embodied two seemingly conflicting ways of looking at the world. But, in fact, almost everything about *Hōkūle'a* had been syncretic from the start. The canoe itself was based on traditional designs that had been recorded in the seventeenth and eighteenth centuries by European observers, interpreted by the Chicago Art Institute–trained Hawaiian artist Herb Kāne, and constructed with modern materials like fiberglass and plywood. The chants and ceremonies surrounding the voyages were a blend of contemporary Hawaiian cultural practices, ceremonies from other parts of Polynesia, and traditional sources recorded in the nineteenth century by men like Abraham Fornander and S. Percy Smith. But the most thrilling example of fusion was the navigational method pioneered by Nainoa and subsequently taught

to navigators all across the Pacific: a mix of Mau's Carolinian knowledge, modern astronomical information, and innovations that the
young Hawaiian had arrived at on his own.

The star compass Nainoa employed was based on that used by
navigators on Satawal—except that it was geometric, with thirty-
two evenly divided segments oriented on the cardinal points. (The
Carolinian compass has irregular segments oriented on the rising
and setting points of important stars.) The names he used for stars,
directions, and constellations were a combination of traditional Hawaiian terms, names of his own devising, and terms used by Western astronomers (which are themselves derived from a mixture of
Arabic, Latin, and Greek). Some of Mau's methods proved impossible for him; he, not surprisingly, found *etak* "a difficult concept,"
and maintained his orientation over the length of the voyage in
relation to a predetermined "reference course" instead. He relied
heavily on bird signs for landfinding and, by his own admission,
found it challenging to learn how to read swells. But his long hours
in the planetarium paid off in the discovery of a new technique for
determining latitude using the rising and setting times of particular pairs of stars.

Nainoa has often remarked that in the beginning he relied more
on geometry and analytic mathematics because he didn't know
how to navigate the way Mau did. It was not just that he lacked
Mau's vast store of experiential knowledge, but that he had been
raised to think in a different way. Both Nainoa and Lewis described
being struck by the differences between the way they were accustomed to thinking about geographic problems and the way traditional navigators saw them. To illustrate this, Lewis described a
conversation he had with the Carolinian navigator Hipour. Lewis
was trying to establish the location of an island known as Ngatik.
No maps or charts of the area existed, and no one from Hipour's
island had been to Ngatik in generations. But because it was used
as an *etak* reference island, its star bearings were known. Using this
information, Lewis drew a diagram "to illustrate that Ngatik must

necessarily lie where these *etak* bearings intersected." Hipour, he wrote, "could not grasp this idea at all. His concept was the wholly dynamic one of moving islands, and possibly this is why he several times asked me how islands got onto charts."

It has been observed that Lewis's framing of this question involved certain assumptions about "the relation of the problem solver to the space in which the problem is being solved." The diagram Lewis drew for Hipour takes a bird's-eye view of the situation, a point of view that is actually impossible to achieve unless you are up in the sky looking down. Nevertheless, it is the point of view that Western navigators are most accustomed to—so much so that, as Lewis reminded us, "it is easy for us to forget . . . how much of an abstraction a chart really is." The Carolinian navigational system is also quite abstract—*etak* is, after all, an abstraction of "a rather high order"—but it is constructed around a different point of view. The Carolinian navigator's perspective is "egocentric," that is, it occupies a "real point of view on the real local space" and envisions everything else—stars, islands, reference objects—only as it exists in relation to the viewer. Thus, "the star bearings of the *etak* island radiate out from the navigator himself" and cannot be triangulated to give the location of the island, because the only place they ever meet is him.

This may seem like an odd way of thinking about geography. But one could argue that the "egocentric" point of view is actually the default perspective even in societies where map use is common. There is an intriguing experiment in which a group of New Yorkers were asked to describe the layouts of their apartments. Their accounts fell into one of two categories, described by the researchers as the "map" and the "tour." In a map account, the apartment dweller might describe his or her apartment like this: "The kitchen is next to the dining room and across the hall from the coat closet." In a tour account, by contrast, he or she might say something like "You come into the hall and turn left into the living room." The vast majority of the New Yorkers surveyed described their apartments in tour terms; only a minuscule 3 percent described them in terms of a map.

Tour thinking is sometimes understood to differ from map thinking in the same way that orality differs from literacy. And one can see how features of non-instrumental navigation overlap with other systems for managing knowledge in an oral culture: the first-person perspective, the emphasis on experience, the encoding of information in narrative form. Mau, who came from an essentially oral culture, had learned much of his technical knowledge—star paths, bearings, names of swells—in the form of oral narratives, and sometimes, when he wanted to recall something specific, he would chant to himself "to 'revisit information.'"

A number of traditional chants of the type used by Carolinian navigators—narratives with names like "Catching the Sea Bass," "Aligning the Weir," "The Lashing of the Breadfruit Picker"— have been recorded. These chants are presented as stories, but their primary function is to arrange large volumes of navigational information into "manageable inventories of knowledge." A typical example, called "Reef Hole Probing," describes the movements of a parrotfish that lives in a hole in the reef on a particular island. When a stick is stuck into the hole, the fish is frightened and escapes to the next island, where it hides in a new reef hole. Again comes the stick, and again the fish flees to the next island, and so it goes, all the way around the chain, until finally the fish returns to the first island, where it is caught. Each time the fish swims away, it does so "under the appropriate star bearing for the next island," and in this way the chant—a quite explicit "tour"—provides the navigator with the directions he needs to travel throughout the archipelago.

To those in Hawai'i, Mau's wayfinding ability—his infallible sense of direction, his ability to predict weather, his vast storehouse of general knowledge about the sky and the sea—seemed almost uncanny. Some tried to explain it by invoking a spiritual dimension; others suggested that Mau might have some kind of sixth sense. But the term most frequently employed was "intuition," an inscrutable form of knowing that does not rely on evidence or reason.

Almost from the beginning, Nainoa had concluded that his success as a navigator was contingent upon developing this sense of intuition. He tells an interesting story about a night on his maiden voyage as a navigator, in 1980. The canoe was in the doldrums, the sky was pitch black, it was pouring, and a twenty-five-knot wind was coming first from one direction and then another. The crew were looking to him for direction, but Nainoa was exhausted and had lost any clear sense of which way to go. Then, "I suddenly felt this warmth come over me," he writes. "The sky was so black, I couldn't see the moon, but I could feel where it was. . . . I directed the canoe on a new course and then, just for a moment, there was a hole in the clouds and the light of the moon shone through—just where I expected it to be."

Nainoa describes this as the moment when he realized he could tap into something "beyond the analytical, beyond seeing with my eyes," something he could not explain "from a scientific point of view." One might demystify this as an example of "skill in guessing well"—which is another way of thinking about intuition—but for Nainoa it was more like *knowing in a different way*. He cites the Hawaiian term *na'au*, which means, literally, "entrails" or "gut" and refers to the part of the body that, in some Polynesian traditions, is viewed as the "immediate organ of sensation" and the place "where all impressions are first received." For Nainoa, the idea that he was reaching a more intuitive level of understanding about the physical world—that he was thinking not just with his conscious mind but with his body, in some sense *feeling* his way across the ocean—was a sign that he was coming closer to navigating in "the ancient way."

BRINGING THESE TWO ways of knowing together turned out to be, as Finney put it years later, "more rewarding than we had ever dreamed." Over the next few decades, *Hōkūle'a* would go on to make a series of spectacular voyages, beginning, in the mid-1980s, with a two-year "Voyage of Rediscovery," sailing the length and breadth of Polynesia, from Hawai'i to Tahiti and the Cook Islands, then on to Aotearoa (New Zealand), Tonga, and Samoa. It then sailed what has long been considered one of the most perplexing of the ancient sea routes: eastward against the trades from Samoa to Tahiti. (The solution, it turned out, was just as Tupaia had described it to Cook: wait for the west wind, which did, in fact, occasionally blow.)

Everywhere the canoe went, it was met by crowds of enraptured islanders, inspiring so much enthusiasm throughout the Pacific that by the mid-1990s, seven more voyaging canoes had been built—in Hawai'i, Tahiti, the Cook Islands, and Aotearoa—and enough navigators trained to marshal a pan-Polynesian fleet, which sailed en masse from the Marquesas to Hawai'i in 1995. In 1999, *Hōkūle'a* closed the triangle by making the difficult passage to Rapa Nui (Easter Island). This was followed by voyages in 2007 to Micronesia and Japan and, finally, in 2013–2017, the ultimate challenge: the *Mālama Honua* voyage around the world. Although the arrival of European shipping in the eighteenth and nineteenth centuries had put an end to the isolation of many Polynesian societies, the voyages of *Hōkūle'a* reunited them in a different way. As one woman put it when the canoe finally reached Rapa Nui: "You have not closed the triangle, you have opened it for us!"

On the research front, too, it almost seemed as though the quest had been concluded—here it was, the end of the story: *They did it after all!* In fact, the voyages of *Hōkūle'a* did not—indeed, could not—prove anything about what had actually happened in the distant past. What they did prove was the robustness of noninstrumental navigation as a method and the feasibility of voyaging in general. They demonstrated—conclusively—that a trained and capable navigator, using nothing but the stars, winds, and swells, could hold a course, calculate the distance traveled, hit a small target with sufficient accuracy, and incorporate all the necessary information into a mental construct that was both flexible enough to allow for adaptation and systematic enough to be passed on. Initially framed as a response to skeptics like Andrew Sharp, the experimental voyaging movement quashed any lingering suspicions about the technical abilities of prehistoric navigators— whether they had been capable of traversing the long seaways of the Pacific; whether they could sail against the prevailing winds; whether, having ventured out into the unknown, they could return to their home islands. If Sharp had "demoted" Polynesians from seafarers to castaways, the Polynesian Voyaging Society re-elevated them to navigators and explorers.

# Part VI

## WHAT WE KNOW NOW

## (1990–2018)

*In which we review some of the latest scientific findings and think about what it takes to answer big questions about the deep past.*

# THE LATEST SCIENCE
## *DNA and Dates*

*Excavations by the Canterbury Museum Archaeological Group
at Wairau Bar, New Zealand, 1964.*
PHOTO BY DON MILLAR, COURTESY SANDY MILLAR.

**THE ERA OF** experimental voyaging left everyone with a clear sense
of the plausibility of long-distance prehistoric travel in the Pacific,
showing persuasively *how* it could have been done. But it added
nothing to the eternal debates about *who* (in the sense of ancestry) the first voyagers were or *when* any of this happened. There
were other issues, too, that remained unsettled: How large or small
were the original colonizing populations? In what order were the
islands settled? Did Polynesians in fact make it to South America?
These were all questions that had been asked before, but during
the last decades of the twentieth century, advances in two areas in
particular—genetics and radiocarbon dating—promised progress
on several of these fronts.

When it comes to the question of *who* Polynesians are—that is, who they are in terms of large global populations—the issue had ultimately boiled down to the question of whether their strongest affinities were with Asian or Melanesian populations, the idea of their being closely related to Native American populations having been largely rejected. The problem, as anthropologists saw it, could be articulated in terms of competing migration theories. One theory, popularly known as the "express train to Polynesia" (a phrase coined by the well-known biologist and geographer Jared Diamond), or sometimes "out of Taiwan," argued that the precursors of the Polynesians had originated in the islands of Southeast Asia and had swept through Melanesia, carrying all their cultural belongings—their foods and plants and language and customs—with them on their way to the remote Pacific.

This, however, did not seem all that plausible to some, including the anthropologist John Terrell, who proposed an alternative known as the "entangled bank." Terrell argued that the express train model did not reflect the way human history actually plays out. Borrowing Darwin's image of "an entangled bank, clothed with many plants of many kinds, with birds singing on the bushes, with various insects flitting about, and with worms crawling through the damp earth," he argued that the settlement history of Remote Oceania, like other large-scale human movements, was "an interlocking, expanding, sometimes contracting and ever-changing" set of interactions, a chaos of "interdependence and complexity."

From a biological standpoint, these two theories implied quite different genetic inheritances. In the express train model, the Austronesian people who ultimately became Polynesians sped through the intermediate region of Melanesia so fast that there was no genetic mixing. The entangled bank model, on the other hand, considered these two populations—the migrating Austronesians and the local Melanesians—so thoroughly intertwined that they were hard to tell apart, and envisioned the Polynesians as having emerged out of this tangle of cultures and peoples. At its heart, this was essentially the same problem that had vexed somatologists like Louis R.

Sullivan and Te Rangi Hiroa in the 1920s and '30s: How much of a connection was there between Polynesians and Melanesians? Were they entirely distinct groups? Or were they more like cousins? And how significant was the Asian/Austronesian component? The hope was, of course, that with the sequencing of the human genome, the matter would be settled once and for all.

THE FIRST RESEARCH into Polynesian genetics involved variations in mitochondrial DNA, a unique kind of DNA inherited exclusively from the maternal line. By the early 1990s it had become clear that virtually all Polynesians carry a distinctive combination of mitochondrial DNA mutations known as the "Polynesian motif," which can be traced back to the islands of Indonesia and the Philippines. This discovery lent credence to the express train model, but just a few years later it was contradicted by researchers using a different genetic method.

If mitochondrial DNA is inherited exclusively from the mother, Y chromosomes, which are found only in males, are indicative of descent through the paternal line. Unlike Polynesian mitochondrial DNA, Polynesian Y chromosomes did not suggest an "out of Asia" story but instead pointed to an ancestral source inside Melanesia. (An earlier study from the 1980s had also found evidence for Melanesian input into Polynesian genes in the form of a mutation associated with malaria resistance. This mutation, which crops up with surprisingly high frequency among Polynesians, was unexpected, because Polynesia is not a malarial region. Melanesia, however, is.)

These conflicting results prompted researchers to propose yet a third migration model, sometimes known as the "slow boat." According to this model, the ancestors of the Polynesians had originated in Asia, but instead of shooting through on their way to Remote Oceania, they had dawdled, "leaving behind their genes and incorporating many Melanesian genes," before moving on to the wider Pacific. Incidentally, it is not immediately obvious why there should be this discrepancy between the maternal and paternal inheritances of Polynesians. But one possibility is that migrating Austronesian populations may have tolerated the incorporation of outsider males while keeping females within the community, a pattern that was also seen during the colonial period.

These early genetic studies were based on the DNA of living Polynesians, but it is important to recognize that the genes of modern populations may not tell us everything we want to know about people in the past. Over the course of many hundreds of years, Polynesians have undergone a number of genetic bottlenecks, periods when the population was suddenly and dramatically reduced. This would have happened any time a small group of people set off from one island to colonize another; it might have happened as a result of natural disasters; it definitely happened in the colonial era in places like the Marquesas, where the population crashed. As a result, the full genetic diversity of the original colonists may no longer be represented in the DNA of people now living, some strands of their genetic history having been lost along the way.

One solution to this problem is to look directly at the genes of ancient Polynesians. But this has been difficult to do in the Pacific for a variety of reasons, not least of which is that the warm, wet tropics are a bad environment for the preservation of ancient DNA. Sites containing suitable genetic material are few and far between, which is why the discovery, in 2003, of the oldest cemetery in the Pacific was such a big deal. The site, known as Teouma, was accidentally discovered by a bulldozer driver who was quarrying soil for a prawn farm in an abandoned coconut plantation on the island of Éfaté, in Vanuatu. What he saw, sticking out of the ground, was not a bone but a large piece of decorated pottery, which he passed along to a friend who had worked for the Vanuatu Cultural Centre and who immediately recognized it for what it was. Thus, Teouma revealed itself as not only one of the great repositories of Lapita ceramics—flat-bottomed dishes, cylinder stands, and large, elegantly shaped vessels—but a burial ground containing nearly seventy inhumations.

Of course, what everyone wanted to know was what the DNA of these ancient skeletons could tell us, and the results, when they finally appeared, were somewhat surprising. The first ancient DNA results from Teouma showed that all three of the individuals tested—all women—carried the "Polynesian motif" and were genetically similar to indigenous populations from the Philippines and Taiwan. But they also showed that these early Lapita people had essentially no Melanesian ancestry. What this seemed to suggest was that the Polynesians had acquired their Melanesian inheritance at some later point. But where and when and how remains unknown.

STUDYING HUMAN DNA can be difficult, for reasons that are not purely technical. The history of biological research on indigenous communities is not a particularly happy one, and many of these communities have expressed skepticism about DNA research, feeling that they have been treated as "specimens" for quite long enough, and doubting whether any of the benefits of such work would ever flow back to them. Also, in many parts of Polynesia, there is a high degree of cultural sensitivity surrounding anything having to do with ancestors and the dead. One place where this has all come together fairly dramatically is the so-called moa-hunter site at Wairau Bar.

Much of the archaeological material uncovered by Jim Eyles and Roger Duff at Wairau Bar in the 1940s and '50s, including moa eggs, adzes, ornaments, and *kōiwi tangata*, or human remains, was handed over to the Canterbury Museum for "security and long-term preservation" by the site's owners and lease holders at the time. Duff claimed to have had the cooperation of the local Māori tribe, Rangitāne o Wairau, but over time Rangitāne came to resent the disturbance of their *tūpuna*, or ancestors, and the removal of *taonga*, or treasures. And in the late 1960s they embargoed the site, denying all further requests for excavations.

This meant that all through the 1970s, '80s, and '90s—a period of significant scientific advances in both genetics and radiocarbon dating—the evidence of Wairau Bar was essentially off-limits. Then, in 2008, the Rangitāne tribal authority made a deal with the University of Otago and the Canterbury Museum. In keeping with a worldwide trend toward the repatriation of artifacts, art objects, and especially human remains, the museum would return the *kōiwi tangata* (though not the ornaments or the tools). In exchange, Rangitāne would permit a full biological assessment of the skeletal material and the removal of small samples of bone and teeth for DNA analysis before the remains were formally reinterred. Rangitāne would recover their *tūpuna* and lay them to rest, and the anthropologists would get a new opportunity to see what could be discovered.

One finding that pleased local members of the Rangitāne tribe was the discovery that several of them shared a direct genetic link with some of the *kōiwi tangata*, including a seven-hundred-year-old woman known as "Aunty." But another interesting revelation was that the people buried at Wairau Bar—still the oldest site ever discovered in New Zealand—were much more genetically diverse than anyone had imagined. This, in turn, suggested that New Zealand's founding population was larger than expected—not just a few canoeloads of closely related families but perhaps hundreds of unrelated immigrants—and that the source populations in Tahiti and the Cook Islands were also large and genetically diverse. After a century of steadily shrinking expectations—the presumption of fewer and fewer voyages, smaller and smaller founding populations, more and more isolation, less and less interaction—this pushed the story back in the direction of the "heroic" narratives of the nineteenth century, with their frequent return voyages and their colonizing fleets.

THERE IS A clever alternative to working with human DNA, however, that obviates many of these problems. Pioneered by a University of Otago anthropologist named Elizabeth Matisoo-Smith, it involves looking at the genes of what are known as "commensal" animals, that is, animals that travel in company with humans and whose history of movement can be used as a proxy for the movement of their human hosts. Polynesians brought an assortment of such creatures with them when they sailed into the Pacific, including pigs, dogs, chickens, and rats. Of these, the ideal animal for study turns out to be *Rattus exulans*, the "wandering" Pacific rat.

*Rattus exulans* cannot get to islands except in the company of humans. It does not interbreed with the rats introduced to the Pacific by Europeans—*Rattus rattus*, the black rat, and *Rattus norvegicus*, the Norwegian. And since it dislikes wet places, it is thought unlikely to have traveled in the holds of European ships. Taken together, what this means is that the Pacific rats living on the islands today are very likely the direct descendants of rats that were brought by the first Polynesian voyagers. Best of all, there are plenty of rat bones in Polynesian archaeological sites, and no one minds if you dig them up or destroy them to extract their DNA.

Studies of rat DNA confirm that the Societies, the Australs, and the Cooks were a "general homeland region" for the islanders of the central and eastern Pacific—the Hawaiki from which the Māori, Marquesans, Rapa Nui, and Hawaiians set out on the final legs of their great journeys. They also show that rats in New Zealand were—like the *kōiwi tangata* from Wairau Bar—surprisingly genetically diverse, meaning that they were likely to have been introduced multiple times, by lots of different canoes carrying lots of different rat populations. On Easter Island, however, the rat story is quite different. Easter Island rats show so little genetic variation that they might have been introduced to the island just once—perhaps even by a single canoeload of people who then became effectively marooned.

So far, genetics has in some cases confirmed what we thought we already knew; in others it has begun to alter narratives that had seemed settled. But we are just at the very dawn of these discoveries, and the one thing that seems irrefutable at this point is the enormous potential of this research. As one DNA researcher recently put it, "It's like turning on an electric light in a dark cave where before there were only small wavering candles."

THE OTHER AREA that has attracted quite a bit of attention in recent years is the question of *when* the islands of Remote Oceania were first settled. When radiocarbon dating was first developed, in the late 1940s and '50s, it was a spectacular breakthrough: the first objective, verifiable means of establishing chronologies for periods of human history for which there was no written record. But, as with any technology, there was room for improvement, and significant technological advances have been made in the decades since. It is now possible to date something as small as an individual seed, which means that the process is much less destructive. The new methods are also increasingly precise, with error ranges a mere fraction of what they once were, and there is a much better understanding of the potential sources of error. All these improvements—but particularly the last—have led to a major shift in thinking about when the islands of Polynesia were first settled.

Back in the 1950s, when the first radiocarbon results were coming in from Polynesia, a number of very early dates were obtained for archipelagoes in the central and eastern Pacific. These included Suggs's tantalizing date of 150 B.C. from charcoal in a Marquesan hearth and Emory's A.D. 124 from a dune on the Big Island of Hawai'i. Early dates are inherently exciting—lighting up the dimmest recesses of the past—and these findings were doubly significant, representing, as they did, the first scientific answers to the question of when human beings had first colonized the remote Pacific. Together with a cluster of later dates, they formed the basis of an orthodox chronology that went something like this: the arrival of the Lapita people in the Tonga/Samoa region, around 1000 B.C., followed by a roughly one-thousand-year pause, and the gradual expansion into the Polynesian Triangle in the first few centuries A.D. It was a narrative that seemed to make sense, allowing plenty of time for Polynesian culture to "set" in the Samoa/Tonga region—

that is, for the Lapita people to become Polynesians—as well as sufficient time for the Polynesians to explore the widest, emptiest, and most navigationally challenging reaches of the Pacific Ocean.

But then, in the early 1990s, a group of revisionist archaeologists began to question this timeline. By this point, a large number of radiocarbon dates from Polynesia had accumulated, but they had been produced under widely varying conditions—at different times and in different places, by different researchers using different standards and employing different laboratories, which also used different protocols. The moment had come, these archaeologists argued, to reassess this corpus of dates, "to weed out" those that could not be relied upon, and "to build a secure chronology with those that remain." They referred to this plan, with dry archaeological humor, as a program of "chronometric hygiene."

They began by suggesting that all the radiocarbon dates from the 1950s and '60s should be treated with "considerable caution." They rejected any date for fish, human, or animal bone, sea urchin spines, land snails, freshwater shells, and anything else that could be "grossly affected by the uptake of old carbon." They rejected dates based on charcoal from long-lived species of trees, as well as all the early run dates from the Gakushuin University radiocarbon laboratory in Japan (on the grounds that they were weirdly inconsistent, both too early and too late). They rejected samples made up of more than one substance, like charcoal and burnt earth, or sugarcane, ti tree, and reeds; as well as samples without any clear cultural context, such as random chunks of charcoal not associated with any human activity. They also tossed out dates that did not overlap at two standard deviations with other dates from the same context; stratigraphically inverted dates; and dates that were anomalous in some other way.

It was a lot to get rid of, and many of the dates on which the orthodox chronology had been built were summarily swept away. Of the one hundred nine Hawaiian dates, only twenty-one were thought good enough to keep; from the Marquesas and Easter

Island, just ten from a total of twenty-three survived. Out went
Suggs's groundbreaking early dates from the Marquesas; out went
Duff's dates from Wairau Bar; out went Emory's early dates from
Hawai'i; out went Heyerdahl's Easter Island dates. When they surveyed what was left, the story looked quite different. The Lapita
people were still envisioned as having reached Samoa and Tonga
in the neighborhood of 900 B.C., but the initial settlement of central
and eastern Polynesia had moved much closer to the present. According to the new orthodoxy, none of the archipelagoes of central
and eastern Polynesia (the Society Islands, Hawai'i, the Marquesas,
Easter Island, the Cooks) is thought to have been settled before the
*end* of the first millennium A.D., while the discovery and settlement
of New Zealand was pushed as far forward as A.D. 1200.

The implication of these much later dates is curious. Coming
hard on the heels of the lightning-fast Lapita expansion, the long
pause in Tonga/Samoa now seems even more mysterious. Having
reached so far out into the Pacific, what kept them sitting there
for nearly two thousand years? While it is certainly true that the
ocean gets emptier east of Samoa, the voyages they had already
made were far from trivial. Clearly, they had the technology; what
they do not seem to have had is the desire or the need. And then,
as though they had been suddenly pricked into action, what made
them set out and conquer the ten million square miles of the Polynesian Triangle? And how did they do that in just a few hundred
years?

There have been some intriguing attempts to explain this new
timeline in terms of climatic variation—changes in weather that
might have enabled or impeded voyaging during different spans
of time. One computer simulation investigates the role that the El
Niño/Southern Oscillation might have played in Polynesian voyaging: warmer El Niño conditions reduce precipitation in the western
Pacific, making it easier to travel eastward (say, from Samoa to Tahiti), while cooler La Niña years favor movement from the central

Pacific southwest toward New Zealand. A second study suggests that there may have been "climate windows," lasting a century or more, during which the weather in the Pacific shifted in such a way as to facilitate sailing over certain notoriously difficult routes.

Another implication of this shorter chronology is that much less time must have elapsed between the Polynesian discovery of some of these islands and the arrival of the first European eyewitnesses—in the case of New Zealand, perhaps as little as four hundred years. But is this long enough to fully populate the islands, alter their landscapes (in some cases dramatically), extirpate a wide variety of creatures, adapt horticultural practices to local conditions (drought-prone Easter Island, chilly New Zealand), develop a distinct range of customs and languages, give up long-distance voyaging, lose geographic knowledge, and become the homebodies they appeared to be when the Europeans first arrived? One does not *feel*, reading the accounts of the early European explorers, as though the people they discovered in the islands of Polynesia had only just gotten there. But the math can be made to work: a founding population of 250 people (say, five canoes) with a growth rate of 1.5 percent per year would reach a population of nearly 100,000 in four hundred years.

But perhaps the single most interesting thing about the new orthodoxy is the way it appears to corroborate the chronologies extracted from Polynesian oral traditions. Both Abraham Fornander and S. Percy Smith developed timelines for the settlement of Oceania based on Polynesian genealogies recorded in the nineteenth century. Both describe a two-step settlement scenario, with a vague and poorly substantiated early discovery phase followed by a well-defined period of colonization around the end of the first millennium A.D. Fornander specifically noted an efflorescence of tales about "bold expeditions, stirring adventures, and voyages undertaken to far-off lands," from which he deduced an era of "national unrest" and "tribal commotion" right around the year 1000. Smith similarly proposed a muddled early settlement phase for New Zealand, but his dates for the arrival of the first named Māori ancestors were 1150 and 1350, exactly straddling the date proposed for the settlement of New Zealand in the cleaned-up radiocarbon chronology. Thus, you might say, the new science, having displaced the old science, agrees surprisingly well with the pre-science.

# CODA

## *Two Ways of Knowing*

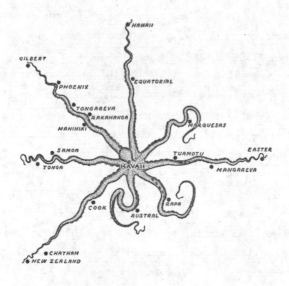

*Map of Polynesia, in* Vikings of the Sunrise
*by Peter H. Buck (Christchurch, 1954).*
COURTESY WHITCOULLS CO., AUCKLAND, NEW ZEALAND.

SHOULD WE BE surprised that the latest science brings us closer to
the oral history of the Polynesians? It has been about a hundred
years since these chants and tales were last taken as seriously by
Europeans as they were by Polynesians themselves. For most of the
twentieth century, they were largely dismissed by scholars, who
were inclined to view Polynesian traditions as "mythical fictions
composed for just about any purpose *other* than memorializing actual events." They were seen as literature or religion or political
tracts, as metaphors or symbols or allegories, but never simply as
documentary accounts.

In part, this was the consequence of a general pivot toward science in the twentieth century: a semi-repudiation of the nineteenth century's romantic tendencies and a gravitation to the provable and quantifiable, toward numbers and calculations. But it also had something to do with the way the traditions—and the world they represented—were receding in time. Nineteenth-century Europeans, for all their foibles, had been close to this material and to the people who created it. But after about the 1930s, one can feel this knowledge, this intimacy, slipping away. The hard turn toward skepticism—regarding both the usefulness of the traditions and the voyaging capacity of the Polynesians themselves—that we see in the 1950s and '60s is a measure of this drift.

The prestige of Polynesia's oral traditions as sources for history was further eroded in the 1970s by studies that showed just how much editing and shaping these narratives had undergone and raised new questions about their authenticity. And the situation was only aggravated by postmodernists who claimed that, since people were always inventing their own histories, there was really no such thing as an authentic tradition anyway—an argument that was deeply resented by many indigenous scholars.

The success of the experimental voyaging movement, however, provided a powerful counterbalance to these trends. At a practical level, the voyages of *Hōkūleʻa* and the other canoes validated traditional Polynesian and Micronesian bodies of knowledge and approaches to problem-solving. And, while they did not prove that Kupe or Moʻikeha or Hotu Matua or any other legendary figure had actually sailed the sea roads of the Pacific, they strongly supported the idea that, as Finney put it, the traditions "could actually reflect an era when Polynesian mariners did sail back and forth."

The past few years have seen a resurgence of interest in Polynesian myths—witness the popularity of Disney's *Moana*—which can also be traced pretty much directly to the success of the experimental voyaging movement. But even among scientists the tide has turned, and it is now common for even the most abstruse academic papers on, say, the geochemical sourcing of lithic artifacts by X-ray fluorescence to reference some piece of traditional lore. Whether or not such gestures are always meaningful at a literal level, their symbolism is important, suggesting as it does the possibility of convergence between quite different ways of thinking not just about *what* but about *how* we know.

The problem of Polynesian origins has never been an easy one to solve, and there are questions remaining. For instance, it is unlikely that we will ever know how some of the remotest archipelagoes were initially discovered or how many canoes were lost in the course of this long and arduous colonizing process. To the extent that this history has been disentangled, however, it has been thanks to input of radically different kinds. At one end of the spectrum are the mathematical models: the computer simulations, chemical analyses, statistical inferences—science with all its promise of objectivity and its periodic lapses into error. At the other, the stories and songs passed from memory to memory: the layered, subtle, difficult oral traditions, endlessly open to interpretation but unique in their capacity to speak to us, more or less directly, out of a precontact Polynesian past.

These two angles of inquiry are in many ways opposed, and for much of the past two centuries the debate has oscillated between them, as first one and then the other was held up as the avenue to truth. In fact, both have been crucial to the unfolding of a credible history of the Polynesian migrations, as have the bold experiments in voyaging that bookend this story: the sixteenth-, seventeenth-, and eighteenth-century explorers whose accounts give us a glimpse of Polynesia as it was, and the twentieth-century experimental voyagers who set out to rediscover what the very first explorers of the great ocean must have known.

In short, it has taken all different kinds of people using all different kinds of tools, and even then the way has been rife with misdirection and dead ends. Some of the best ideas were had way back at the beginning (Cook's early insight about the Asian origin of

the Polynesians), while some of the worst looked great at the time
(the notion that Polynesians had Indo-European roots). This should
remind us how easy it is to get the wrong end of the stick, and how
hard it can be, in the moment, to tell the right end from the wrong.
But, looking back on three centuries of inquiry, it is interesting to
note that many of the most compelling insights have arrived at
moments of convergence, when two different ways of looking at a
problem—practical and abstract, ancient and modern, humanistic
and scientific, European and Polynesian—intertwine.

I have always loved the image of Tupaia in the great cabin of
the *Endeavour* with Captain Cook (however much they were said
to have gotten on each other's nerves; both haughty men, accustomed to power—how could it have been any other way?). I like
to think of them standing there at the table, with the charts and
maps spread out before them, trying to find some common navigational ground. Or Abraham Fornander, up late at night in the
port of Lahaina, poring over his Hawaiian texts, dreaming up
wildly improbable solutions—*the key to all mythologies!*—while
his half-Hawaiian daughter slept nearby. Or the physician-sailor
David Lewis, hunkered down on the deck of his yacht, studying the
navigator Tevake, trying to see the swells, the birds, the loom of an
island through the other man's eyes. Or, to take what may be the
paramount example, Te Rangi Hiroa, who *embodied* the problem of
divergent perspectives and who, while he often spoke about being
a "blend" of two cultures, tended to describe his experience not as
a fusion or synthesis but as an oscillation between two contrasting,
even irreconcilable, points of view. What he had, as he once put it,
was the ability to "detach" himself from one side or the other—to
be Māori or to be European, but never exactly to be both. When, in
truth, both is exactly what he was.

IT HAS BEEN fashionable in recent decades to say that the "problem
of Polynesian origins" was always a European quest, "an ongoing
vehicle for investigating the European past, present and future,"

and that the question was never so much "Where did they come from?" as "What does their existence imply for us?" And there is certainly some truth to this. We can never escape the fact that this inquiry has unfolded within the colonial period, or that it involves questions that could only ever have been asked by people who came to the Pacific from someplace else. Questions about who Polynesians are would never have been asked by Polynesians themselves in the days before outsiders arrived in the Pacific. Queries about origins would have been answered by myths—*We are the people from Te Pō, from Te Tumu, from Taʻaroa; we come from Hawaiki*—and there would have been no point of view from which to ask, *What are the geographic limits of Polynesia?* or *Which people are Polynesians most closely related to?* Indeed, there would hardly have been any way to frame such inquiries, there being no term for—or even concept of—what we mean by "Polynesian."

The whole project presupposes an outsider perspective. It also arises from an intellectual tradition in which events of the past—the facts of history—are essentially up for grabs. History, in the post-Enlightenment European tradition, is made up of elements that are theoretically available to anyone to do with as they see fit. But this idea conflicts with what one might call a "traditional" Polynesian perspective about things that happened in the past. According to the Polynesian view, history is not an assortment of data points to be cherry-picked at will but something much closer to a kind of intellectual property. Polynesian histories may be fluid, but not everyone is equally entitled to make use of them. As the Māori scholar Tipene O'Regan puts it: "To inquire into my history or that of my people, you must inquire into my whakapapa [genealogy]. My tupuna [ancestors] may be dead but they are also in me and I am alive. . . . My past is not a dead thing to be examined on the post-mortem bench of science without my consent. . . . I am the primary proprietor of my past."

This position presents difficulties for European scholars, effectively denying them "any absolute right" to study the history of the Polynesian peoples. And it is hard *not* to have some sympathy for the idea that the past "belongs first to those on whom it impinges"—particularly in cases like this, where there has been a good deal of conflict and where one group has suffered at the hands of another. How can Europeans be trusted to tell the story of a people they have subjugated and dispossessed? And even beyond the question of willful distortion or suppression, how can anyone be trusted to tell a story they may not fully understand?

Writing about these difficulties, the historian Judith Binney concluded that there are contradictions here that simply cannot be resolved. "We cannot translate other histories into our own," she wrote. "We can merely juxtapose them." There will always be a sense in which this is a European story and a sense in which it is a Polynesian one as well. The best we can do is to acknowledge this complexity, and, as the anthropologist Kenneth Emory once put it, "keep our minds as sensitive as we can to every little breeze of thought that flows."

When I look at this history, what I see is not so much the steady march of knowledge toward some final point of truth, but the complicated process of trying to figure things out—a twisting, braided rope of intersecting narratives, a set of conversations between different people with different bodies of knowledge, different ways of thinking, and different reasons for wanting to know. At some point, it dawned on me that the whole thing was a kind of contact story, a story about people trying to peer, if not always to leap, across a cultural divide. This was certainly true of both Cook and Tupaia; it was true of the priests and chiefs, many nameless, who entrusted Europeans with their most sacred lore, and of the missionaries, travelers, and colonial officials who painstakingly wrote it all down. It was true, almost by definition, of the anthropologists whose very job it is to try to crack the code of someone else's way of thinking, and true, perhaps most obviously, of the experimental voyagers who, in pursuit of prehistory's secrets, quite literally put their lives on the line.

Will Kyselka once said of Nainoa Thompson that he "chose to be puzzled," and this, it seems to me, is the tonic note. For what, after all, do we see when we look back at Tupaia, who sailed away from his homeland out of—one can only assume—overwhelming curiosity; or Willowdean Handy, with her Marquesan sketchbook; or Gifford and Shutler, with their shovels and pails? Fornander, in particular, seems to me a man who, within the limits of his era, made remarkable efforts to grapple with what he could barely understand. But even poor, ill-fated Sullivan, with his taxonomic muddle, or Tregear, with his mad Aryan cow tales, share this commitment to inquiry, this unshakable enthusiasm for the as yet unknown.

Virtually everyone who has ever thought about the problem of Polynesian origins has been attracted to the subject by two different things: first, by the sheer wondrousness, the improbability, of these migrations—all those thousands of miles of open ocean, the landfalls so few and far between—and, second, by the intellectual puzzle, the question of how such a story can ever really be known. For them, as for me, the appeal of this history is that it combines the romance of a great human adventure with a cool, cerebral awareness that it is only by sifting through volumes of evidence that we will ever get close to knowing what happened in the dim, unreachable, mesmerizing, endlessly entrancing past.

I BEGAN THIS story in Kealakekua Bay because it was there that I first really grasped the full significance of the Polynesian Triangle and what it meant for my husband and sons, whose deep genealogy I was trying to fathom. It was one of many sites that taught me something important about Polynesia, but of all the places I have visited, the one I go back to in my mind is a bay on the north side of Nuku Hiva known as Anaho.

Anaho is that rarest of rare things in the Marquesas: a sheltered bay with a long, creamy sickle of sand and a stretch of clear, shallow water. Tucked into the lee of a headland, it is protected from both wind and ocean surge, sheltered on its eastern flank by a long, snaking ridge of barren rock. There is no road in, and the only way to get there is by sea, or by foot along the trail over the ridge from the neighboring village of Hatiheu. The ridge rises some seven hundred feet, and from its crest you can see the bay spread out below you, the long, branching arms of the island reaching out to the sea, and the deep blue clefts of water in between. Farther out, the ocean glints like burnished metal, and away in the distance, where sky and water meet, lies the vast, empty curve of the horizon at the edge of the visible world. From there, the track plunges down again through a dry forest, the leaves crunching underfoot and the light coming, dim and dappled, through the canopy. At the bottom, you come suddenly out into the open and find yourself on a broad, grassy verge planted out in banana and coconut palms, with the beach just a stone's throw away.

In 1888, Robert Louis Stevenson dropped anchor in Anaho Bay. He was on a valedictory tour of the South Pacific in a chartered ninety-four-foot schooner called the *Casco*, and the Marquesas were his first stop. His health, never good, had been in decline, and he believed, as he later wrote, that he "was come to the afterpiece of life, and had only the nurse and the undertaker to expect." In fact, he was not far wrong; he would live only another six years. But the South Seas revived him, and he was well enough to take a boundless pleasure in this, his first port of call. "I have watched the morning break in many quarters of the world," he wrote, "and the dawn that I saw with most emotion shone upon the bay of Anaho." As the sun came up on that first morning, he watched the glow light up the mountains that overhung the bay. "Not one of these but wore its proper tint of saffron, of sulphur, of the clove, and of the rose. The lustre was like that of satin; on the lighter hues there seemed to float an efflorescence; a solemn bloom appeared on the more dark."

Anaho is today almost exactly as Stevenson described it in 1888: a scattering of houses and canoe sheds, some gardens, a little hamlet at the western end. To the east is the spot where he liked to spend his days, standing in the shallows with the warm sea bubbling up to his knees and the shells and pebbles tumbling between his feet. In the perfect stillness of midday, the sun shines hot and bright, the palms lean drunkenly out over the sand. From time to time a bird pipes somewhere in the forest; the sea heaves gently in and out. At such moments, Stevenson wrote, "the face of the world was of a pre-historic emptiness; life appeared to stand stock-still, and the sense of isolation was profound." It was an illusion, of course; he was not even alone on the beach, never mind the island. But it is easy to feel in Anaho as though one has slipped through a fissure in time, back to when a primeval stillness *had* reigned over the Marquesas, a time of wind and waves and the harsh, high call of seabirds, a time lasting hundreds of thousands, even millions, of years.

I sat on the beach in Stevenson's favorite spot and thought about the perplexing history of Polynesia. Seven had gone for a walk over the ridge to the east, to the bay where Robert Suggs found his five miraculous pieces of pottery. The boys were out in the water, with their snorkels and masks. I thought about all the many bits and pieces of history—the chants, bones, fishhooks, chromosomes, charcoal—and how all we can do is to try to fit them together like the fragments of a smashed and scattered urn. I thought about how the deep history of Polynesia—perhaps like all of human time—lives in that interesting place between knowledge and imagination, how it is a story not just of facts but of interpretations, which are the imaginative extensions of what can be known. We had chosen the Marquesas as our first stop because they were the first Polyne-sian islands to be discovered by Europeans and because of Suggs's interesting discovery of pottery where there ought to have been none. What I had not anticipated, though, was the power of the place itself to cast me back beyond the archaeological digs and the missionary journals, beyond the arrival of the first eyewitnesses, beyond the centuries of settled Polynesian life, back to the very dawn of the story, to a time of rattling palm fronds and the beach-ing of the first canoes.

For ages upon ages, the islands of the remote Pacific—tips of volcanoes, rings of coral, remnants of ancient Gondwana—remained
secluded, far beyond the reach of man. No one set foot on their sun-
bleached shores or penetrated their forests. Wind and rain eroded
their mountains; coral grew up and encircled their shores; birds
and plants, floating on sea wrack or blown by the wind, arrived
and took root, evolving in curious and unexpected ways. The islands were eminently habitable, much more so than many of the
places where people had already settled. They were warm and lush,
rarely subject to storm, and the seas around them teemed with life.
But their location in the middle of the world's largest ocean kept
them isolated, out of reach of human beings for tens of thousands
of years. Then, one day, a canoe appeared, emerging out of the haze
on the horizon. No one saw it from the beach—there was no one to
see it. No one documented its arrival; no one knows who it was. But
one moment the sounds of the island were those of wind and sea
and the cries of birds, and the next, the air was filled with voices
and the thud of feet and the scrape and rumble of hulls being run
up the shore.

# Acknowledgments

I WANT TO begin by acknowledging how very indebted I am to a handful of scholars in the fields of Pacific history and anthropology, first among them, the anthropologist Patrick Kirch, whose many lucidly written books on Polynesian archaeology provided the scaffolding for this project, and the New Zealand historian K. R. Howe, whose view from thirty thousand feet helped clarify many critical connections. I have also turned frequently to the works of J. C. Beaglehole, O. H. K. Spate, Anne Salmond, and Nicholas Thomas for orientation, while the overviews of M. P. K. Sorrenson and Alan Howard were invaluable in helping me sort out the story's different threads. I benefited greatly from the linguistic work of Malcolm Ross, Andrew Pawley, and Meredith Osmond of the Oceanic Lexicon Project at the Australian National University. And I also made use of a number of biographical and autobiographical works, including the engaging memoirs of Thor Heyerdahl, Robert Suggs, Willowdean Handy, and Ben Finney, and can only wish that more experts would undertake to write popular accounts of their experiences. In this same vein, I especially want to thank the documentary filmmaker Sam Low for sharing his book *Hawaiki Rising* with me; those who have read it will see how heavily I leaned on him in places.

Although I am essentially an armchair theorist, it was important, especially in the beginning, to get out into the field, and I want to acknowledge the generous assistance of several individuals who helped us way back at the start: Shelley Madsen at Aspire Downunder for executing an extremely complicated itinerary; Laura Thompson for her openheartedness in Hawai‘i; Sateki and Fine Uasike and the late Ana Uasike for their unexpected kindness in Tonga; Matthew Spriggs and Stuart Bedford for showing me around the dig at Teouma; Robert Hammar for the use of his house in Mo‘orea; Rose Corser for advice and assistance in the Marquesas; the extended Parangi family for their always-warm welcome in New Zealand; Ann, Joel, Isabel, and David for companionship in Hawai‘i; Katy and Linzee Crowe and the late Barbara Martin for getting us launched; and Tessa and Daniel Fisher for providing a much-needed crash pad on our return. Also my late mother, who waited for us; my brother who watched over things while we were away; my sons Aperahama, Matiu, and Daniel, for being good sports; and, of course, Seven, for undertaking the journey with me and, as always, for helping me see things in a different way.

This book has taken a long time to write, and several institutions provided critical assistance along the way. For grants supporting the original research—enabling me to visit places I would never otherwise have seen—I want to thank both the National Endowment for the Arts and the Australia Council for the Arts. I also wish to express my deep gratitude to the National Endowment for the Humanities for granting me a Public Scholar Award in 2015; I think I never would have reached the finish line without that year's release from my other professional responsibilities. I am also extremely grateful to the Librarians of Houghton Library, William Stoneman and Tom Hyry, for generously allowing me to take leave, and to Chloe Garcia Roberts, Laura Healy, and the rest of the team at *Harvard Review* for keeping the wheels turning while I was gone.

Many friends and colleagues have assisted me in ways both large and small: first, the members of my longtime writing group, Elizabeth Greenspan, Greg Harris, and Sarah Stewart Johnson, who read more versions of more chapters than anyone should have to. I also want to thank Susan Faludi and David Armitage for their support at a critical moment, and the many experts—Robert Suggs, Glyn Williams, Matthew Spriggs, Michael Levison, Elizabeth Matisoo-Smith, Kevin McGrath—who answered my often naïve questions. Several faculty members at Harvard generously allowed me to sit in on their classes, including Rowan Flad, Jason Ur, Michael Witzel, Jeremy Rau, David Armitage, and John Huth. I sometimes say that I taught myself a number of disciplines in the course of writing this book, but actually it was they who taught me what I needed to know.

I could never have written this book without the phenomenal resources of the Harvard University library system. I can count on one hand the number of obscure texts, among the hundreds I consulted, that were not held in one of Harvard's repositories, and these were immediately procured for me through interlibrary loan. I had additional research help from a number of individuals, including John Delaney of the Historic Maps Collection at Princeton; Diana Zlatanovski of Harvard's Peabody Museum; Jan Rensel at the University of Hawai'i's Center for Pacific Islands Studies; John Overholt and Susan Halpert at Houghton Library; and Cristina Monfasani, my hardworking Harvard Extension School faculty aide. Fred Hagstrom at Carleton College has been an unflagging supporter of my work over many years, for which I am truly grateful.

Many people were generous when it came to permissions: Benedict Fitzgerald, Christophe Sand, Sandy Millar, Carol Ivory, Henry Lawrence, Na'alehu Anthony, and Dennis Kawaharada of Kalamaku Press. And I would like to acknowledge the generosity of several institutions, including the Polynesian Society at the University of Auckland, the Story of Hawaii Museum, Princeton University Library, the Dunedin Public Library, the *Honolulu Star-Bulletin*, and Whitcoulls, New Zealand. Both Sonja Swenson Rogers at the Polynesian Voyaging Society and Tia Reber at the Bernice P. Bishop Museum answered innumerable questions about images. Rachel Ahearn was hugely generous with her time in helping prepare the graphics for publication. I owe a debt of gratitude—yet again—to

C. Scott Walker of the Harvard Map Collection for providing me with maps and to my longtime friend and collaborator Laura Healy for designing them.

I want to thank my brother, Elliott Thompson, for serving as an early reader and Patrick Kirch for checking the manuscript for mistakes. Of course, there will still be errors, and for these I am entirely to blame. Finally, to my perennially optimistic agent, Brettne Bloom, and my firm, clear-sighted editor, Gail Winston, I have only this to say: Without you the whole thing would have been but a wisp of sea mist, a dream of islands and nothing more. Thank you to the Book Group, the entire team at Harper, and to the members of my family, who know how much they had to put up with for how long.

# Notes

## Prologue: Kealakekua Bay

5 "all the Shore of the bay": James Cook, *The Voyage of the* Resolution *and* Discovery, *1776–1780*, vol. 3 of *The Journals of Captain James Cook on His Voyages of Discovery*, ed. J. C. Beaglehole, 4 vols. (London: Cambridge University Press, 1967), part 1, 491.

5 There have been varying interpretations: See Gananath Obeyesekere, *The Apotheosis of Captain Cook: European Mythmaking in the Pacific* (Princeton, NJ: Princeton University Press, 1992), and Marshall Sahlins, *How "Natives" Think* (Chicago: University of Chicago Press, 1995).

7 "amused them with Lies": Quoted in Anne Salmond, *The Trial of the Cannibal Dog* (New Haven, CT: Yale University Press, 2003), 409.

11 "spread themselves over": James Cook, *The Voyage of the* Resolution *and* Adventure, *1772–1775*, vol. 2 of *The Journals of Captain James Cook on His Voyages of Discovery*, ed. J. C. Beaglehole, 4 vols. (London: Cambridge University Press, 1969), 354.

11 "Could the story of the Polynesian voyagers": Elsdon Best, *Polynesian Voyagers: The Maori as a Deep-Sea Navigator, Explorer, and Colonizer* (Wellington: R. E. Owen, Government Printer, 1954), 15.

## A Very Great Sea: The Discovery of Oceania

19 They had words for lash: See Malcolm Ross, Andrew Pawley, and Meredith Osmond, *The Lexicon of Proto Oceanic: The Culture and Environment of Ancestral Oceanic Society*, vol. 2 (Canberra: ANU E Press and Pacific Linguistics, 2007), chaps. 4, 8. See also Patrick Vinton Kirch, *The Lapita Peoples: Ancestors of the Oceanic World* (Malden, MA: Blackwell, 1999), esp. chaps. 1, 7.

20 They probably had names for parts: See Rev. J. M. Osmond, "The Birth of New Lands after the Creation of Havai'i (Raiatea)," *Journal of the Polynesian Society* 3, no. 3 (1894): 136.

20 It was *tasik*: Ross, Pawley, and Osmond, *Lexicon of Proto Oceanic*, 2:88–89.

22 "a sea so vast": J. C. Beaglehole, introduction to *The Voyage of the* Endeavour, *1768–1771*, vol. 1 of *The Journals of Captain James Cook on His Voyages of Discovery*, ed. J. C. Beaglehole (London: Cambridge University Press, 1955), xxxv.

22 "If our Lord": Antonio Pigafetta, *Magellan's Voyage: A Narrative Account of the First Circumnavigation*, trans. R. A. Skelton (New York: Dover, 1994), 57.

26 "fall to destruction": Quoted in Glyndwr Williams and Alan Frost, "Terra Australis: Theory and Speculation," in *Terra Australis to Australia*, eds. Glyndwr Williams and Alan Frost (Melbourne: Oxford University Press Australia, 1988), 4.

26  Almost from the beginning: See Williams and Frost, "Terra Australis," 4, n. 9.
27  "as great as all *Europe*": Alexander Dalrymple, *An Account of the Discoveries Made in the South Pacifick Ocean* (1767; repr., Sydney: Hordern House, 1996), 2–3; Quirós quoted in Williams and Frost, "Terra Australis," 10.
27  "the sea with its labouring waves": Joseph Conrad, *Lord Jim* (1900; repr., Harmondsworth, UK: Penguin, 1957), 185.

## First Contact: Mendaña in the Marquesas

30  "At all hours": Robert Louis Stevenson, *In the South Seas* (1896; repr., Rockville, MD: Arc Manor, 2009), 69.
31  But archaeological sites: Patrick Vinton Kirch, *The Evolution of the Polynesian Chiefdoms* (Cambridge: Cambridge University Press, 1984), 89.
31  "thickly inhabited": Pedro Fernández de Quirós, *The Voyages of Pedro Fernandez de Quiros, 1595 to 1606*, trans. Sir Clements Markham, 2 vols. (London: Hakluyt Society, 1904), 1:20.
31  As the Frenchman: See "Le Voyage Autour du Monde du Capitaine Étienne Marchand," in *Bulletin de Géographie Historique et Descriptive* (Paris: Imprimerie Nationale, 1896), 280. The exact passage is: "Mon dessein était de prendre possession de l'île Marchand . . . au nom de Roi, quoique je n'aie jamais pu concevoir comment et de quel droit une nation policée pouvait s'emparer d'une terre habitée sans le consentement de ses habitants."
32  "half a pint of water": Quoted in O. H. K. Spate, *The Spanish Lake* (Canberra: Australian National University Press, 1979), 125.
32  "sunk in a religious stupor": Spate, *Spanish Lake*, 127, 130.
33  "pressed" on the water: Quirós, *Voyages*, 1:16.
33  the development of the outrigger: I. C. Campbell, "The Lateen Sail in World History," *Journal of World History* 6, no. 1 (1995): 12.
33  "with much speed and fury": Quirós, *Voyages*, 1:16–17.
33  "a friendly bit of advice": Robert C. Suggs, *The Hidden Worlds of Polynesia* (London: Cresset Press, 1963), 31.
33  "They looked at the ships": Quirós, *Voyages*, 1:17–18.
34  "It was a sight to behold": Ibid., 1:17–18.
34  The encounters between: Ibid., 1:29, 21, 24.
35  "exquisite beyond description": Quoted in Greg Dening, *Islands and Beaches: Discourse on a Silent Land, Marquesas, 1774–1880* (Chicago: Dorsey Press, 1988), 126.
35  "as fine a race": Cook, *Journals*, 2:373.
36  This, of course, was tattooing: Willowdean Chatterson Handy, *Tattooing in the Marquesas* (Honolulu: Bishop Museum, 1922), 14.
36  "than the ladies of Lima": Quirós, *Voyages*, 1:152.
37  "They gave us to understand": Ibid.
37  "islands which are supposed": Quoted in E. S. Craighill Handy, *The Native Culture in the Marquesas* (Honolulu: Bishop Museum, 1923), 19.
37  "some country where": G. S. Parsonson, "The Settlement of Oceania," in *Polynesian Navigation*, ed. Jack Golson, 3rd ed. (Wellington: A. H. & A. W. Reed, 1972), 30–31.

38 "the Land": Dening refers to the Marquesas as *Henua te Enata*, but there are two dialects: in the north the islands are called *Te Henua 'Enana*, and in the south they are known as *Te Fenua 'Enata*. Dening, *Islands and Beaches*.

38 "other islands which lye": Quoted in Parsonson, "Settlement of Oceania," 12–13.

## Barely an Island at All: Atolls of the Tuamotus

42 "manning the foreshrouds": Baron George Anson, *Anson's Voyage Round the World in the Years 1740–44*, ed. Richard Walter (New York: Dover, 1974), 75.

42 "this tempestuous ocean": William Bligh, *A Voyage to the South Sea* (Dublin: H. Fitzpatrick, 1792), 48.

43 "sailing on some variant": Beaglehole, introduction to *Journals of Captain James Cook*, 1:xxxiv.

44 "as flat as a plate": Stevenson, *In the South Seas*, 95.

44 "A long and brilliantly white beach": Charles Darwin, *The Voyage of the Beagle* (1839; repr., New York: Dutton, 1979), 386, 447.

44 "animalcules": See D. R. Stoddart, "Darwin, Lyell, and the Geological Significance of Coral Reefs," *British Journal for the History of Science* 9, no. 2 (1976): 200.

45 "On what have the reef-building corals": Darwin, *Voyage of the Beagle*, 449.

45 One theory popular at the time: See Stoddart, "Darwin, Lyell," 204.

47 What they did manage to observe: See Quirós, *Voyages*, 1:204; Jacob Le Maire, *The East and West Indian Mirror*, trans. J. A. J. de Villiers (London: Hakluyt Society, 1906), 192; Charles de Brosses, *Terra Australis Cognita; or, Voyages to the Terra Australis, or Southern Hemisphere, During the Sixteenth, Seventeenth, and Eighteenth Centuries*, 3 vols. (Edinburgh: Hawes, Clark, and Collins, 1766), 2:237; Jacob Roggeveen, *The Journal of Jacob Roggeveen*, ed. Andrew Sharp (London: Oxford University Press, 1970), 97.

47 "both sides were in the dark": De Brosses, *Terra Australis Cognita*, 2:236.

47 "roving migratory habits": Quoted in Parsonson, "Settlement of Oceania," 30.

48 "from within the island": Gaspar de Leza, quoted in Quirós, *Voyages*, 2:336.

48 "by far the oldest complete hull": A. C. Haddon and James Hornell, *Canoes of Oceania* (Honolulu: Bishop Museum Press, 1975), 65.

49 "exceedingly well wrought": Quoted in Haddon and Hornell, *Canoes of Oceania*, 80.

49 "reminders of the courage": Katharine Luomala, *Voices on the Wind: Polynesian Myths and Chants* (Honolulu: Bishop Museum Press, 1955), 173.

49 "many small pieces of wood": Roggeveen, *Journal*, 91–92, n. 1.

## Outer Limits: New Zealand and Easter Island

52 Two of New Zealand's three bat species: See Timothy Fridtjof Flannery, *The Future Eaters* (Melbourne: Reed Books, 1994), 64.

52 "ecological equivalent of giraffes": Flannery, *Future Eaters*, 55.

54 "*groot hooch verheven landt*": "Tasman's Journal or Description," trans. M. F. Vigeveno, in *Abel Janszoon Tasman and the Discovery of New Zealand* (Wellington: Department of Internal Affairs, 1942), 33, 45.

55 "a rough loud voice": Ibid., 49

55 "since there was good anchoring-ground": Ibid., 50.

56 *Māori* is a common Polynesian word: See *An Encyclopaedia of New Zealand*, ed. A. H. McLintock (Wellington: R. E. Owen, Government Printer, 1966), https://www.teara.govt.nz/en/1966/maori-pakeha-pakeha-maori.

56 "over which some planks": Abel Janszoon Tasman, *The Journal of Abel Janszoon Tasman*, ed. Andrew Sharp (London: Oxford University Press, 1968), 121–22.

56 "very cleverly": "Tasman's Journal or Description," 50.

57 "detestable deed": Ibid., 53.

57 "painted Black from the middle": Tasman, *Journal*, 153–56.

58 For "hog" they had recorded: See James Burney, *A Chronological History of the Discoveries in the South Sea or Pacific Ocean*, 5 vols. (London: L. Hansard, 1803–1817), 2:440–45.

59 "the precursor of the extended coast": Roggeveen, *Journal*, 89–93.

60 Although Roggeveen found: See Jared Diamond, *Collapse* (New York: Viking, 2005), 103–7.

61 "the most extreme example": Ibid., 107.

61 One argument points: See Diamond, *Collapse*, chap. 2, for a full statement of this argument.

61 "heating, drying, wind, and rain": Jared Diamond, "Easter Island Revisited," *Science* 317 (September 21, 2007): 1692.

61 Others—partly in response: See Terry Hunt and Carl Lipo, *The Statues That Walked* (New York: Free Press, 2011), esp. chap. 2. For thoughts on cutting down the last palm tree, see Diamond, *Collapse*, 114.

62 "in all respects similar": Roggeveen, *Journal*, 138n., 151.

63 "To make an end and conclusion": Ibid., 154.

## Tahiti: The Heart of Polynesia

67 "visitations": O. H. K. Spate, *Paradise Found and Lost* (Rushcutters Bay: Australian National University Press, 1988), 204–8.

69 "one of the spoilt children of fortune": Beaglehole, introduction to *Journals of Captain James Cook*, 1:cxii.

70 "The island of Tahiti": J. C. Beaglehole, *The Life of Captain James Cook* (Stanford, CA: Stanford University Press, 1974), 132–33.

70 Tahiti is the largest: The Society Islands were named, by Captain Cook, not for the Royal Society, as is often claimed, but in recognition of their close proximity to one another.

71 "made us all very uneasy": George Robertson, *The Discovery of Tahiti*, ed. Hugh Carrington (London: Hakluyt Society, 1948), 136.

71 Estimates of the pre-contact populations: Donald Denoon, "Lives and Deaths," in *Cambridge History of the Pacific Islanders* (Cambridge: Cambridge University Press, 1997), 113.

71 "at a Moderate Computation": Robertson, *Discovery of Tahiti*, 154.

71 "nothing could be hade without blows": Ibid., 142.

72 "a Little surly": Ibid., 136–38.

72 "some supposed that it was a floating island": W. N. Gunson, "Cover's Notes on the Tahitians, 1802," *Journal of the Polynesian Society* 15, no. 4 (1980): 220.

73 "by any standard of objective discourse": Greg Denning, "Possessing Tahiti,"

*Archaeology and Physical Anthropology in Oceania* 21, no. 1 (1986): 107. See also Anne Salmond, "Their Body Is Different, Our Body Is Different," *History and Anthropology* 16, no. 2 (2005).

73 But it seems likely: See Salmond, "Their Body Is Different," 171.

73 "opened a pathway to Te Po": Anne Salmond, *Aphrodite's Island* (Berkeley: University of California Press, 2009), 54.

74 "drew all our people": Robertson, *Discovery of Tahiti*, 154.

74 "all our Decks was full": Ibid., 154. See also Joan Druett, *Tupaia: Captain Cook's Tahitian Navigator* (Santa Barbara, CA: Praeger, 2011), 17.

74 "terror and amazement": Gunson, "Cover's Notes," 220.

74 At this, the Tahitian armada: See Robertson, *Discovery of Tahiti*, 156; John Hawkesworth, *An Account of the Voyages Undertaken by the Order of His Present Majesty: For Making Discoveries in the Southern Hemisphere*, 2nd ed., 3 vols. (London: W. Strahan and T. Cadell, 1773), 1:225.

75 "The mildness of the climate": Louis-Antoine de Bougainville, *The Pacific Journal of Louis-Antoine de Bougainville, 1767–1768*, trans. and ed. John Dunmore (London: Hakluyt Society, 2002), 63.

76 "I was transported": Louis-Antoine de Bougainville, *A Voyage Round the World: Performed by the Order of His Most Christian Majesty, in the Years 1766, 1767, 1768, and 1769*, trans. John Reinhold Forster (London: J. Nourse, 1772), 228–29, 244, 269, 239.

## A Man of Knowledge: Cook Meets Tupaia

78 "soft and comfortable": Joseph Banks, *The Endeavour Journal of Joseph Banks, 1768–1771*, ed. J. C. Beaglehole, 2 vols. (Sydney: Angus and Robertson, 1962), 1:235.

79 "All the birds we saw": Richard Pickersgill quoted in Cook, *Journals*, 1:65, n. 2.

79 "March'd along the shore": Ibid., 1:70.

80 "any thing that is made": Ibid., 1:76

80 "groves of Cocoa nut": Banks, *Journal*, 1:252.

80 "a most proper man": Ibid., 1:312.

81 "an extraordinary genius": Quoted in Salmond, *Aphrodite's Island*, 36, 175.

81 "Man of Knowledge": Banks, *Journal*, 1:381.

81 The Tahitian word is *tahu'a*: See E. S. Craighill Handy, *Polynesian Religion* (Honolulu: Bishop Museum, 1927), 149.

81 "the names and ranks": Banks, *Journal*, 1:381.

81 an "indigenous intellectual": Nicholas Thomas, *Cook: The Extraordinary Voyages of Captain Cook* (New York: Walker and Co., 2003), 21.

82 "a S[outh]-Sea dog": Banks, *Journal*, 1:343, 335, 348.

82 "if we may credit the reports": Ibid., 1:366.

83 The name Fenua Ura: Beaglehole, *Life of Cook*, 174, n. 1; Cook, *Journals*, 1:291–94. See also Anne Salmond, "Voyaging Exchanges: Tahitian Pilots and European Navigators," in *Canoes of the Grand Ocean*, ed. Anne Di Piazza and Erik Pearthree (Oxford: Archaeopress, 2008), 38–46.

83 They might be islands: See Salmond, *Aphrodite's Island*, 203–4; Paul Geraghty, "Pulotu, Polynesian Homeland," *Journal of the Polynesian Society* 102, no. 4 (1993): 362.

84 Some of the names begin: See H. A. H. Driessen, "Outriggerless Canoes," *Journal of Pacific History* 19, no. 4 (1984): 27.

84  "nothing he ever did": Beaglehole, *Life of Cook*, 69.
85  "vague and uncertain": Cook, *Journals*, 1:138, 117.
85  "Tupia the Indian": Salmond, *Aphrodite's Island*, 175; Druett, *Tupaia*, xi.
86  "cosmopolites by natural feeling": Horatio Hale, *Ethnography and Philology*, vol. 6 of *United States Exploring Expedition during the Years 1838, 1839, 1840, 1841, 1842* (Philadelphia: Lea and Blanchard, 1846), 14.
86  "Thank heaven": Banks, *Journal*, 1:312–13.
87  "the likeliest person to answer": Cook, *Journals*, 1:117.
87  "Launchd out into the Ocean": Banks, *Journal*, 1:329.

### Tupaia's Chart: Two Ways of Seeing

89  *"etopa"*: Banks, *Journal*, 1:329, n. 2.
90  "we cannot find": Cook, *Journals*, 1:157.
90  "All these kind of birds": Ibid., 1:159.
91  "not the least visible sign": Ibid., 1:161.
91  "Now do I wish": Banks, *Journal*, 1:396.
91  "caused to be engraved": Johann Reinhold Forster, *Observations Made during a Voyage round the World*, eds. Nicholas Thomas, Harriet Guest, and Michael Dettelbach (Honolulu: University of Hawai'i Press, 1996), 310–11.
92  Even before they left: Salmond, *Aphrodite's Island*, 204–5.
92  "opaque with trans-cultural confusion": Gordon R. Lewthwaite, "The Puzzle of Tupaia's Map," *New Zealand Geographer* 26 (1970): 1.
93  "though not accurately": Hale, *Ethnography and Philology*, 122.
93  The key terms here: Ross, Pawley, and Osmond, *Lexicon of Proto Oceanic*, 2:136–37.
93  "they concluded naturally": Hale, *Ethnography and Philology*, 122.
96  a mosaic: Anne Di Piazza and Erik Pearthree, "A New Reading of Tupaia's Chart," *Journal of the Polynesian Society* 116, no. 3 (2007): 321, 324. See also Geraghty, "Pulotu, Polynesian Homeland," 354–55.
96  "segmenting the circle": C. Frake, quoted in Edwin Hutchins, *Cognition in the Wild* (Cambridge, MA: MIT Press, 1995), 99.
97  Using a model of this kind: Di Piazza and Pearthree, "A New Reading," 327.

### An Aha Moment: A Tahitian in New Zealand

99   "some in heaps": Banks, *Journal*, 1:395–97.
100  "many great smoaks": Ibid., 1:400.
101  "About an hundred": Cook, *Journals*, 1:169, n. 2.
101  "prodigious advantage": Ibid., 1:291.
102  "their antiquity and Legends": Banks, *Journal*, 1: 454, 462–63.
102  "There remains," he wrote: Ibid., 2:37.
103  "It is extraordinary": Cook, *Journals*, 2:354.
104  "the same language": Ibid., 2:373, 275.
104  "affinity": William T. Jones, quoted in Benjamin W. Fortson IV, *Indo-European Language and Culture* (Malden, MA: Blackwell, 2004), 8.
106  The Greek stem: See Calvert Watkins, *How to Kill a Dragon: Aspects of Indo-European Poetics* (New York: Oxford University Press, 1995), 4; Fortson, *Indo-European Language*, 1.

107 "very soft and tuneable": Banks, *Journal*, 1:370.

108 The number two: See Fortson, *Indo-European Language*, 131.

108 Banks's chart: See Banks, *Journal*, 1:371.

108 Today Tongan is spoken: See Robert Blust, *The Austronesian Languages* (Canberra: Research School of Pacific and Asian Studies, Australian National University, 2009), 44.

108 Here the linguistic picture: See John Lynch, *Pacific Languages* (Honolulu: University of Hawai'i Press, 1998), map 9.

109 "That the people who inhabit": Banks, *Journal*, 1:371.

109 more than a thousand languages: See Lynch, *Pacific Languages*, 45.

110 "longer Voyages": Joseph Banks, quoted in Salmond, *Aphrodite's Island*, 212.

## Drowned Continents and Other Theories: The Nineteenth-Century Pacific

116 The major stops: See I. C. Campbell, *Worlds Apart: A History of the Pacific Islands* (Christchurch, NZ: Canterbury University Press, 2003), 73–74.

118 Poets like Keats: See Richard D. Fulton, "The South Seas in Mid-Victorian Children's Imagination," in *Oceania and the Victorian Imagination*, eds. Richard D. Fulton and Peter H. Hoffenberg (Burlington, VT: Ashgate, 2013).

119 "if the inhabitants": Cook, *Journals*, 1:288, 154.

120 "easier to populate": Quoted in K. R. Howe, *The Quest for Origins* (Honolulu: University of Hawai'i Press, 2003), 123.

120 As early as 1775: See Forster, *Observations*, 190.

120 Other observers, coming along a bit later: See J. A. Moerenhout, *Travels to the Islands of the Pacific Ocean*, trans. Arthur R. Borden Jr. (1837; repr., Lanham, MD: University Press of America, 1983), 411. See also Alan Howard, "Origins and Migrations," *Polynesian Culture History: Essays in Honor of Kenneth P. Emory*, eds. Genevieve A. Highland et al. (Honolulu: Bishop Museum Press, 1967), 49.

120 An English missionary by the name of William Ellis: See William Ellis, *Polynesian Researches during a Residence of Nearly Six Years in the South Sea Islands*, 2 vols. (1829; repr., Cambridge: Cambridge University Press, 2013), 2:49.

121 "abode of fire": Julien Marie Crozet, *Crozet's Voyage to Tasmania, New Zealand, the Ladrone Islands, and the Philippines in the Years 1771–1772*, trans. H. Ling Roth (London: Truslove & Shirley, 1891), 70–71.

121 "supposing a remnant": William Wyatt Gill, *Life in the Southern Isles* (London: Religious Tract Society, 1876), 21.

121 there has never been any scientific evidence: Even now there are reports from time to time of evidence of a lost continent in the Pacific, including the recent discovery of the underwater continent known as Zealandia. This is a fragment of the ancient supercontinent of Gondwana, which has now been found to extend farther underneath the ocean than was previously believed. This continent has nothing to do with the volcanic islands of the mid-Pacific, however, and predates the human settlement of the Pacific by tens of millions of years. See, for example, "Scientists Claim Existence of Drowned Pacific Ocean Continent," Reuters, February 18, 2017, https://www.reuters.com/article/us-new-zealand-continent/scientists-claim-existence-of-drowned-pacific-ocean-continent-idUSKBN15X044.

121 "merchant adventurer": Borden, preface to *Travels to the Islands*, xi.

122 "suddenly destroyed by the waters": Moerenhout, *Travels to the Islands*, 390.

122  "Mr. Moerenhout come now!": Ibid., 189–90.

123  "In the state of mind": Ibid., 191.

124  "it was only by dint": Ibid., 194.

124  "He was (or there was)": Ibid., 210.

124  "extreme elevation": Ibid., 382–83.

### A World without Writing: Polynesian Oral Traditions

127  The advent of writing: See, for example, Walter J. Ong, *Orality and Literacy* (New York: Routledge, 2002), chaps. 3, 4.

128  "and that at a very advanced age": S. Percy Smith, *Hawaiki: The Original Home of the Maori*, 4th ed. (Auckland: Whitcombe & Tombs, 1921), 16– 17.

129  "close to the living human lifeworld": Ong, *Orality*, 49.

129  "A circle would be called": Ibid., 50–51.

130  "abstractly sequential": Ibid., 8–9.

130  "science-like elements": John Huth, "Losing Our Way in the World," *New York Times*, July 20, 2013, Sunday Review, 6.

130  But simply that, by enabling: See Ong, *Orality*, 45.

130  "subjective and objective reactions": Handy, *Polynesian Religion*, 6.

131  Tregear was an Englishman: See K. R. Howe, "Tregear, Edward Robert," *Dictionary of New Zealand Biography*, first published in 1993, *Te Ara—The Encyclopedia of New Zealand*, https://teara.govt.nz/en/biographies/2t48/tregear -edward-robert.

131  "no white man has ever yet seen": Edward Tregear, "Thoughts on Comparative Mythology," *Transactions and Proceedings of the New Zealand Institute* 30 (1897): 56–57. See also Margaret Orbell, *Hawaiki: A New Approach to Maori Tradition* (Christchurch, NZ: Canterbury University Press, 1991), 1–2.

132  "the enquiry became general": Niel Gunson, *Messengers of Grace: Evangelical Missionaries in the South Seas, 1797–1860* (Melbourne: Oxford University Press, 1978), 192–93.

134  "I do not know": Elsdon Best, *Maori Religion and Mythology*, part 1 (1924; repr., Wellington: Te Papa Press, 2005), 60.

135  "At the time that turned": Martha Warren Beckwith, ed. and trans., *The Kumulipo: A Hawaiian Creation Chant* (Chicago: University of Chicago Press, 1951), 7, 44–45.

135  "*Te Po-nui*": Best, *Maori Religion and Mythology*, part 1, 59.

136  "realm of potential being": Māori Marsden, quoted in Agathe Thornton, *The Birth of the Universe* (Auckland: Reed Books, 2004), 226.

136  "Ideas of infinity": Thornton, *Birth of the Universe*, 225.

136  "first generation of growth": Teuira Henry, *Ancient Tahiti* (1928; repr., Millwood, NY: Kraus Reprint, 1985), 341, 340. This chant has been reformatted slightly to make it easier to read.

137  In Hawai'i: See Beckwith, *Kumulipo*, 58.

137  "Grove by copulating": Alfred Métraux, *Ethnology of Easter Island* (Honolulu: Bishop Museum, 1940), 321.

138  There were mixed motives: D. R. Simmons and B. G. Biggs, "The Sources of 'The Lore of the Whare-Wananga,'" *Journal of the Polynesian Society* 79, no. 1 (1970): 24.

*The Aryan Māori: An Unlikely Idea*

139  According to this popular Māori myth: See, for example, Sir George Grey, *Polynesian Mythology and Ancient Traditional History of the New Zealand Race, as Furnished by Their Priests and Chiefs*, 2nd ed. (Auckland: H. Brett, 1885; repr., Elibron Classics, Adamant, 2005), 1–3.

140  "the layer above them": Henry, *Ancient Tahiti*, 411, 347.

140  "lift on high": Homer, *Odyssey*, trans. Robert Fagles (New York: Penguin Classics, 1997), Book I, lines 63–64. In the Vedic tradition, the demiurge Indra is similarly tasked with propping up the sky, and one might even suggest a Norse echo of the concept in the image of Yggdrasil, the World Tree.

140  They were also entirely familiar: See E. J. Michael Witzel, *World Mythology: The Origins of the World's Mythologies* (Oxford and New York: Oxford University Press, 2013), 129.

140  "And the earth": Gen. 1:2 (AKJV).

140  "Before the ocean": Ovid, *Metamorphoses*, trans. Brookes More (Boston: Cornhill, 1933), 3.

141  Other scholars: Hesiod, "Theogony," *The Homeric Hymns and Homerica*, trans. Hugh G. Evelyn-White (London: William Heinemann, 1920), 87: "Verily at the first Chaos came to be, but next wide-bosomed Earth, the ever-sure foundations of all . . . From Chaos came forth Erebus and black Night; but of Night were born Aether and Day." Rigveda, quoted in Witzel, *Origins*, 107–9: "There was neither 'being' nor 'nonbeing' then, nor intermediate space, nor heaven beyond it. What turned around? Where? In whose protection? Was there water?—Only a deep abyss." Snorre, *The Younger Edda*, trans. Rasmus B. Anderson (1901), Project Gutenberg, http://www.gutenberg.org/files/18947/18947-h/18947-h.htm, chap. IV: "It was Time's morning, / When there nothing was; / Nor sand, nor sea, / Nor cooling billows. / Earth there was not, / Nor heaven above. / The Ginungagap was, / But grass nowhere."

141  Another intriguing proposition: Witzel, *Origins*, 410.

141  "great natural turn": M. P. K. Sorrenson, *Maori Origins and Migrations* (Auckland: Auckland University Press, 1979), 14–15.

142  "until in the lapse": Rev. Richard Taylor, *Te Ika a Maui, or New Zealand and Its Inhabitants* (London: Wertheim and Macintosh, 1855), 12, 8.

142  "the mother of modern civilization": Edward Tregear, *The Aryan Maori* (Wellington: George Didsbury, Government Printer, 1885), 6.

143  It could be inferred: Fortson, *Indo-European Language*, 16–44.

144  "To learn": Tregear, *Aryan Maori*, 5.

145  "remnants of a race": John Rae, quoted in K. R. Howe, "Some Origins and Migrations of Ideas Leading to the Aryan Polynesian Theories of Abraham Fornander and Edward Tregear," *Pacific Studies* 11, no. 2 (1988): 71.

145  "Strange as it may sound": Quoted in Howe, "Some Origins," 73.

146  "of a pastoral people": Quoted in K. R. Howe, *Singer in a Songless Land: A Life of Edward Tregear, 1846–1931* (Auckland: Auckland University Press, 1991), 40.

146  An English example: Tregear, *Aryan Maori*, 27.

146  "Knowing that the Maoris": Quoted in Howe, *Singer*, 41.

146  Combing the Māori lexicon: Tregear, *Aryan Maori*, 28.

146  "cloak of heaven": See Tiaki Hikawera Mitira, *Takitimu* (Wellington: Reed,

1972), 131, http://nzetc.victoria.ac.nz/tm/scholarly/tei-MitTaki-t1-body-d2-d10 .html.

147  "crotchety but highly intelligent": Howe, *Singer*, 56–57. See A. S. Atkinson, "The Aryo-Semitic Maori," *Transactions and Proceedings of the New Zealand Institute* 19 (1886): 556–76; Howe, "Some Origins," 68.

148  "cradle in Central Asia": Sorrenson, *Maori Origins*, 18; review of *An Account of the Polynesian Race*, vol. 1, by Abraham Fornander, *Saturday Review of Politics, Literature, Science and Art* 45 (February 9, 1878): 180–81.

148  "primitive aliens": Howe, *Quest for Origins*, 168.

149  "seeking new homes": Tregear, *Aryan Maori*, 82.

### *A Viking in Hawai'i: Abraham Fornander*

151  a rugged and daring tribe: R. J. McLean, *A Book of Swedish Verse* (London: Athlone Press, 1968), 57.

151  "I will say nothing of the hardships": Eleanor Harmon Davis, *Abraham Fornander: A Biography* (Honolulu: University of Hawai'i Press, 1979), 32, 31.

151  In 1847, he took: Davis, *Abraham Fornander*, 49–51.

152  "I have a native wife": *Honolulu Times*, December 13, 1849, quoted in Helen Geracimos Chapin, *Shaping History: The Role of Newspapers in Hawai'i* (Honolulu: University of Hawai'i Press, 1996), 49.

152  "holiest memory": Quoted in Davis, *Abraham Fornander*, 123.

153  The pandemic: See Alfred W. Crosby, *America's Forgotten Pandemic: The Influenza of 1918* (New York: Cambridge University Press, 1989), 235, 256.

153  As early as the 1830s: See William Ellis, *Polynesian Researches during a Residence of Nearly Eight Years in the Society and Sandwich Islands*, 4 vols. (New York: J. & J. Harper, 1833), 1:89–93.

154  "there not being persons": Quoted in Robert C. Schmitt and Eleanor C. Nordyke, "Death in Hawai'i: The Epidemics of 1848–1849," *Hawaiian Journal of History* 35 (2001): 1–3.

154  From a high: See Stephen J. Kunitz, *Disease and Social Diversity: The European Impact on the Health of Non-Europeans* (New York: Oxford University Press, 1994), appendix 3-1. See also Dening, *Islands and Beaches*, 239.

154  Robert Louis Stevenson: Stevenson, *In the South Seas*, 26–27.

154  "death coming in like a tide": Ibid., 24.

154  "as a reminder": Abraham Fornander, *An Account of the Polynesian Race: Its Origins and Migrations*, 3 vols. (1877–1884; repr., Rutland, VT: Charles E. Tuttle, 1969), dedication.

154  "bearing upon the ancient history": Ibid., 1:iv.

155  "maintain the greatest reserve": Ibid., 1:v.

155  "to a 'common man'": Edward Shortland, *Maori Religion and Mythology* (London: Longmans, Green, 1882; repr., New York: AMS Press, 1977), viii; Michael Reilly, "John White, Part Two: Seeking the Elusive Mohio: White and His Maori Informants," *New Zealand Journal of History* 24, no. 1 (1990): 47.

155  "in olden times": Quoted in Jane McRae, "Maori Oral Tradition Meets the Book," in *A Book in the Hand: Essays on the History of the Book in New Zealand*, eds. Penny Griffith, Peter Hughes, and Alan Loney (Auckland: Auckland University Press, 2000), 5–6.

156 "embalm": Michael Reilly, "John White: The Making of a Nineteenth-Century Writer and Collector of Maori Tradition," *New Zealand Journal of History* 23, no. 2 (1989): 167.

156 "the isolation and oblivion": Fornander, *Account*, 1:ix.

156 "a chip of the same block": Ibid., 1:iv.

156 "peculiarly Cushite outgrowth": Ibid., 1:iv, 43.

156 "the manner or the occasion": Ibid., 2:3–4.

157 "Polynesian folklore": Ibid., 2:6.

157 "migratory wave swept": Ibid., 1:198.

158 "almost impenetrable jungle": Ibid., 2:v.

158 There are cyclical calendars: See Ross, Pawley, and Osmond, *Lexicon of Proto Oceanic*, 2:287.

159 Even the much more common: The length of time that orally transmitted information can be accurately passed on is thought to be about two hundred years. This is often referred to as "three-generation reachback." See, for example, Elizabeth Vandiver, *Herodotus: The Father of History*, The Great Courses, The Teaching Company Limited, 2000, compact disc.

159 "to the rocks, trees": Beckwith, *Kumulipo*, 7.

160 "undertaken purposely": Fornander, *Account*, 2:19–20, 8–9.

160 "the Icelandic folklore": Ibid., 2:20.

## Voyaging Stories: History and Myth

162 At the same time: Teuira Henry and Others, *Voyaging Chiefs of Havai'i*, ed. Dennis Kawaharada (Honolulu: Kalamaku Press, 1995), 54–56.

162 "first procure choice food": Henry, *Ancient Tahiti*, 481, 492, 493; Smith, *Hawaiki*, 216.

162 "The Canoe Song of Ru": Henry, *Ancient Tahiti*, 459–65. In an early version, it is only the islands of the Society group that are discovered; according to a later tradition, collected in 1854 and thus potentially influenced by new information, Ru and Hina discover all the island groups of Polynesia.

163 A similar sequence: Martha Beckwith, *Hawaiian Mythology* (1940; repr., Honolulu: University of Hawai'i Press, 1970), 169.

163 Stories of Rata: Henry, *Ancient Tahiti*, 502–3; Beckwith, *Hawaiian Mythology*, 263–75.

163 But the human cost: The place name is cognate with Rarotonga, a name made up of the words *raro*, meaning "down" or "under" (i.e., "downwind"), and *tonga*, meaning "south."

164 "We have come": Karl von den Steinen, *Von den Steinen's Marquesan Myths*, trans. Marta Langridge, ed. Jennifer Terrell (Canberra: Target Oceania and the Journal of Pacific History, 1988), 13.

164 "We are Pepeu": Von den Steinen, *Marquesan Myths*, 18–19, 14. The different star names in this account are not easy to identify, but one—Taku'ua—is a term applied to many bright guiding stars, as in Takurua-i-te-ahiahi, the Evening Star (Venus), and Takurua-to-vae-nga-rangi, "star in the middle of the heavens" (Pollux). See Maud Worcester Makemson, *The Morning Star Rises: An Account of Polynesian Astronomy* (New Haven, CT: Yale University Press, 1941), 254–55, 259–60.

164 "Twenty died": Von den Steinen, *Marquesan Myths*, 15.

165 Like Tregear: See M. P. K. Sorrenson, "A Short History of the Polynesian Society," The Polynesian Society, http://www.thepolynesiansociety.org/history .html.

165 "all tradition is based": Smith, *Hawaiki*, dedication, 13.

166 In cosmogonies from: Henry, *Ancient Tahiti*, 344; Antony Alpers, *Legends of the South Seas* (New York: Thomas Y. Crowell, 1970), 100, 139; Orbell, *Hawaiki*, 14; von den Steinen, *Marquesan Myths*, 17, 73.

167 "key-word": Hale, *Ethnography and Philology*, 120–21.

167 Hale believed: In the westerly islands of Samoa and Tonga, this cluster of ideas—otherworldliness, a land of plenty, the destination of the dead—goes by the name of Pulotu rather than Hawaiki. In stories from Tonga, men go to Pulotu in search of children or to procure the wood of a certain tree or to get red feathers or yams or houses made of human bones. It is as though, when you reach Samoa and Tonga, the trail of Hawaikis goes cold, but it is possible to pick up a trail of Pulotus leading still farther west. See Edward Winslow Gifford, *Tongan Myths and Tales* (Honolulu: Bishop Museum, 1924), 153–80; Geraghty, "Pulotu, Polynesian Homeland," 343–84.

168 Smith's story: See S. Percy Smith, *The Lore of the Whare-wananga*, 2 vols. (1915; repr., New York: AMS, 1978), 2:57–59; H. W. Williams, "The Maruiwi Myth," *Journal of the Polynesian Society* 46, no. 3 (1937): 110–11; Henry, *Ancient Tahiti*, 123.

168 "of the marvelous": Smith, *Hawaiki*, 216.

169 Thus the rhetorical question: Orbell, *Hawaiki*, 28.

169 "the most famous event": Te Rangi Hiroa, *The Coming of the Maori* (Wellington: Whitcombe & Tombs, 1949), 36.

169 "The *tapu* sea": Orbell, *Hawaiki*, 17.

170 Oral narratives: See Agathe Thornton, *Maori Oral Literature, As Seen by a Classicist* (Otago, NZ: University of Otago, 1987), 69, charts 2 and 4.

170 "terse, cryptic": McRae, "Maori Oral Tradition," 7.

170 In a close textual study: D. R. Simmons, *The Great New Zealand Myth* (Wellington: A. H. & A. W. Reed, 1976), 3, 59, 58, 108, 316.

171 "facts" over "rumors": Hiroa, *Coming of the Maori*, 41.

## Somatology: The Measure of Man

176 "fundamentally a field problem": Herbert E. Gregory, "Progress in Polynesian Research," *Science*, New Series 56, no. 1454 (1922): 529.

176 "the first comprehensive attack": "Polynesian Origins: Results of the Bayard Dominick Expedition," *Journal of the Polynesian Society* 32, no. 4 (1923): 250.

178 "as repositories of information": Willowdean C. Handy, *Forever the Land of Men* (New York: Dodd, Mead, 1965), 5.

178 "a great liar": Ibid., 70–71.

179 "covered every feature": Ibid., 55.

179 Willowdean was often flummoxed: Ibid., 56.

181 Johann Blumenbach's classic: See Alfred C. Haddon, *History of Anthropology* (London: Watts & Co., 1934), 17–18.

181 including a census: Haddon, *History*, 28.

181 In biology and anthropology: Yasuko I. Takezawa, "Race," *Encyclopedia Britannica*, http://www.britannica.com/topic/race-human.

181 Genetic research: A somewhat more nuanced view is that "there are nontrivial average genetic differences across populations in multiple traits" but that "the race vocabulary is too ill-defined and too loaded with historical baggage to be helpful." See David Reich, *Who We Are and How We Got Here: Ancient DNA and the New Science of the Human Past* (New York: Pantheon, 2018), 253.

182 "combined to make": Gregory, "Progress in Polynesian Research," 527.

182 "a hybrid people": Louis R. Sullivan, *Marquesan Somatology with Comparative Notes on Samoa and Tonga* (Honolulu: Bishop Museum, 1923), 212–15.

183 "European racial affinities": Louis R. Sullivan, *A Contribution to Samoan Somatology* (Honolulu: Bishop Museum, 1921), 18, 20.

183 When it came to the Tongans: Louis R. Sullivan, *A Contribution to Tongan Somatology* (Honolulu: Bishop Museum, 1922), 3.

184 All of Sullivan's calculations: Patrick Kirch, personal communication.

185 "no doubt that at least two": Sullivan, *Marquesan Somatology*, 19.

186 "There is only one way": Peter H. Buck (Te Rangi Hiroa), *Vikings of the Sunrise* (New York: Frederick A. Stokes, 1938), 13.

## *A Māori Anthropologist: Te Rangi Hiroa*

188 His father was: J. B. Condliffe, *Te Rangi Hiroa: The Life of Sir Peter Buck* (Christchurch: Whitcombe & Tombs, 1971), 51, 55.

189 "an internal struggle": Quoted in ibid., 54.

189 "the inside angle": Ibid., 151; *Na to Hoa Aroha, From Your Dear Friend: The Correspondence Between Sir Apirana Ngata and Sir Peter Buck, 1925–50*, 3 vols., ed. M. P. K. Sorrenson (Auckland: Auckland University Press, 1986–1988), 1:48.

189 "the taboo precincts": Buck, *Vikings*, 14. The author of this notice was almost certainly the anatomy professor J. H. Scott, who in 1893 had written a paper on the osteology of the Māori, which was published, somewhat bizarrely, in the "Zoology" section of the *Transactions and Proceedings of the New Zealand Institute*.

190 Borrowing a Flower's craniometer: Hiroa, "Maori Somatology: Racial Averages," *Journal of the Polynesian Society* 31, no. 1 (1922): 37–38.

191 "With all my love": Hiroa, *Coming of the Maori*, 36, 48, 38, 43; Buck, *Vikings*, 25.

191 He believed that theorizing: Condliffe, *Te Rangi Hiroa*, 209.

191 "objects which people": Te Rangi Hiroa, *Coming of the Maori*, 2.

191 "but the fingers": Buck to Ngata, Nov. 20, 1928, *Na to Hoa*, 1:146.

191 "the atrocities that could": Condliffe, *Te Rangi Hiroa*, 178, 182–83.

192 "the best way to describe": Ibid., 189, 109.

192 "packed store-houses of facts": Ngata quoted in ibid., 190; see also 205.

193 "atoll-studded route": Buck, *Vikings*, 307, 49.

193 "a parsimonious explanation": Patrick Vinton Kirch, *On the Road of the Winds* (Berkeley: University of California Press, 2002), 26.

194 "the one more fair": Forster, *Observations*, 153.

194 "*la race cuivrée*": Jules-Sébastien-César Dumont d'Urville, "Sur les Isles du Grand Océan," *Bulletin de la Societé de Géographie* 17 (1832): 5–6. D'Urville also included Australia in this region, but subsequent writers have tended to separate Australia from Melanesia as a separate cultural region.

194   "as the wolf": Hale, *Ethnography and Philology*, 50. See also Nicholas Thomas,
      "The Force of Ethnology: Origins and Significance of the Melanesia/Polynesian
      Divide," *Current Anthropology* 30, no. 1 (1989): 31.

195   "We know the Maoris": John H. Scott, "Contribution to the Osteology of the
      Aborigines of New Zealand and of the Chatham Islands," *Transactions and Pro-
      ceedings of the New Zealand Institute* 26 (1893): 5; Louis R. Sullivan, "The Racial
      Diversity of the Polynesian Peoples," *Journal of the Polynesian Society* 32, no. 21
      (1923): 83. See also Moira White, "Dixon, Skinner and Te Rangi Hiroa," *Journal
      of Pacific History* 47, no. 3 (2012).

195   "I am binomial": Buck, *Vikings*, 260; Te Rangi Hiroa quoted in John S. Allen,
      "Te Rangi Hiroa's Physical Anthropology," *Journal of the Polynesian Society* 103,
      no. 1 (1994): 20.

195   "the Pakeha [European] attitude": Buck to Ngata, Feb. 11, 1934, *Na to Hoa*, 3:126.

196   "the Polynesian idea of beauty": Te Rangi Hiroa, "Maori Somatology: Racial
      Averages, III," *Journal of the Polynesian Society* 31, no. 4 (1922): 164; Te Rangi
      Hiroa, "Maori Somatology," 39; see also Buck, *Vikings*, 15.

196   "the more antient inhabitants": Forster, *Observations*, 187.


## The Moa Hunters: Stone and Bones

199   For a long time: See Kirch, *On the Road of the Winds*, 20–23.

200   "large fossil ossifications": Joel S. Polack, quoted in Roger Duff, *The Moa-
      Hunter Period of Maori Culture*, 2nd ed. (Wellington: Government Printer,
      1956), 291–92.

200   "a certain monstrous animal": Rev. William Colenso, quoted in Duff, *Moa-
      Hunter Period*, 293. See also T. Lindsay Buick, *The Mystery of the Moa* (New
      Plymouth, NZ: Thomas Avery, 1931), 52.

200   "such as is brought to table": Quoted in Buick, *Mystery of the Moa*, 65–72.

201   "as if a hole": W. B. D. Mantell, quoted in Duff, *Moa-Hunter Period*, 251.

202   "the huge *pachydermata*": Julius von Haast, "Moas and Moa-Hunters. Address
      to the Philosophical Institute of Canterbury," *Transactions and Proceedings of
      the New Zealand Institute* 4 (1872): 67.

202   Haast believed that these: Haast, "Moas and Moa-Hunters," 67, 84.

202   He argued that: Quoted in Duff, *Moa-Hunter Period*, 250, 298, 306–7, 331–32.

203   "remarkably perfect": James Hector, "On Recent Moa Remains in New Zea-
      land," *Transactions of the New Zealand Institute* 4 (1872): 110–11.

203   "the very word": Duff, *Moa-Hunter Period*, 298, 333.

204   According to Smith's account: Smith, *Lore of the Whare-wananga*, 2:71–75.

204   "many of the rich collections": Janet Davidson, *The Prehistory of New Zealand*
      (Auckland: Longman Paul, 1984), 6.

205   They noted their use: David Teviotdale, "The Material Culture of the Moa-
      Hunters in Murihuku," *Journal of the Polynesian Society* 41, no. 2 (1932): 102–3.

206   "type-site of the earliest phase": Hallie R. Buckley et al., "The People of Wairau
      Bar: A Re-examination," *Journal of Pacific Archaeology* 1, no. 1 (2010): 1.

206   "during the ages": Duff, *Moa-Hunter Period*, 22–23.

206   Eyles's find generated: Jim R. Eyles, *Wairau Bar Moa Hunter* (Dunedin, NZ:
      River Press, 2007), 64.

207   About twelve inches below: Duff, *Moa-Hunter Period*, 33, 35.

207 "a chance, isolate find": Eyles, *Wairau Bar*, 81.

207 These "enigmatical" objects: Duff, *Moa-Hunter Period*, 2, 6.

209 "a single canoe-load": Davidson, *Prehistory of New Zealand*, 56–57.

## Radiocarbon Dating: The Question of When

210 "a godsend": Colin Renfrew, *Before Civilization: The Radiocarbon Revolution and Prehistoric Europe*, 2nd ed. (New York: Cambridge University Press, 1979), 48.

211 The rate at which: Ibid., 49–52, 266; see also R. E. Taylor and Ofer Bar-Yosef, *Radiocarbon Dating: An Archaeological Perspective*, 2nd ed. (Walnut Creek, CA: Left Coast Press, 2014), 19–23.

211 "closed system": Renfrew, *Before Civilization*, 50–51.

212 "I shall be very much interested": Taylor and Bar-Yosef, *Radiocarbon Dating*, 284.

213 "the color of Marguerite's skin": Bob Krauss, *Keneti* (Honolulu: University of Hawai'i Press, 1988), 170–71.

213 "be safe from bombs": Ibid., 293.

213 Not long after America's entry: Ibid., 295–96.

214 Enthusiasm for Emory's little book: Ibid., 297–98.

215 "a whole new vista": Ibid., 338.

216 "poor man's IBM": Ibid., 359–60.

217 "few opportunities": Ralph Linton, *Archaeology of the Marquesas Islands* (Honolulu: Bishop Museum, 1925), 3.

217 "We were seldom out of sight": Suggs, *Hidden Worlds*, 3.

218 "hibiscus tangle": Ibid., 81–82.

218 "some very peculiar stone adzes": Ibid., 104–7.

219 They suggested that: Harry L. Shapiro and Robert C. Suggs, "New Dates for Polynesian Prehistory," *Man* 59 (1959): 12–13.

219 "According to the most trustworthy": Robert Carl Suggs, *The Archaeology of Nuku Hiva, Marquesas Islands, French Polynesia* (New York: American Museum of Natural History, 1961), 174.

219 "a few fragmentary": Suggs, *Hidden Worlds*, 87–89.

220 "the complexion of Polynesian": Suggs, *Archaeology of Nuku Hiva*, 95–96.

220 "The big question now": Suggs, *Hidden Worlds*, 88.

## The Lapita People: A Key Piece of the Puzzle

221 "I, poor hermit": Quoted in Kirch, *The Lapita Peoples*, 6.

222 Cook's naturalists: Georg Forster, *A Voyage Round the World*, 2 vols. (London: B. White, 1777), 1:471. See also Cook, *Journals*, 2:451.

222 "highly porous, lightly fired": W. C. McKern, *The Archaeology of Tonga* (Honolulu: Bishop Museum, 1929), 116–17.

222 An amateur ornithologist: Patrick V. Kirch, "E. W. Gifford and Pacific Prehistory: An Appreciation," in *L'Expédition Archéologique d'Edward W. Gifford et Richard Shutler Jr. en Nouvelle-Calédonie au Cours de l'Année 1952*, by Christophe Sand and Patrick V. Kirch (Nouméa, New Caledonia: Service des Musées et du Patrimoine de Nouvelle-Calédonie, 2002), 25; Wilhelm G. Solheim II, "Edward Winslow Gifford," *Journal of the Polynesian Society* 68, no. 3 (1959): 177.

223   "succession of cultures": E. W. Gifford, *Archaeological Excavations in Fiji* (Berkeley: University of California Press, 1951), 189, 225.

223   Like New Zealand: Flannery, *Future Eaters*, 43–48.

224   "coastal kitchen middens": E. W. Gifford and Dick Shutler Jr., *Archaeological Excavations in New Caledonia* (Berkeley: University of California Press, 1956), 1.

224   "I am afraid": Christophe Sand, "Petites et Grandes Histoires Autour de l'Expédition Archéologique de 1952 en Nouvelle Calédonie," in Sand and Kirch, *L'Expédition Archéologique*, 174–75, n. 1.3.

225   "peaceful uses": "The Michigan Memorial Phoenix Project," University of Michigan Energy Institute, http://energy.umich.edu/about-us/phoenix-project.

225   "of considerable significance": E. W. Gifford, "A Carbon-14 Date from Fiji," *Journal of the Polynesian Society* 61 (1952): 327.

225   "vastly superior": Gifford and Shutler, *Archaeological Excavations in New Caledonia*, 75.

225   Richly and completely decorated: See Maurice Piroutet, *Études Stratigraphique sur la Nouvelle Calédonie* (Mâcon, France: Imprimérie Protat, 1917), 260; M. H. Lenormand, "Découvert d'un Gisement de Poteries a l'Ile des Pins," *Bulletin Periodique de la Société d'Études Mélanésiennes* 3 (1948): 57.

226   "Lapita was name": Sand, "Petites et Grandes Histoires," 146.

226   In his final report: Gifford and Shutler, *Archaeological Excavations in New Caledonia*, 94. For the complex history of who realized what when, see also Lenormand, "Decouvert d'un Gisement de Poteries," and Jacques Avias, quoted in Gifford and Shutler, *Archaeological Excavations in New Caledonia*, 94.

226   Dates from these sites: Kirch, *On the Road of the Winds*, 93–97.

228   No one has ever uncovered: Kirch, *Lapita Peoples*, 98–99.

228   The splitting off: Ross, Pawley, and Osmond, *Lexicon of Proto Oceanic*, 1:2. See also Blust, *Austronesian Languages*, 23–28.

229   they had terms: Ross, Pawley, and Osmond, *Lexicon of Proto Oceanic*, 2:310–14, 126–31, 166–70; see also vol. 1.

229   Not all these concepts: Ibid., 2:89, 189; Arthur Grimble, quoted in ibid., 2:191.

230   One salient feature: R. C. Green, "Near and Remote Oceania—Disestablishing 'Melanesia' in Culture History," in *Man and a Half: Essays in Pacific Anthropology and Ethnobiology in Honour of Ralph Bulmer*, ed. A. Pawley (Auckland: Polynesian Society, 1991), 499.

231   "portmanteau biota": Alfred W. Crosby, *Ecological Imperialism: The Biological Expansion of Europe, 900–1900* (Cambridge: Cambridge University Press, 1986), 89; Kirch, *Lapita Peoples*, 218–19.

231   "the most extreme example": David W. Steadman, "Extinction of Birds in Eastern Polynesia: A Review of the Record, and Comparisons with Other Pacific Island Groups," *Journal of Archaeological Science* 16 (1989): 201; Kirch, *Lapita Peoples*, 222–25.

232   "pulled" into the unknown: Kirch, *On the Road of the Winds*, 97; Peter Bellwood, "Hierarchy, Founder Ideology and Austronesian Expansion," in *Origins, Ancestry and Alliance: Exploration in Austronesian Ethnography*, eds. James J. Fox and Clifford Sather (Canberra: ANU E Press, 1996), 29.

233   "would have been heirs": Bellwood, "Hierarchy," 30–31.

Kon-Tiki: *Thor Heyerdahl's Raft*

237 "most preposterously": John Dunmore Lang, *View of the Origins and Migrations of the Polynesian Nation* (London: Cochrane and M'Crone, 1834), 79–82.

238 "the chains": Thor Heyerdahl, *Fatu Hiva* (Harmondsworth, UK: Penguin, 1976), 11.

238 "It's queer": Thor Heyerdahl, *The Kon-Tiki Expedition* (Harmondsworth, UK: Penguin, 1963), 12.

239 "accompanied by the muffled roar": Ibid., 13.

239 "a figure or design": Handy, *Native Culture*, 244–45; Handy, *Polynesian Religion*, 121.

240 "The decisive factor": *Kon-Tiki*, directed by Thor Heyerdahl (Sweden: Artfilm, 1950).

242 "Whether it was 1947": Heyerdahl, *Kon-Tiki*, 130, 89.

242 "waves and fish and sun": Ibid., 121, 130.

243 "curious stationary cloud": Ibid., 165, 169.

243 "the viciousness of the red reef": Ibid., 174.

243 "a question of saving our lives": Ibid., 183, 186, 196.

244 It was described: Arnold Jacoby, *Señor Kon-Tiki* (n.p.: Rand McNally, 1967), 267–68, 278–79.

245 "A nice adventure": Quoted in ibid., 288.

245 "chronologically, archaeologically": Lowell D. Holmes, "An Appraisal of the Kon Tiki Theory," *Oceania* 29, no. 2 (1958): 128.

246 "The author's unquenchable": Ralph Linton, review of *American Indians in the Pacific: The Theory behind the Kon-Tiki Expedition*, by Thor Heyerdahl, *American Anthropologist*, New Series 56, no. 1 (1954): 123.

246 "every straw is seized": Edward Norbeck, review of *American Indians in the Pacific: The Theory behind the Kon-Tiki Expedition*, by Thor Heyerdahl, *American Antiquity* 19, no. 1 (1953): 93.

246 "to avoid reading racism": Ibid., 93.

247 "the poorest natives": Quoted in D. E. Yen, *The Sweet Potato in Oceania* (Honolulu: Bishop Museum Press, 1974), 311.

247 "absolute botanical proof": Ibid., 9.

247 Botanists have long argued: There is still a great deal of debate about this, with new evidence emerging and being disputed all the time. For a summary of the issues, see Terry L. Jones, Alice A. Storey, Elizabeth A. Matisoo-Smith, and José Miguel Ramírez-Aliaga, eds., *Polynesians in America: Pre-Colombian Contacts with the New World* (Lanham, MD: Altamira Press, 2011).

248 Very recently arguments have even been made: See Pablo Muñoz-Rodríguez et al., "Reconciling Conflicting Phylogenies in the Origin of Sweet Potato and Dispersal to Polynesia," *Current Biology* 28, no. 8 (April 23, 2018): 1246–56.e12, https://www.cell.com/current-biology/fulltext/S0960-9822(18)30321-X.

248 "that America was discovered": Heyerdahl, *Kon-Tiki*, 151; Robert Suggs, *The Island Civilizations of Polynesia* (New York: Mentor/New American Library, 1960), 224.

248 "If an opinion poll": Howe, *Quest for Origins*, 122.

249 "the old Polynesians": Heyerdahl, *Kon-Tiki*, 150–51.

249 "systematically underrated": Linton, review of *American Indians in the Pacific*, 124.

*Drifting Not Sailing: Andrew Sharp*

250 "one of the most provocative": K. R. Howe, "The Sharp-Lewis Debate," *Texts and Contexts*, ed. Doug Munro and Brij V. Lal (Honolulu: University of Hawai'i Press, 2006), 66.

250 "no deliberate colonization": Andrew Sharp, *Ancient Voyagers in the Pacific* (Wellington: Polynesian Society, 1956), 2.

251 "Stars do not shine": Sharp, *Ancient Voyagers in the Pacific*, 22–23, 34.

252 "This circumstance": Cook, *Journals*, 3.1:87.

252 "From all the accounts": Ibid., 1:154.

253 "a man tired": Beaglehole, introduction to *Journals of Captain James Cook*, 3.1:cliv.

253 Drawing from the accounts: Sharp, *Ancient Voyagers in the Pacific*, 4, 63, 125, 93, 42, 45.

253 He related in detail: Ibid., 43–44.

254 "re-set their courses": Ibid., 15, 49, 115.

254 "No Polynesian": Ibid., 115, 90, 140.

255 "to ancient prejudices": Parsonson, "Settlement of Oceania," 24.

255 "My first reaction": Pei Te Hurinui Jones, "A Maori Comment on Andrew Sharp's 'Ancient Voyagers in the Pacific,'" *Journal of the Polynesian Society* 66, no. 1 (1957): 131.

255 "I stand before you": Howe, *Quest for Origins*, 99.

255 "upwards of a hundred": Andrew Sharp, *Ancient Voyagers in Polynesia* (Sydney: Angus and Robertson, 1963), preface.

256 "Polynesians," he argued: Sharp, *Ancient Voyagers in the Pacific*, 85, 84; Orbell, *Hawaiki*, 29–30.

256 "echoed the doubts": L. M. Groube, review of *Ancient Voyagers in Polynesia*, by Andrew Sharp, *Journal of the Polynesian Society* 75, no. 1 (1966): 143.

257 "the inner thought": Te Rangi Hiroa, "The Value of Tradition in Polynesian Research," *Journal of the Polynesian Society* 35 (1926): 187.

257 "precision and definiteness": Robert W. Williamson, "Origins of Polynesian Culture," in *Essays in Polynesian Ethnology*, by Robert W. Williamson, ed. Ralph Piddington (Cambridge: Cambridge University Press, 1939), 286.

258 "an unqualified yes or no": Michael Levison, R. Gerard Ward, and John W. Webb, *The Settlement of Polynesia: A Computer Simulation* (Minneapolis: University of Minnesota Press, 1973), 11.

258 "All sorts of people": Michael Levison, personal communication; Michael Levison, "Computing in the Humanities: The Early Days," unpublished manuscript, 2016.

259 "risk probability table": Levison, Ward, and Webb, *Settlement of Polynesia*, 20–21. See pp. 13–27 for a full description of the model.

259 "mammoth task": Ibid., vi.

259 "Once a week": Michael Levison, personal communication.

259 Out of more than 120,000: Levison, Ward, and Webb, *Settlement of Polynesia*, 50, 42.

260 Then there were the islands: Ibid., 53.

260 Nor would a drifting canoe: Ibid., 55, n. 52.

260 As for Easter Island: Ibid., 54, 46–48.

261 "good chances of successfully crossing": Ibid., 8, 60, 62.

### The Non-Armchair Approach: David Lewis Experiments

262 "stultified by shortage": David Lewis, *We, the Navigators: The Ancient Art of Landfinding in the Pacific*, 2nd ed. (Honolulu: University of Hawai'i Press, 1994), 12.

263 "Most scholars are landlubbers": Ben Finney, *Hokule'a: The Way to Tahiti* (New York: Dodd, Mead, 1979), 12.

263 "trailing my toes luxuriously": Lewis, *We, the Navigators*, 18.

263 "hampered by too theoretical": Ibid., 18, 19.

264 "star and sun steering": Ibid., 21, 23.

264 "a most unusual fellowship": Finney, *Hokule'a*, 59.

264 "an old and wrinkled man": Lewis, *We, the Navigators*, 31, 30.

265 "a mosaic of fragments": Ibid., 24.

266 "the sinking Pollux": Ibid., 90.

266 Navigators could steer: Ibid., 123, n. 3.

267 "with a slow, swelling": Ibid., 126.

267 passed "through each other": Ibid., 127–28.

267 Lewis reported: Ibid., 133.

268 "some large and some small": William Wyatt Gill, *Myths and Songs from the South Pacific* (London: Henry S. King, 1876), 319–20.

268 "Picture yourself": Thomas Gladwin, *East Is a Big Bird* (Cambridge, MA: Harvard University Press, 1970), 182.

269 In some stories: See Bacil F. Kirtley, *A Motif-Index of Traditional Polynesian Narratives* (Honolulu: University of Hawai'i Press, 1971), 319; Martha Warren Beckwith, ed., *Kepelino's Traditions of Hawaii* (Honolulu: Bishop Museum, 1932), 189; Beckwith, *Hawaiian Mythology*, 71–72.

269 "expanding the target": Lewis, *We, the Navigators*, 252, 205, 207.

270 "downright affectionate": Gladwin, *East Is a Big Bird*, 197.

270 "as if stuck": Lewis, *We, the Navigators*, 216–20.

270 "a pale, shimmering column": Ibid., 222; on underwater lightning, see John Huth, *The Lost Art of Finding Our Way* (Cambridge, MA: Harvard University Press, 2013), 422–27.

270 Islanders also speak: Lewis, *We, the Navigators*, 291.

271 As one anthropologist: Quoted in Ben Finney, "Nautical Cartography and Traditional Navigation in Oceania," in *Cartography in the Traditional African, American, Arctic, Australia, and Pacific Societies*, ed. David Woodward and G. Malcolm Lewis, vol. 2, book 3 of *The History of Cartography* (Chicago: University of Chicago Press, 1998), 485.

271 "Europeans had no corresponding": Lewis, *We, the Navigators*, 248.

272 "that if one landfall": Levison, Ward, and Webb, *Settlement of Polynesia*, 63–64. They note that this idea was first suggested to them by the anthropologist Roger Green.

272 "a unity": Lewis, *We, the Navigators*, 48.

272 "When a Puluwatan": Gladwin, *East Is a Big Bird*, 34, 33.

273 "All over Oceania": Lewis, *We, the Navigators*, 298; Gladwin, *East Is a Big Bird*, 37.

273 "sweet burial": Raymond Firth, *We, the Tikopia*, 2nd ed. (New York: Routledge, 2011), 32.

273 "simply paddled out": Lewis, *We, the Navigators*, 356.

## Hōkūleʻa: *Sailing to Tahiti*

274  "All this seemed absurd": Finney, *Hokuleʻa*, 13.

275  "for the graceful way": Ibid., 15.

275  "skidding sideways": Ibid.

276  "an exercise in 'experimental archaeology'": Quoted in Sam Low, *Hawaiki Rising* (Waipahu, HI: Island Heritage Publishing, 2013), 31.

276  "The canoe was the center": Quoted in ibid., 61, 66.

277  "No one could foresee": Dave Lyman, quoted in ibid., 78.

277  "a professor who seemed to embody": Ibid., 82.

278  "There was something about Mau": Shorty Bertelmann, quoted in ibid., 57.

278  "I made that trip": Mau Piailug in "The Navigators: Pathfinders of the Pacific," directed by Sam Low (Educational Resources, 1983), YouTube, uploaded by maupiailugsociety, https://www.youtube.com/watch?v=uxgUjyqN7FU; Ben Finney, "Hawaiʻi to Tahiti and Back," Voyaging Traditions, Polynesian Voyaging Society, http://archive.hokulea.com/holokai/1976/ben_finney.html.

278  "Before we leave": Quoted in Low, *Hawaiki Rising*, 89.

278  "Tommy Holmes": "Tommy Holmes, a Founder (1945–1993)," Hawaiian Voyaging Traditions, Polynesian Voyaging Society, http://archive.hokulea.com/index/da_crew/tommy_holmes.html; Lewis, *We, the Navigators*, 333–34; Finney, *Hokuleʻa*, 194.

279  "Our strategy": Finney, "Hawaiʻi to Tahiti and Back."

279  "A medieval Tahitian": Lewis, *We, the Navigators*, 317.

280  "Once this background": Ibid., 318; see also Finney, *Hokuleʻa*, 127.

280  "a red giant": Finney, *Hokuleʻa*, 121, 119.

280  "you can tell the experienced navigators": Gladwin, *East Is a Big Bird*, 2.

280  "looks the part": Finney, *Hokuleʻa*, 122.

281  "smoothed to a vast skin": Low, *Hawaiki Rising*, 91, 95.

281  "calmly confident": Finney, *Hokuleʻa*, 223.

281  "they were everywhere": Ibid., 251–53; Low, *Hawaiki Rising*, 101–2.

282  "When we leave from Maui": Quoted in Finney, *Hokuleʻa*, 260–61; Low, *Hawaiki Rising*, 104–5.

283  "I could see what we were doing": Quoted in Low, *Hawaiki Rising*, 51.

283  "to understand my place": Quoted in ibid., 43.

283  "The more I learn": Quoted in ibid., 134.

284  "We thought we could do without one": Quoted in ibid., 157.

284  "It was blowing like shit": Harry Ho and Ben Finney, quoted in ibid., 159.

284  "It just happened": Snake Ah Hee and Nainoa Thompson, quoted in ibid., 163.

285  "We're tired": Stuart Holmes Colman, *Eddie Would Go: The Story of Eddie Aikau, Hawaiian Hero and Pioneer of Big Wave Surfing* (New York: St. Martin's, 2001), 222.

285  "to see Tahiti": Nainoa quoted in ibid., 211, 246.

## Reinventing Navigation: *Nainoa Thompson*

286  "if the canoe's legacy": Quoted in Low, *Hawaiki Rising*, 181–82.

287  Three thousand years ago: See Ross, Pawley, and Osmond, *Lexicon of Proto Oceanic*, vol. 2, chap. 6, esp. 189–91.

287  "Knowledge alone": Will Kyselka, *An Ocean in Mind* (Honolulu: University of Hawai'i Press, 1987), 53, 56, 58.

287  "I will train you": Nainoa Thompson, "Recollections of the 1980 Voyage to Tahiti," Polynesian Voyaging Society, http://archive.hokulea.com/holokai/1980 /nainoa_to_tahiti.html.

287  "You need to define": Quoted in Low, *Hawaiki Rising*, 182, 193.

289  "I was in near trauma": Thompson, "Recollections of the 1980 Voyage."

289  "naïve" to think: Finney, *Hokule'a*, 37; see also Ben Finney, *Voyage of Rediscovery: A Cultural Odyssey through Polynesia* (Berkeley: University of California Press, 1994), 93.

289  The canoe itself: See Ben Finney, *Sailing in the Wake of the Ancestors: Reviving Polynesian Voyaging* (Honolulu: Bishop Museum Press, 2003), 62–74.

290  The Carolinian compass: Finney notes that the points on the Carolinian compass are sometimes depicted as evenly spaced and sometimes not, a difference that may "simply reflect the differing approaches of the researchers"; see Finney, "Nautical Cartography and Traditional Navigation in Oceania," 464.

290  "to illustrate that Ngatik": Lewis, *We, the Navigators*, 184.

291  "the relation of the problem solver": Hutchins, *Cognition in the Wild*, 80–81.

291  "it is easy for us to forget": Lewis, *We, the Navigators*, 184

291  "a rather high order": Gladwin, *East Is a Big Bird*, 220.

291  "real point of view": Hutchins, *Cognition in the Wild*, 80–81.

291  There is an intriguing experiment: Experiment by C. Linde and W. Labov, described in Michel de Certeau, *The Practice of Everyday Life* (Berkeley: University of California Press, 1984), 119. See also C. Linde, "The Organization of Discourse," in *Style and Variables in English*, ed. Timothy Shopen and Joseph M. Williams, Center for Applied Linguistics (Cambridge, MA: Winthrop, 1981), 104–6.

292  Tour thinking: See Woodward and Lewis, introduction to *Cartography in the Traditional African, American, Arctic, Australian, and Pacific Societies*, 4, n. 9.

292  "to 'revisit information'": Thompson, "Recollections of the 1980 Voyage."

292  "manageable inventories": Saul H. Riesenberg, "The Organisation of Navigational Knowledge on Puluwat," *Journal of the Polynesian Society* 81, no. 1 (1972): 19–22.

293  "I suddenly felt": Thompson, "Recollections of the 1980 Voyage."

293  "immediate organ of sensation": Elsdon Best, *Maori Religion and Mythology*, part 2 (Wellington: Te Papa Press, 2005), 45.

293  "the ancient way": Thompson, "Recollections of the 1980 Voyage"; Kyselka, *An Ocean in Mind*, 206.

293  "more rewarding": Finney, *Voyage of Rediscovery*, 309.

294  "You have not closed": Finney, *Sailing in the Wake*, 147.

295  "demoted": Ibid., 8.

## The Latest Science: DNA and Dates

300  "express train to Polynesia": Jared M. Diamond, "Express Train to Polynesia," *Nature* 336, no. 24 (1988): 307–8. Diamond credits Peter Bellwood with the essential idea, but the catchphrase appears to be his.

300  "entangled bank": John Terrell, "History as a Family Tree, History as an Entangled

Bank: Constructing Images and Interpretations of Prehistory in the South Pacific," *Antiquity* 62 (1988): 642–57.

301 An earlier study: David Addison and Elizabeth Matisoo-Smith, "Rethinking Polynesian Origins: A West-Polynesia Triple-I Model," *Archaeology in Oceania* 45 (2010): 3.

301 "leaving behind their genes": Manfred Kayser et al., "Melanesian Origin of Polynesian Y chromosome," *Current Biology* 10 (2000): 1237.

302 genetic bottlenecks: See Elizabeth Matisoo-Smith and K. Ann Horsburgh, *DNA for Archaeologists* (Walnut Creek, CA: Left Coast Press, 2012), 133.

302 The site, known as Teouma: Stuart Bedford, Matthew Spriggs, and Ralph Regenvanu, "The Teouma Lapita Site and the Early Human Settlement of the Pacific Islands," *Antiquity* 80 (2006): 822; Stuart Bedford and Matthew Spriggs, "Birds on the Rim: A Unique Lapita Carinated Vessel in Its Wider Context," *Archaeology in Oceania* 42 (2007): 12–21.

303 The first ancient DNA: See Pontus Skogland et al., "Genomic Insights into the Peopling of the Southwest Pacific," *Nature* 538 (October 27, 2016): 510–13; Mark Lipson et al., "Population Turnover in Remote Oceania Shortly after Initial Settlement," *Current Biology* 28, no. 7 (April 2, 2018): 1157–65, https://doi.org/10.1016/j.cub.2018.02.051.

303 Where and when and how: Frédérique Valentin et al., "Early Lapita Skeletons from Vanuatu Show Polynesian Craniofacial Shape: Implications for Remote Oceanic Settlement and Lapita Origins," *Proceedings of the National Academy of Sciences* 113, no. 2 (January 12, 2016): 292–97.

304 One finding: Elena McPhee, "Marlborough Rangitane o Wairau Iwi Related to Wairau Bar Ancestors," *Marlborough Express*, December 5, 2016, https://www.stuff.co.nz/national/87142104/marlborough-rangitane-o-wairau-iwi-related-to-wairau-bar-ancestors.

304 But another interesting revelation: Thomas Higham, Atholl Anderson, and Chris Jacomb, "Dating the First New Zealanders: The Chronology of Wairau Bar," *Antiquity* 73 (1999): 425–26; Elizabeth Matisoo-Smith, "The Human Landscape: Population Origins, Settlement and Impact of Human Arrival in Aotearoa/New Zealand," in *Atlantis Advances in Quaternary Science: Landscape and Quaternary Environmental Change in New Zealand*, ed. J. Shulmeister (Paris: Atlantis Press, 2017), 305.

305 *Rattus exulans*: See Elizabeth Matisoo-Smith, "The Commensal Model for Human Settlement of the Pacific 10 Years On—What Can We Say and Where to Now?," *Journal of Island and Coastal Archaeology* 4 (2009): 151–63.

305 Studies of rat DNA: Matisoo-Smith, "Human Landscape," 296.

305 On Easter Island: S. S. Barnes, E. Matisoo-Smith, and T. L. Hunt, "Ancient DNA of the Pacific rat (*Rattus exulans*) from Rapa Nui (Easter Island)," *Journal of Archaeological Science* 33, no. 11 (2006): 1536–40; Matisoo-Smith, "Human Landscape," 305; Higham, Anderson, and Jacomb, "Dating the First New Zealanders," 425–26.

306 "It's like turning on an electric light": Stephanie Dutchen, "Coming Into Focus," interview with David Reich, Harvard Medical School, February 21, 2018, https://hms.harvard.edu/news/coming-focus.

306 These included: Patrick V. Kirch, "When Did the Polynesians Settle Hawai'i?

A Review of 150 Years of Scholarly Inquiry and a Tentative Answer," *Hawaiian Archaeology* 12 (2011): 9–11.

307 "to weed out": Matthew Spriggs, "The Dating of the Island Southeast Asian Neolithic: An Attempt at Chronometric Hygiene and Linguistic Correlation," *Antiquity* 63 (1989): 590.

307 "chronometric hygiene": Spriggs claims to have lifted the term from Wilfred Shawcross, who, he says, "ad-libbed" it; see Matthew Spriggs, "Archaeology and That Austronesian Expansion: Where Are We Now?," *Antiquity* 85 (2011): 510.

307 "considerable caution": Spriggs, "Dating of the Island Southeast Asian Neolithic," 604.

307 They rejected samples: Matthew Spriggs and Atholl Anderson, "Late Colonization of East Polynesia," *Antiquity* 67 (1993): 207.

307 Of the one hundred nine Hawaiian dates: Ibid., 208–10; Atholl Anderson, "The Chronology of Colonization in New Zealand," *Antiquity* 65 (1991): 783.

308 According to the new orthodoxy: Kirch, "When Did the Polynesians," 16–18; Anderson, "Chronology of Colonization," 792. More recent work puts these dates even later, at A.D. 1000 and 1300, respectively. See, for example, Matisoo-Smith, "Human Landscape."

308 One computer simulation: Álvaro Montenegro, Richard T. Callaghan, and Scott M. Fitzpatrick, "Using Seafaring Simulations and Shortest-Hop Trajectories to Model the Prehistoric Colonization of Remote Oceania," *Proceedings of the National Academy of Sciences* 113, no. 45 (November 2016): 12685–90, https://doi .org/10.1073/pnas.1612426113.

309 A second study: Ian D. Goodwin, Stuart A. Browning, and Atholl J. Anderson, "Climate Windows for Polynesian Voyaging to New Zealand and Easter Island," *Proceedings of the National Academy of Sciences* 111, no. 41. (October, 2014): 14716–21.

309 "bold expeditions": Fornander, *Account*, 2:6.

310 the new science: Thanks to Greg Harris for this clever formulation.

## Coda: Two Ways of Knowing

311 "mythical fictions": Finney, *Voyage of Rediscovery*, 317–18.

312 "could actually reflect an era": Ibid., 318.

314 to "detach" himself: Allen, "Te Rangi Hiroa's Physical Anthropology," 14.

314 "an ongoing vehicle": Howe, *Quest for Origins*, 36.

315 "What does their existence": Brian Durrans, "Ancient Pacific Voyaging: Cook's Views and the Development of Interpretation," in *Captain Cook and the South Pacific*, ed. T. C. Mitchell (London: British Museum, 1979), 139.

315 "To inquire into my history": Tipene O'Regan, "Who Owns the Past?," in *From the Beginning: The Archaeology of the Maori*, ed. John Wilson (Auckland: Penguin, 1987), 142.

316 "belongs first to those": Greg Dening, "Respectfulness as a Performance Art: Way-finding," *Postcolonial Studies*, 11.2 (2008): 149.

316 "We cannot translate": Judith Binney, "Maori Oral Narratives, Pakeha Written Texts," in *The Shaping of History*, ed. Judith Binney (Wellington: Bridget Williams Books, 2001), 13.

316   "keep our minds as sensitive": Krauss, *Keneti*, 249.
317   "chose to be puzzled": Kyselka, *An Ocean in Mind*, 235.
318   "was come to the afterpiece": Stevenson, *In the South Seas*, 9.
318   "I have watched the morning": Ibid., 20.
319   "the face of the world": Ibid., 21.

# Index

Page numbers of illustrations and their captions appear in italics.

# About the Author

**CHRISTINA THOMPSON** is the editor of *Harvard Review* and the author of *Come On Shore and We Will Kill and Eat You All: A New Zealand Story*. Her awards include the Australian Prime Minister's Literary Award, a National Endowment for the Humanities Public Scholar Award, and fellowships from the National Endowment for the Arts and Australia Council. A dual citizen of the United States and Australia, she lives outside of Boston with her family.